THE
JIHADI
NEXT DOOR

Dan

Thanks for the

wine.

[signature]

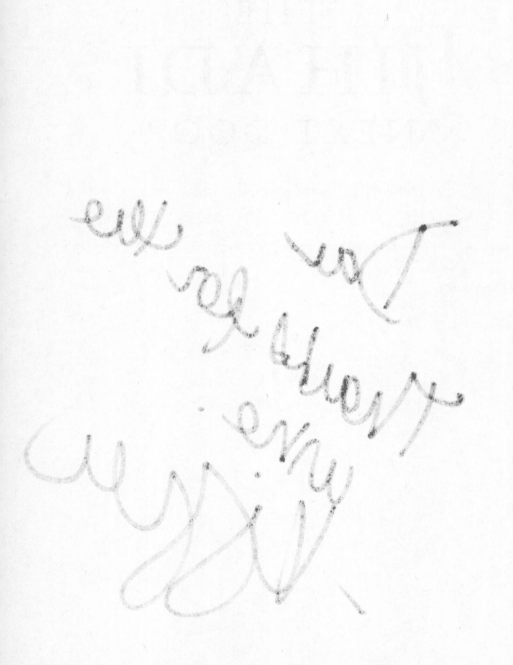

THE JIHADI NEXT DOOR

HOW ISIS IS FORCING, DEFRAUDING, AND COERCING YOUR NEIGHBOR INTO TERRORISM

DR. KIMBERLY MEHLMAN-OROZCO

Foreword by Chris Sampson

Skyhorse Publishing

Skyhorse Publishing books may be purchased in bulk at special discounts for sales promotion, corporate gifts, fund-raising, or educational purposes. Special editions can also be created to specifications. For details, contact the Special Sales Department, Skyhorse Publishing, 307 West 36th Street, 11th Floor, New York, NY 10018 or info@skyhorsepublishing.com.

Skyhorse® and Skyhorse Publishing® are registered trademarks of Skyhorse Publishing, Inc.®, a Delaware corporation.

Visit our website at www.skyhorsepublishing.com.

10 9 8 7 6 5 4 3 2 1

Library of Congress Cataloging-in-Publication Data is available on file.

Cover design by Brian Peterson
Cover photo credit: iStockphoto

ISBN: 978-1-51073-286-5
Ebook ISBN: 978-1-51073-287-2

Printed in the United States of America

For all the parents who have lost a child to terrorism.

CONTENTS

PART IV

FOREWORD

Why would anyone join ISIS—the terrorist offspring of al-Qaeda?

While much has been written on the roots of the organization and the violent tactics used by the group, more understanding is needed on what brought these terrorists to the world stage. People are not recruited to commit murder simply as a result of watching a propaganda video or from a belief in a particular religion. It is a process known as radicalization.

By selectively targeting vulnerable individuals, terrorists use a series of techniques to lower the recruits' inhibitions, increase a strong sense of grievance, and build a feeling of community. To understand this process, we look at cases and testimony from those who have taken this path to destruction and learn from the choices they made. In this book, Dr. Kimberly Mehlman-Orozco applies her experience in criminology to lay out an understanding of what it takes to draw people from the fabric of society into a world of extremism and, ultimately, terrorism.

Understanding these lures assists counterextremist efforts in exposing the lies used by recruiters. Targeted conscripts are pulled in by promises of being made heroes—of being useful and relevant. Recruits come from various backgrounds and many seem surprising at first glance.

For example, Colleen LaRose of Detroit became a high-profile recruit to ISIS, yet her background seemed at odds with what many people conceived as the type of person who would join the terrorist group. However, as the book will show, she had all the conditions necessary to be at risk of radicalization. All her recruiter needed to do was give her a role that she had failed to achieve in her life thus far. She had an opportunity to become someone else—someone important, valued, and cherished. With the terrorists who recruited her, LaRose felt her abusive upbringing, repeated mistreatment, failed relationships, and drug-addicted life could be things of the past. She reinvented herself as Fatima LaRose—an aspiring suicide bomber— before becoming internationally notorious as Jihad Jane.

This pattern isn't isolated in one country, either. *The Jihadi Next Door* highlights stories of men and women, young and old, from around the world, who joined ISIS based on promises of change, community, and heroic adventure. Despite many differences on the surface, most recruits shared common characteristics in their lack of social acceptance, engagement, and successes.

The range of their personal attributes reflected a clear pattern of ISIS targeting. They wanted to bring in people from the Muslim world as part of their effort to hijack the religion. They sought to recruit people from outside the Muslim world who didn't understand the Arabic language, the deep roots of the Islamic culture, or the religion so they could carry out their death cult view of Islam. They sought out people from various sectors of society to fill organizational needs. For grunt fighters, ISIS worked to lure young men who would fight to the death for their so-called caliphate. For breeding another generation, they sought women who desired husbands and a sense of fulfillment. To lure these groups in, they targeted recruits who would focus on promises of brides and husbands. They sought bright, computer-savvy people like Junaid Hussain and Siful Sujan from the UK to hack and engage in social engineering. They pursued people in marginalized groups of societies and fed their need to belong.

As the caliphate crumbled underneath them in recent years, ISIS fanned out into other fragmented countries that were at the outer perimeter of their reach. After they lost territory in Syria and Iraq they retreated to failed countries like Yemen, Libya, and Afghanistan. ISIS efforts in Boko Haram, the Sinai Peninsula, and the Philippines remained ongoing crises even after the losses in Syria and Iraq. It must be stated that though ISIS failed to hold its grip on Syria and Iraq in the second half of 2018, they still have an estimated thirty thousand fighters in the organization at the time of this publication.

Terrorists thrive on resentment and ignorance. The examples in this book are a guide for those who wish to understand the inception of extremism through the stages of radicalization to the acts of terror, which can be equally applied to other groups. Gangs, white supremacists, neo-Nazis, and other extreme political organizations follow many of the same patterns as we've seen used by ISIS. *The Jihadi Next Door* does well at covering specific examples of recruitment and can serve future scholars as a window into the radicalization process, which needn't be limited to ISIS.

—Chris Sampson
Terrorism Analyst
Coauthor of *Hacking ISIS: How to Destroy the Cyber Jihad*

AUTHOR'S NOTE

You will soon realize that the title of this book is paradoxical, which was my intention. I will argue that the term "jihadi" should not be used interchangeably with the nouns "terrorist" and "extremist."

Jihad is a religious word, which is referenced in the Qur'an. It literally means a struggle or effort—to live out the Muslim faith as well as possible, to build a good Muslim society, and to defend Islam, with force if necessary, but with rules of engagement.[1]

Terrorists do not engage in religiously sanctioned or legal warfare with proper rules of engagement; they are criminals who commit horrific acts of violence with cowardice and deceit. Their leadership is truly motivated by money and power, not religion. Therefore, despite their self-proclamations, I try not to describe them as "jihadists" or as engaging in "jihad." Instead, I have attempted to more accurately refer to them as "terrorists" or *irjafiyyun* (singular *irjafi*), extremists, and criminals.[2]

Likewise, a *mujahid* is someone who engages in jihad, which terrorists don't do; and a martyr is someone who is killed because of their religious beliefs. Terrorists are suicide bombers, not martyrs.

Although this may seem like I am quibbling over semantic distinction for the sake of political correctness, I will argue that this confounding use of language reflects a larger issue that undermines the efficacy of counterterrorism interventions.

Words matter, especially because:

A lie told often enough becomes truth.
—Vladimir Lenin

INTRODUCTION

Close your eyes and imagine a criminal.

Now visualize a law-abiding citizen.

Whom did you see?

Over the last ten years, I've taught undergraduate criminology classes at two top-ranked universities. Each semester, I have my students do this exercise and collect their anonymous responses. Despite teaching diverse groups of educated young people, the reactions to this assignment are usually, stereotypically patterned. The "criminal" is most frequently described as being a young black male.[1] Even if my students are politically correct enough to refrain from remarking on the particular race of the person they imagined, the "criminal" is still described in "dark" places, with "dark" features (e.g., eyes or hair), and "dark" clothing.

On the other hand, the "law-abiding citizen" is most frequently described as being an old white woman. Again, even if the student omits the race of the "law-abiding citizen," this person is still described in "light" places, with "light" features (e.g., white teeth), and "light" clothing, such as a sundress.

These stereotypes exist, whether we admit to them or not. Naturally, people will develop heuristics based on the information they are exposed to. The reason why young black men are stereotyped as criminals is that the media disproportionately portrays them as such.[2] Moreover, our criminal justice system has perpetually suffered from disproportionate minority contact and sentencing. This means that although the likelihood of engaging in crime is similar across different races, young people of color are more likely to be stopped, searched, arrested, and incarcerated based solely on their skin hue.[3]

Similar patterns exist when discussing terrorism and who is profiled as a terrorist.

When I ask my students to envision a terrorist, many of them describe a "Muslim-looking" man with a "turban and long beard." Some even believed that "Allahu Akbar" is "something that terrorists say," despite the fact that it literally translates to "God is greater" or "God is the greatest."[4]

In response, I would try to challenge their preconceived notions. Is it even possible to *see* someone's criminality? Why would saying, "God is great," in Arabic be considered "a sign of terrorism," but not when said in English?

"I didn't know that's what Allahu Akbar means, I just heard that's what terrorists shout before killing people," one student explained.

The information that we are exposed to shapes our assumptions on criminality in a way that is often divergent from reality. The same holds true for persons recruited into terrorism. To us, we are the freedom fighters, and they are the terrorists killing civilians. To them, we are the crusaders who invaded their country, and they are the freedom fighters.

Given the instability in certain regions in Iraq and Syria, ISIS leadership and recruiters want people to believe that they are protecting their community and killing people in accordance with Islam, under the will of Allah, but that's a lie.

Violence in the name of God results from the perversion of religion to exploit marginalized people for money and power. Religion is just another veneer under which criminal enterprises can operate.

ISIS leadership is comprised of nothing more than sacrilegious opportunists who are using Islam for their own personal gain and selfish motives—what many would consider a sin. The criminals who run ISIS and other terrorist organizations manipulate their interpretation of the religion in order to use it to force, defraud, and coerce exploitable people into fighting and dying for them.

Many of you may not believe this reality now, but by the end of this book, my hope is that you will understand why exposing this falsehood is key to counterterrorism.

PART I

1

Drawing Parallels

Allow me to introduce myself. My name is Dr. Kimberly Mehlman-Orozco. I am a mother of four children—two girls, two boys—and a social scientist, with an expertise in human trafficking.

I've spent nearly a decade researching human trafficking by serving on task forces; attending related conferences and summits; and collecting qualitative data from convicted human traffickers, human trafficking survivors, commercial sex consumers, and consenting sex workers. I've written extensively on the topic of trafficking in persons—one book; two magazine features; four peer-reviewed scholarly journal articles; and over two dozen opinion editorials, all before the age of thirty-five. At the time of this writing, I have served as a human trafficking expert witness on approximately one dozen criminal and civil court cases, across multiple states, and I've been interviewed over two dozen times by reporters writing pieces on human trafficking.

Given my area of expertise, you may be wondering why am I writing a book about a seemingly unrelated topic—terrorism. The explanation begins more than six years before this publication.

After graduating in the summer of 2012 with my PhD in criminology, law, and society from George Mason University, I took a position as an instructor in the criminology department of a top-ranked university. I was on a nine-month teaching contract and instructed four classes per semester, with over 500 students. My introductory criminology courses were in large lecture halls that could fit 250 students at one time.

Due to the size of those classes, I normally didn't know any of the students by name. However, there was an interesting phenomenon that I noticed—undergrads were territorial. No matter the size of the class or lack of seat assignments, they typically sat in the same location, every class, and would become per-turbed if someone took *their* seat.

Given the self-selected and consistent seating structure, I was able to famil-iarize myself with some faces, especially of those students who regularly attended class. I'll call one of them Amal.[1]

Amal was in the very first class[2] I taught after earning my PhD. She didn't sit in the front row or actively participate in class discussion, but she never missed a lecture and always sat in the same location—middle row, in the seat closest to the isle on my right. I also noticed her because of her clothing, as she was one of the few female criminology students at the time who wore a *hijab*.

I had become familiar with the significance of the *hijab* nearly ten years earlier in a psychology class during my undergraduate coursework. It was in the imme-diate aftermath of 9/11, and one of my classmates wanted to do a presentation on the stigma that she felt had become associated with Muslim veils. This student wore a *hijab*, which is a scarf that covered her head and neck, along with a *niqab*, which concealed her entire face apart from her eyes, and a *jilbab*—a loose fitting garment, which covered her entire body, aside from her hands. During her pre-sentation, she removed the *niqab* and *jilbab*, which shocked everyone in the class, including our professor.

Underneath her *jilbab*, she dressed in jeans and a shirt, like any other student in class. After removing the *niqab*, she revealed a naturally beautiful, make-up-less face. The student explained that she didn't wear the *niqab*, *jilbab*, or *hijab* during high school but had made the choice to start wearing these veils once she started college. She believed that the Qur'an called for modesty, and wearing the *hijab*, *niqab*, *jilbab*, or other veils fulfilled this commandment. She told us that she wore these garments in order to avoid the gaze of men, which she wanted to reserve only for her future husband and in the comfort of her own home.

Before that moment, I had no idea why some Muslim women chose to wear veils, and I hadn't cared enough to find out. I suppose I had just assumed it was some relic of paternalistic restrictions against females. After listening intently to my classmate's presentation, however, I came to realize that for many women, the choice was left to their discretion and served as a symbol of their commitment toward their current or future partner, as well as to their God.

I remember leaving that class with a positive connotation of the *hijab*. My takeaway was that Muslim women who chose to wear a veil were no different from you or me; they just decided to express their modesty on their own terms, in accordance with their interpretation of religion.

As such, although I noticed Amal because of her *hijab*, I thought nothing of it. She was just another undergrad in my class.

About midway through the semester, Amal approached me after my lecture and asked if she could interview me for her communications course. Her assignment was to interview a professor to gain insight into career paths associated with her major—criminology. I told her that I would be happy to help her out with the assignment and to visit me during office hours.

A few weeks later, Amal knocked at my office door and asked if I had time that day for the interview. I welcomed her into my office and gave her a seat, before shutting the door for privacy. She pulled out a notebook with her interview questions and a tape recorder. After asking my permission to record the interview, she began.

I don't remember all of the questions Amal asked, but I believe there were about ten. They included inquiries about my pathway into the criminal justice field, how I became interested in the subject, where I went to school, and what positions I had before teaching at her university.

After about thirty minutes, she opened up to me about her aspiration: "I want to become an FBI agent."

In every class I've ever taught, I try to look at my students as if they were my own children, so that I can give them genuine advice on how to bring their professional dreams into reality. I responded to Amal the same, by giving her my assessment of what makes a competitive applicant for the FBI, before urging her to seek out one of the many internship opportunities that are available for college students. However, I could tell there was something left unsaid in our conversation, as she didn't respond to the advice as most students did.

"Ummmm," she hesitated, fidgeting in her seat.

Her shyness was palpable, so I encouraged her: "You can ask me anything, I won't judge."

"Okay," she paused. "Can . . . can someone still join the FBI if their family member committed a crime?"

I was taken a bit off guard by her question, as I couldn't imagine how it pertained to her. "I believe so. The most important thing is that you're honest when they perform the background checks. As long as you're honest, there shouldn't be a problem."

"Are you sure? What if . . . if it was a *serious* crime?"

"As long as you weren't involved and are honest on your background and polygraph, I couldn't imagine it would affect you."

"What if it's a *close* family member, like a sibling, does that matter?"

"No, I don't think so, just as long as you weren't involved and you are upfront with it. I don't think you'll have a problem. Did your family member commit a crime?"

"Yes, my brother."

I felt as though she wanted to tell me more but for some reason was refraining.

"If you don't mind me asking, what type of crime?"

A pregnant pause filled the room.

I broke the silence, confused about the impetus for her questions but wanting to give her the opportunity to speak with me without fear of judgment. "You don't have to tell me if you don't want to, but I honestly won't judge, and I think it would help me provide you with a better answer. What type of crime was it?"

She let out a soft sigh, before whispering the word *terrorism.*

After she said it, Amal looked up from her hands, waiting, and watching for my reaction.

I was utterly shocked but tried my hardest not let my facial expression show. I didn't know exactly how to respond but endeavored to academically assess the situation to provide the best advice for this student who sought my counsel. "Well, that might be a little different, depending on how serious it was. Can you tell me what happened?"

In the interest in preserving Amal's anonymity, I won't go into details about her brother's case, but essentially he was convicted of providing material support to terrorists—an increasingly common charge in the United States. According to U.S. Federal Criminal Code, material support includes the provision of any property, tangible or intangible, or service, including currency or monetary instruments or financial securities, financial services, lodging, training, expert advice or assistance, safe houses, false documentation or identification, communications equipment, facilities, weapons, lethal substances, explosives, personnel, or transportation.[3]

Terrorist recruiters targeted Amal's brother online, recognizing his computer programming skills, and asked him to set up a website to facilitate money transfers for the "jihad." Federal agents monitored the exchange and arrested her brother after he complied with the terrorists' request.

Amal began to tear as she recalled them searching her family's home on the day of his arrest and on additional occasions thereafter. Streams were running down her face by the time she told me, "One of the agents, I asked him, and he said I could never be an FBI agent because of what my brother did. And this is all I've wanted to do with my life since I was a little girl. My dreams are crushed because of his mistake."

I tried to console her the best that I could and give her some advice on how to still have a meaningful career, but I was at a loss. Her brother was facing fifteen years in federal prison.

I continued to meet with Amal during my office hours throughout the course of the semester and got to know her and the story of her family more closely. Her parents worked hard to make ends meet and provide the best educational opportunities for Amal and her siblings. They had absolutely no extremist leanings, and were just pursuing the American Dream like everyone else. Their hard work had seemingly paid off when Amal's older brother received a full scholarship to a prestigious university, but it was all washed away with his conviction. After he served five years in federal prison, he was deported back to their home country, and his family chose to self-deport with him to stay united.

After getting to know Amal, I do not believe her brother was destined to become a terrorist sympathizer; he was recruited. Like many high-risk terrorist recruits, her brother was rather isolated, impressionable, and had very few friends. In fact, he was later diagnosed with Asperger syndrome, which is an Autism Spectrum Disorder that, among other things, causes challenges for normal social interactions. He found solace online, chatting with strangers for more than 40 hours per week. Terrorists lured him by providing a sense of belonging that he struggled to find in normal day-to-day relationships. He fed off of their positive reinforcement and failed to realize that they were exploiting him.

There was something incredibly familiar about the manner in which Amal's brother was recruited into terrorism. To me, his story at least was somewhat reminiscent of how human traffickers recruit and control victims.

The way that I conceptualize human trafficking recruitment, in a nutshell, is as follows:

First, the human trafficker identifies a target and determines which of his or her needs are not being met: physiological, safety, love/belonging, esteem, or self-actualization.[4]

Next, the human trafficker typically makes the false promise to fulfill the needs of the target or temporarily meet the needs of the target in order to gain her or his trust and distance them from social support systems.

Once the target is distanced from their social support, the human trafficker often attempts to create a bond and power imbalance with him or her. To the extent possible, the aim is to make the target reliant on the trafficker and distrustful of anyone besides the trafficker, while the target internalizes blame for any negative consequence received.

Ultimately, human traffickers are typically very skilled in making their victims believe they are consenting to their own exploitation, and I have come to find that terrorist recruiters exhibit similar characteristics.

Amal's brother, for example, clearly had a void in his life. The terrorists he met online temporarily filled that void by giving him a sense of belonging that was difficult for him to obtain in normal day-to-day interactions, in part due to his Asperger syndrome. Although he never left his home, Amal's brother became reliant on terrorists for these social interactions and began to believe in their message, because, after all, they were coercing him through positive reinforcement. All the while, they were using him as a means to an end.

I do not believe that Amal's brother was preordained to become a terrorist. Almost through happenstance, extremist recruiters just recognized and exploited his unmet needs, as human traffickers.

Although at this point it may seem like a stretch in my reasoning, this potential parallel was enough for me to develop a new scholarly interest in better understanding terrorist recruitment strategies.

For the purpose of this inquiry, I defined a terrorist as a clandestine agent who provides material support for and/or perpetrates premeditated, politically motivated violence against noncombatant targets. Although this definition certainly encompasses a variety of both foreign and domestic terrorists, I decided to focus on persons who claimed affiliation with the Taliban, al-Qaeda, al-Shabaab, ISIS, and related criminal organizations.[5]

As a first step, I read dozens of peer-reviewed journal articles and published books by renowned counterterrorism scholars. In my research, I noticed that relatively few studies explored the methods of terrorist recruitment.

Of those experts who did publish on the topic, some claimed that recruitment was random and unpatterned, meaning that anyone was at risk of joining extremist groups like ISIS and there was no way to predict or prevent it. Others asserted that only devout religious Muslims were the ones choosing to join, and it was the responsibility of the Islamic community to stop them by alerting authorities. However, I felt that both of these theories were quantitatively and qualitatively unsupported.

Given the dearth of research on terrorist recruitment strategies, I decided to conduct my own mixed-methods, exploratory investigation.

Following my dissertation, I conducted longitudinal qualitative interviews with convicted human traffickers, human trafficking survivors, consenting sex workers, and commercial sex consumers, which were later published in my first book—*Hidden in Plain Sight: America's Slaves of the New Millennium*. I found that interviewing the actors in criminal networks provided nuanced insight into how victims were recruited and controlled. I decided to employ this same methodology by interviewing convicted terrorists. However, gaining access to this population was much more difficult.

Utilizing publicly available materials, I created a list of convicted terrorists incarcerated in the United States.[6] I then referenced the Federal Bureau of Prisons inmate locator tool[7] to find the mailing address for each person I wanted to write.

My initial inquiry was straightforward and unrelated to recruitment. I asked the same four questions on every handwritten notecard:

1. Why did you do what you are convicted of?;
2. If you could tell the world one thing, what would it be?;
3. Why do people commit acts of terrorism?; and
4. What, in your opinion, is the best way for the United States to prevent future acts of terrorism?

I thought the questions were potentially provocative, and I just wanted to see who would respond. However, due to the Special Administrative Measure (SAM) restrictions for convicted terrorists, most of my cards were returned, along with a letter from the US Department of Justice Federal Bureau of Prisons. Each letter was signed by the respective associate warden, stating, "Your correspondence to the above named inmate is being returned. This correspondence was not delivered to the inmate because you are not approved to correspond with this individual."

A SAM is a process under United States law 28 C.F.R. 501.3 that allows the attorney general to direct the Bureau of Prisons to further restrict the terms of incarceration for specific inmates. In layman's terms and in this situation, this means that although most inmates have the first amendment constitutional right to correspond while in prison, there was a compelling government interest to restrict the correspondence of persons convicted of terrorism. Only a few terrorists have had their SAM restrictions lifted, allowing them communication to the outside world.

Given the number of returned cards due to SAM restrictions and the lapse in time following my mailing, I wasn't sure if anyone would respond, but eventually I received my first letter from a convicted terrorist: Richard Colvin Reid a.k.a. "The Shoe Bomber."

Reid was sentenced to life in prison for attempting to blow up American Airlines Flight 63 from Paris to Miami three months after 9/11. During the course of his trial, he claimed that he was a solider of God under the command of Osama bin Laden.

At the time of my correspondence, he had been in prison for over a decade; however, the content of his communications suggested that his extremist perspective had not wavered. From his solitary confinement cell at the maximum-security prison in Florence, Colorado, he wrote:

> Our religion teaches us that if our religion or lands are attacked it is our duty to defend them—if necessary with our lives—so "terrorism" is simply a tactic which has been employed in that regard. . . . If one claims to accept the existence and reality of God then it follows that the ONLY valid reason for taking another life can be if that is done in His name and/or in accordance with His law.

His belief was incredible to me, because, like many convicted terrorists, Reid wasn't born into extremism or Islam, for that matter. In fact, he actually converted as a young adult only a few years before his attempted terrorist attack.

As a mixed-race child in England, Reid felt ostracized from part of his community. He rebelled by spraying graffiti and engaging in petty crimes. At age 16, he dropped out of school to become a career criminal, like his father. While serving a sentence at Feltham Young Offenders' Institution in West London for petty theft, Reid was advised by his father to convert to Islam so that he would receive *better food in jail*.[8] Following his release in 1996, he joined Brixton Mosque. There, militant recruiters targeted him. According to Brixton Mosque chairman, Abdul Haqq Baker, extremists worked on "weak characters," and Reid was "very,

very impressionable."[9] Three years later, Reid traveled from England to Pakistan and Afghanistan, receiving religious and combat training.

Richard Reid's background suggests that he experienced multiple voids in fulfilling the needs in his life, from unstable housing and a broken family to his lack of belonging in the mainstream London community. The idea of Islamic conversion was suggested as a conduit to better meeting his needs while incarcerated and in the free world. Again, I felt that Reid's narrative was reminiscent of the type of people targeted by human traffickers for exploitation: impressionable, in need, and seeking belonging. I wondered, *How many other terrorists fit that profile?*

And so, I continued researching terrorist recruitment strategies by reading and analyzing the content of their propaganda and videos, as well as continuing to write qualitative inquiries to inmates who were imprisoned for terrorism.

In addition to Richard Reid a.k.a. "The Shoe Bomber," I received responses from Colleen LaRose a.k.a. "Jihad Jane," two of the "Fort Dix Five" (Eljvir and Shain Duka), Kevin James and Levar Washington of Jam'iyyat Ul-Islam Is-Saheeh, and ISIS hopefuls Donald Morgan and Michael Wolfe, among others.

Ultimately, my research suggests that from the outside looking into the Islamic State, most people see these men and women as nothing more than evil terrorists with a psychotic penchant for violence. Internally, they perceive themselves as freedom fighters or *mujahideen* who violated the laws of men to protect their *Ummah* (community) according to the will of Allah.

However, neither of these perceptions is based in reality.

While some experts claim that terrorist recruitment is completely random, my analyses of terrorist propaganda and interviews with convicted terrorists suggest that there are clear patterns that can be used to explain how regular people are being conscripted into terrorism and who is at high risk of being targeted.

By laying bare the tactics used by ISIS to deceive and exploit new recruits and exposing the veneer these extremists operate under, the intent of this book is to empower readers with the knowledge needed to prevent future recruitment and thereby to prevent acts of terrorism.

My research and experiential knowledge lead me to wholeheartedly believe that:

> *With guns you can kill terrorists,*
> *with education you can kill terrorism.*
>
> —Malala Yousafzai

2

Archetype

Like many Americans, I can tell you exactly where I was and what I was doing on September 11, 2001. I had graduated from Annandale High School in the spring that year and was working as a receptionist for a prominent law firm in Tysons Corner, Virginia—approximately thirteen miles from the Pentagon. I took a semester gap from school in order to work and save money for college.

I remember sitting at the front desk, like any other day, answering phones, processing invoices, and greeting clients. I tried to be as efficient as possible, so that when I'd have a lull in work, I could play my new favorite video game—Bejeweled—on my computer.

My desk faced the elevators to our floor, and there were hallways to my left and right, leading to dozens of offices and various conference rooms. Most of the time, I sat there quietly, in the black, marble-lined reception area, doing my work, with very little interaction with the attorneys and staff.

In fact, aside from when they were entering or exiting the building, I rarely saw anyone. As such, my curiosity was piqued that morning when shortly after 9:00 a.m., I watched several attorneys and staff briskly walk from one side of the building to the other, crossing my desk. I could tell by their pace and their facial expressions that something was wrong, but I was completely unaware of what troubled them.

Earlier that morning, at 8:46 a.m., American Airlines Flight 11, departing from Logan International Airport in Boston, Massachusetts, had crashed into the North Tower of the World Trade Center in New York.[1] Five Arab men, ranging in age from twenty-two to thirty-three, had taken control of the plane after smuggling box cutters onto the aircraft and charging the cockpit. After gaining control of the Boeing 767 roughly fourteen minutes after takeoff, the terrorists changed course, aiming the airplane at the twin towers, a symbol of American

ARCHETYPE
11

finance, power, and achievement.[2] A mushroom of fire appeared to engulf the top of the building upon impact. Professional news agencies and amateur filmmakers across the city began recording the tower, as black smoke billowed out into the clear blue sky.

Nearly twenty minutes later, another plane approached the towers. A second group of hijacker terrorists from United Arab Emirates and Saudi Arabia purposefully collided United Airlines Flight 175 into the South Tower, resulting in a succeeding fiery explosion, followed by another stream of smoke.

At the time, the details were unknown by the staff and attorneys in my office, but they had likely seen the second attack on the news or heard of the horror from colleagues in New York. The link to terrorism was confirmed by 9:31 a.m., when President George W. Bush addressed the American public from Florida:

> *Today, we've had a national tragedy. Two airplanes have crashed into the World Trade Center in an apparent terrorist attack on our country.*

Much of America watched President Bush's televised statement in shock and horror, while I remained at my desk, unaware.

> *I have spoken to the Vice President, to the Governor of New York, to the Director of the FBI, and I've ordered that the full resources of the federal government go to help the victims and their families and to conduct a full-scale investigation to hunt down and to find those folks who committed this act. Terrorism against our nation will not stand. And now, if you join me in a moment of silence.*

A diverse group of students, teachers, and faculty from Emma E. Booker Elementary School in Sarasota, Florida, stood behind President Bush, all bowing their heads and closing their eyes in silence. After about five seconds, he concluded his brief address: *"May God bless the victims, their families, and America. Thank you very much."*

President Bush received a round of applause as he left the podium and made his way to exit the school. Five minutes later, a third set of terrorists crashed American Airlines Flight 77 into the western façade of the Pentagon.

Although our office was approximately thirteen miles away, I could feel our building shake when the plane hit. My heartbeat quickened with fear. At the time, I remember thinking it was an earthquake. I didn't realize that terrorists perpetrated the act until one of the office managers came out to my desk.

"No visitors are allowed onto our floor, and do *not* accept any packages," she ordered.

"Is everything okay? What's going on?" I asked.

"Terrorists are crashing planes into buildings. There are multiple attacks," she replied. I was speechless. I was only seventeen years old and didn't have any concept of terrorism or war.

"Don't accept any packages, under any circumstance," she reiterated, before walking away.

Roughly one hour after the attack on the Pentagon, I was dismissed early from work. I tried to call my mom and dad from my cell phone, but the lines were busy. In fact, I couldn't reach anyone. I imagine it was because the large volume of calls at that time, driving the phone lines over capacity.

During my commute home, I remember how perfect the weather was. It was exceptionally sunny and comfortably warm, with a slight breeze. But the outdoor silence was deafening. It was almost as if the world had stopped turning in the wake of such a catastrophic loss of life. No birds, no cars, no people—just a void.

When I think of *terrorism*, my mind immediately jumps to the tragedies on September 11, 2001. Watching the video of planes being aimed at the World Trade Center, and piercing the buildings like missiles, will forever be engrained in my mind as my first exposure to premeditated, politically motivated, horrific violence perpetrated against civilians. Watching businessmen and women escape the flames and smoke by jumping, falling like rag dolls, down the length of those buildings was disturbingly surreal and made my heart sink into my stomach. Honestly, there are no words to express how those images changed me. When the building folded in on itself and collapsed into nothing but a cloud of smoke and debris, I became painfully aware of what terrorism is—an awareness that has gripped our citizens, young and old, ever since.

The perpetrators on each flight were eventually identified, but they remained nameless and faceless in my mind. Perhaps I never came to learn or remember their identities because each man was treated like a pawn by both the media and the extremist organization that financed their terrorism—al-Qaeda. None of the men were unique. They were simply interchangeable instruments of mass destruction.

A face and name wasn't paired with the word *terrorist*, until I learned of Osama bin Laden. Osama bin Mohammed bin Awad bin Laden (Anglicized as Osama bin Laden) was the billionaire founder of al-Qaeda, responsible for funding and orchestrating the most catastrophic terrorist attack in the world. After 9/11, his likeness was everywhere—in the news, magazines, and newspapers. Effigies of bin Laden were even sold as targets at American shooting ranges—I know this because I shot at one. For many, a newfound patriotism was forged through a collective hate for this man—a loathing strong enough to wage international war.

Less than one month after 9/11, George W. Bush announced Operation Enduring Freedom. American military offensively entered Afghanistan in an attempt to stamp out the Taliban regime, which had allegedly aided and abetted al-Qaeda in the plot against America. The fear, security changes, and additional attacks seemed to just fold into the counterterrorism milieu post-9/11.

While patriotism appeared to help many Americans cope with the attacks, Islamophobia became rampant and felt wrong.

I remember eating at one of my favorite strip-mall restaurants—Food Corner Kabob—when an older white man came in and began yelling at the employees about terrorism and 9/11. Oddly enough, while the restaurant served Afghan cuisine and was owned by a lovely Afghan family (who were extremely kind, incredibly generous, and welcoming), the employees were all from Central America and spoke very little English. While I was disturbed by the clear racism and religionism of the verbal attack, the workers just smiled, shrugged it off, and kept cooking and serving patrons.

Although the efforts to combat terrorism following the 9/11 tragedies may have been well intentioned, many of them made about as much sense as a white man yelling at Hispanic immigrants about terrorism in an Afghan strip-mall restaurant in suburban Virginia.

The wars in Afghanistan and eventually Iraq were heavily debated, prompting protests across the country. For those in support, they believed that military action would exact retributive justice against those who financed and supported the 9/11 attacks and in turn deter future acts of terrorism. However, the protracted conflicts did not yield such effects, as antiwar demonstrators had cautioned. In fact, the extremist ideas that motivated the 9/11 terrorists appeared to have proliferated, infecting the minds of an increasingly diverse group of young people.

Nearly two decades after 9/11, these young people are whom I now envision when I think of a *terrorist*.

They were lured into extremism following the wars in Afghanistan and Iraq, as terrorist organizations began exploring new outlets for effective propaganda.

The Afghan Taliban began publishing English-language magazines in 2009, starting with *In Fight* (see Image 1).

Al-Qaeda in the Arabian Peninsula followed suit by publishing *Inspire* magazine, beginning in 2010 (see Image 2).

Much of the magazines featured what was presumably inspiration for terrorists—images of Arab children who were killed in war, pictures of wounded American soldiers and funerals, as well as the aftermath of suicide-bomber attacks. While the overwhelming majority of the magazines were made up with nothing more than images of violence and war, a smaller proportion focused on religion. A manipulated interpretation of Islam was used as justification for their crimes:

> . . . But [even so], if there are a hundred of you, patient and persevering, they will vanquish two hundred, and if a thousand, they will vanquish two thousand, with the leave of Allah: for Allah is with those who patiently persevere.[3]

In the propaganda, terrorists would ask readers to pray for the *mujahideen* as follows:

> O Allah, make them and their weaponry a booty for the mujahideen. *You are our support and you are our only victor; By your order we attack; By your order we retreat and by your order we fight. O Allah, the sky is yours; the earth is yours; the sea is yours, so whatever forces they have in the sky, drop them. Destroy all their forces in earth and sink all their forces in sea. O Allah, deal with them for verily they can never disable you. Retaliate upon them, afflict them like you did the Pharaoh and his nation.*
>
> *O Allah defeat them, destroy them O the All-Strong, the All-Mighty Allahu Akbar.*
>
> *Honor, Power and Glory Belong to Allah, His Messenger and the believers, but the hypocrites know not.*[4]

American soldiers were labeled "invaders," "terrorists," or "enemies"; local ally militias and police were called "puppets" or "minions"; and Muslims who did not support terrorism were denounced as "apostates."

Given the success of these online magazines in gaining attention for the plight of terrorists, ISIS did the same, first with *Dabiq* magazine in 2014 (see Image 3), followed by *Rumiyah* magazine in 2016 (see Image 4).

In addition to magazines that boasted of victories and explained the purported ideology behind the group, ISIS also proliferated its message through its notorious and brutally violent videos, disseminated through social media savvy. Even after the horrific crimes on September 11, 2001, these images were a shock to the conscience.

* * *

MESSAGE TO AMERICA

Following a clip of President Barack Obama authorizing military airstrikes against the Islamic State, the video transitioned to a gaunt-looking white man, with a shaved head, kneeling in a desolate desert with his hands bound behind his back. He was wearing a prisoner-orange tunic-and-pant uniform, made to portray him as a criminal. A graphic of the black ISIS flag with white Arabic lettering waved in the top, right-hand corner of the video. At the bottom, there was a white label with the name of the prisoner in thin, black lettering: James Wright Foley.

Foley was a freelance journalist-photographer who was abducted in northwestern Syria while working as a war correspondent for the Global Post. The FBI believed that he was targeted after leaving an Internet café, where he was uploading his last images on November 22, 2012.[5] Armed men sped up behind his vehicle and forced Foley out at gunpoint.[6]

Almost two years after his kidnapping, and following a series of failed hostage negotiations and rescue attempts, Foley's ISIS captors filmed his last moments, as he read from a script:

> *I call on my friends, family, and loved ones to rise up against my real killers, the U.S. Government. For what will happen to me is only a result of their complacency and criminality.*

One of his captors stood next to him, wearing a balaclava mask, jet-black uni-form shirt and pants, with military boots and a brown leather gun holster over his left arm. He waited for his part in the script, with his feet shoulder-width apart and his head slightly tilted.

Foley continued, as the screen split—an image of him before his capture, look-ing healthier, wearing army fatigues and sunglasses to the left and him kneeling in the desert before his execution to the right.

> *My message to my beloved parents—save me some dignity and don't accept any meager compensation for my death from the same people who effectively hit the last nail in my coffin with their recent aerial campaign in Iraq. I call on my brother John, who is a member of the U.S. Air Force.*

Foley paused, seemingly choking back tears at the mention of his brother, prompting his captor to lean in and inch closer toward him, nonverbally intim-idating him to continue:

> *Think about what you are doing. Think about the lives you destroy, including those of your own family. I call on you, John. Think about who made the decision to bomb Iraq recently and kill those people, who-ever they may have been. Think John, who did they really kill? And did they think about me, you, our family when they made that decision? I died that day, John. When your colleagues dropped that bomb on those people, they signed my death certificate. I wish I had more time, I wish I could have the hope of freedom and seeing my family once again, but that ship has sailed. I guess, all in all, I wish I wasn't American."*

The video briefly faded to black before recording a statement from his on-screen captor, who now gripped a large knife with his left fist. He rested his right hand on Foley's upper back and pointed the knife at him. In a British accent, muffled by the mask, he professed, *"This is James Wright Foley, an American citizen of your country."* The terrorist turned his knife, pointing toward the camera, before continuing:

> *As a government, you have been at the forefront of the aggression towards the Islamic State. You have plotted against us and gone far*

out of your way to find reasons to interfere in our affairs. Today,
your military air force is attacking us daily in Iraq.

Again, he pointed the knife toward the camera for violent emphasis.

Your strikes have caused casualties amongst Muslims. You are no
longer fighting an insurgency. We are an Islamic army, a state that
has been accepted by a large number of Muslims worldwide. So
effectively any aggression towards the Islamic State is an aggression
to Muslims of all walks of life who have accepted the Islamic caliph-
ate as their leadership. So any attempt by YOU, Obama, to deny
Muslims their safety of living under the caliphate will result in the
bloodshed of your people.

The ISIS spokesman stepped directly behind Foley, who remained stoic with
his chest held high. He wrapped his right arm around Foley's head, placing
his hand tightly over his chin and mouth, took the knife in his left hand, and
began vigorously sawing on his neck.

The sounds of the knife cutting against him were gruesome. Although it was
only a few seconds, the noise reverberated until it was replaced with gurgling and
the video again faded to black.

The recording returned with the aftermath of the attack—James Foley's lifeless body lying in the desert sand, with his fully decapitated and bloodied head
resting on his back and handcuffed hands, facing the camera. A pool of blood
soaked the sand under his neck and chest. I had never seen someone commit such
a horrific crime, with a soulless and unflinching disregard for humanity. *This* was
a terrorist.

The video concluded by filming the masked murderer, who now gripped the
orange jumpsuit collar of another victim—Steven Joel Sotloff—as he kneeled in
the desert, also looking haggard with a shaved head.

"The life of this American citizen, Obama, depends on your next decision," he
ominously warned.

The world later learned that the man who perpetrated this horrific crime was
named Mohammed Emwazi. Although he was born in Kuwait, he moved to
the United Kingdom at age six and was raised in a middle-class neighborhood
in West London.[7] Emwazi was considered a member of the "Beatles of ISIS"—a

four-person terror cell of British ISIS recruits: Junaid Hussain from Birmingham, Mohammed Emwazi from London, Cardiff-born Reyaad Khan, and Raymond Matimba from Manchester.[8] As a member of the group, Emwazi was given the moniker "Jihadi John" by the Western media.

After the video of him beheading James Foley was disseminated to the world, Emwazi became the face of ISIS for a short time, which was particularly frightening because there was no apparent catalyst or explanation for his recruitment.

According to media reports, Emwazi had a relatively normal childhood, being raised in the United Kingdom by his Kuwaiti immigrant parents. His teachers described him as "a quiet young man and reasonably hardworking."[9] In school, he had some issues with bullies—girls making fun of the way he walked or his breath—but nothing extreme or out of the ordinary for primary school. He aspired to be a soccer player, liked French fries, pop music, and *The Simpsons*[10]—for all intents and purposes, he was a regular kid.

Emwazi eventually graduated with a degree in computer sciences from the University of Westminster, while also engaging in some minor delinquency and petty crime. He attempted to get his life back on track by planning to get married and securing a new job in his native country of Kuwait, but British authorities blocked his travel.[11] As a result, his fiancée called off their engagement.

Following these travel restrictions and encounters with law enforcement, Emwazi expressed frustration regarding what he perceived as the injustices toward and oppression of Muslims worldwide. In 2013, he disappeared, and his parents reported him as missing. The following year, he resurfaced in Islamic State beheading videos.

After brutally murdering James Foley on August 19, 2014, Emwazi went on to behead Israeli-American journalist Steven Sotloff and British aid workers David Haines and Alan Henning for ISIS propaganda.

When I first watched the footage of 9/11 and the beheading of James Foley, my initial reactions were based in *lex talionis*—the law of retaliation. I wanted the offenders—these terrorists—to be met with a punishment that was equivalent to the severity of the offenses they had committed. However, after further reflection, I questioned what affect that would have in preventing future acts of terrorism.

Prima facie, I, like many Americans, felt that the indiscriminate murder of civilians was an action that could only be committed by an evil person—whether by nature or nurture, someone who was or had become profoundly immoral and malevolent. Yet, each time I began researching the biographies of these terrorists, there was no discernible pattern of evil behaviors or lifelong religious extremism prior to their recruitment into terrorism.

For example, Mohammed Emwazi, like many terrorists, was an easily impressionable loner[12] who had expressed suicidal ideation in the past. Well before joining ISIS, Emwazi felt that British authorities were unfairly targeting him, preventing him from returning to his home country of Kuwait. In order to escape how he was being treated, he threatened to take as many pills as he could, so that he could sleep forever. He expressed that he felt like a "dead man walking,"[13] but instead of committing suicide, he was given a sense of belonging and purpose, albeit extreme and brutally violent, when he was recruited to join ISIS.

While in the United Kingdom, Emwazi was mentored by extremists who groomed him to be used like a puppet. Despite his evil acts, he wasn't the mastermind; he was a pawn. Preceding his recruitment, he did not hold particularly religious beliefs. In support of that fact, several news sources pointed out how Emwazi had smoked drugs and drunk alcohol during his adolescence, while neglecting to pray.

Religion is the veneer used by war profiteers and opportunists to recruit disposable people into terrorism. When examining the methods of terrorist recruitment, profiles of recruited terrorists, and the content of propaganda, it is clear that ISIS uses force, fraud, coercion, and deception to lure marginalized people into a position of exploitation.

Thoughts of a terrorist or terrorism elicit feelings of hate, disgust, and retribution for many people. In particular, the crimes committed on 9/11 and the murder of James Wright Foley provoke those feelings in me. However, that response is not how future acts of terrorism will be prevented.

"An eye for an eye" is the almost instinctive reaction to terrorism, but it is an instinct shared with the same terrorists who perpetrate these heinous crimes. In fact, terrorist propaganda advocates, by name, for *lex talionis* (see Image 5).[14]

As such, when crafting effective counterterrorism polices, the following should be considered:

> *An eye for an eye makes the whole world blind.*
> —Mahatma Gandhi

3

Entrapped

I was twenty-three years old when I first heard about the "Fort Dix Six."

I distinctly remember watching Chris Christie, who was the US Attorney for the District of New Jersey at the time, in a press conference outside of the Camden Federal Courthouse building, describing the thwarted terrorist attack. It was all over television. "The philosophy that supports and encourages jihad around the world against Americans, came to live here in New Jersey and threatened the lives of our citizens through these defendants. Fortunately, law enforcement in New Jersey was here to stop them," Christie said, while flanked by more than one dozen white male police officers, federal agents, and staff. My heart welled up with pride at the thought of American heroes stopping the bad guy terrorists and saving the day.

More than twenty microphones were lined up in front of him, while TV crews from the Associated Press, CNN, NBC, CBS, ABC, and Univision, among others, recorded. A flutter of cameras shuttered as he continued. "We brought criminal complaints today against six defendants involved in a plot to bring a violent attack on military and civilian personnel at Fort Dix, here in the state of New Jersey."

Christie told the reporters that three of the men, brothers, were "illegally here in the United States"—Eljvir, Dritan, and Shain Duka. Increased border security was a huge point of contention in the wake of 9/11, so many conservative politicians and pundits later used the illegal immigration status of these men as an anecdote to support their border security agenda.

What they failed to mention was the fact that these three men were nonimmigrant visa overstayers, meaning they didn't cross the border without documentation, and as such, any border wall or increase in border security would not have prevented them or others like them from coming to the United States and

Figure 3.1 Foreign National Typologies.

Legal	Illegal
Immigrant: Legal *permanent* resident or green card recipient; An immigrant can eventually apply to become a naturalized U.S. Citizen.	**Illegal Immigrant**: Violated the terms of entry by committing a crime of moral turpitude, becoming deportable under the Illegal Immigration Reform and Immigrant Responsibility Act (IIRIRA) of 1996.
Nonimmigrant: Legal *temporary* visitor and visa recipient; A nonimmigrant may include guest workers, tourists, students, and other short-term visitors to the United States.	**Illegal Nonimmigrant:** Violated the terms of entry by committing a crime of moral turpitude *or* overstaying a temporary visa, becoming deportable.
	Undocumented Migrant: Crossed the border by completely evading immigration checkpoints *or* entered through other fraudulent means, such as using another person's travel documentation. Immediately deportable.

Source: Mehlman-Orozco, Kimberly. 2017. *Hidden in Plain Sight: America's Slaves of the New Millennium.* ABC-Clio.

overstaying their visa. Politicians often used the arrests of legal permanent residents, nonimmigrants, and visa overstayers to support laws that impact undocumented migrants—an entirely different population (see Figure 3.1).

Christie went on to explain that a fourth defendant, Mohamad Shnewer, was recorded on tape as saying, "My intent is to hit a heavy concentration of American soldiers, light up four or five Humvees full of soldiers."

A fifth defendant, Serdar Tatar, allegedly prepared for the attack by using his knowledge of the base, which included a detailed map of Fort Dix. According to Christie, Tatar was recorded describing where they could hit the base to cause a power outage, which would make it easier for them to "kill as many American soldiers as possible"—a threat that reverberated across the media.

The lede from the *New York Times* read, "Six Muslim men from New Jersey and Philadelphia were charged Tuesday with plotting to attack Fort Dix with automatic weapons and possibly even rocket-propelled grenades, vowing in taped conversations 'to kill as many soldiers as possible.'"[1]

The *Associated Press* wrote, "Six foreign-born Muslims were arrested and accused Tuesday of plotting to attack Fort Dix and slaughter scores of US soldiers—a scheme the FBI says was foiled when the men asked a store clerk to copy a video of them firing assault weapons and screaming about jihad."[2]

NPR reiterated, "Six foreign-born Muslims have been arrested for plotting an attack on the Fort Dix Army base in New Jersey. Investigators say the men planned to 'kill as many soldiers as possible.'"[3]

Within the first few words of each news story on the Fort Dix Six, the author seemed to always describe the men as being Muslim and foreign-born. According to the media accounts, the group of male friends and relatives rented a house in the Poconos in Pennsylvania in late December 2006, where they recorded video of themselves skiing, hiking, joking around, and shooting guns.[4] Following the trip, the youngest Duka brother, Burim, who was not charged in the case, took the 8mm video to Circuit City to convert it into a DVD. The Circuit City clerk who converted the video saw what he thought were illegal, fully automatic weapons and claimed to have heard the words *jihad* and *Allahu Akbar*, which prompted him, after some thought, to alert local law enforcement.

Given the nature of the potential threat, which was perceived as terrorists training for an attack, the FBI quickly became involved, and two informants were implanted to gain additional information from the group. The recordings from the informants were the primary basis for the arrests. According to Christie, the recordings included Tatar saying that he was "prepared to die in service of Allah," as well as conversations between Shnewer and Tartar on how they had missed an opportunity to kill even more military personnel at the Army-Navy game in Philadelphia.

On May 7, 2007, the FBI set up a sting operation, which involved Dritan and Shain Duka making arrangements to purchase three AK-47s and four M-16 fully automatic machine guns, as well as four handguns. According to Christie, the purchase of these weapons would have completed their preparation for the attack on Fort Dix, if it were not for law enforcement apprehending them and extinguishing the danger.

A year and a half later, five[5] of the men—Shain, Eljvir, and Dritan Duka; Mohamad Shnewer; and Serdar Tatar—were convicted of conspiring to kill American soldiers. Dritan and Shain Duka were sentenced to life in prison plus thirty years, Eljvir Duka and Mohamad Shnewer were sentenced to life, and Serdar Tatar was sentenced to thirty-three years in federal prison."[6] Like many Americans, I didn't question the guilt of these men and (at least initially) celebrated their convictions as victories in preventive policing against terrorism.

I don't remember hearing anything more about their case or even really thinking about it until six years later, when I decided to write them. Memories of their highly publicized arrest and conviction had stayed with me, and I wanted to gain insight on how they perceived their crimes and how they were recruited into extremism. Their responses, however, were very different from what I expected.

Eljvir Duka, the youngest of the three incarcerated brothers, was the first to respond. From his high security prison cell in Terre Haute, Indiana, he wrote:

(1) Why did you do what you are convicted of?

I received your greeting card and don't mind to respond. I kind of take your first question[7] with a smile because I understand how you can automatically believe that because I/we have been convicted, therefore we actually did it. We are actually innocent of the charges and didn't do anything that the gov't accuses us of doing. If you actually are shown the evidence, you will see that actually we say the opposite of what the gov't claimed. I and my two brothers with me actually stated in the government's secret recordings that we are not involved in any plot or even plan on harming anyone in the uniformed services or otherwise. Now, part of those recordings never made it before the jury because the judge prevented us from doing so. There are many lawyers and other activists who have actually seen the evidence in our case and have strongly spoken against our wrongful convictions. But I must admit that the prejudice in so-called terrorism cases is indeed very hard to overcome. So that's that. We have to live with this so far.

(2) If you could tell the world one thing, what would it be?

If you are asking about one thing I would tell the world in regards to my case, that is "We are innocent!" and what happens in courtrooms on so-called terrorism cases is not justice. Rather injustice. All geared to play upon prejudices, the public's emotions, and misconceptions which already exist in the public and not upon facts. And worst of all, especially with their informants (who are mostly actual criminals whom the government has caught and forces them to cooperate or otherwise face long and harsh punishments) they lie. Their testimony is tailored through the tutoring of FBI agents and the U.S. attorneys to lie and say the things, which fill in the holes in their case just to gain convictions. It's not about truth and justice. It's only about "How we can win this one."

(3) Why do people commit acts of terrorism?

It's a very hard question to answer, as I do not know what goes on in people's hearts and minds. Some people have exploited their reasons by themselves, so I guess no person can say it better than themselves. I've actually read the self-published manifesto of that former African American cop in California who killed several people last year or two.[8] Others have done the same. So I guess several reasons of different people are already known. All we can do is speculate.

(4) What is the best way for the United States to prevent future acts of terrorism?

This is a very broad question because many groups of people are involved. But in my opinion—to try and put it simply—Justice! Justice is key to life. Also what is important is to keep to yourself. We find that this is a key factor in our own personal lives in avoiding problems.

Hopefully your questions have been answered. I appreciate your card sent to me. Feel welcomed.

Best Regards,
Eljvir Duka

Shain Duka, the second oldest of the incarcerated brothers, responded four days later:

> *Upon receiving your letter (card) and read [sic] the contents in it, my first response was anger and unbelief how one can send such a letter. The reason for this instant emotion is because I have spent nearly 7½ years in prison—nearly 6 years spent in solitary confinement—for a crime that I did not commit. Being stripped from my family, sent to the supermax prison—the ADX in Florence, Colorado—and labeled as a terrorist solely for political reasons. In addition to that I have a life plus 30 years sentence. But only God knows my true sentence.*
>
> *I immediately dropped the letter and tried to ignore it. I began pondering and thought of the ignorance of how people have a*

tendency to listen to one side and automatically assume one is guilty if they have been convicted. I began thinking some more and understood that these questions have been stuck in your head enough to drive you to inquire about them. That's when I decided that, "let me write to maybe break the ignorance and dig deeper upon these so called terrorism cases." This is the reason why I am writing back.

As stated above, I am innocent! I've claimed my innocence since day one and hold to that claim. I am not a terrorist so I can't answer or satisfy your questions. I urge you though to dig deeper and have another look at my case. You should be able to Google my name or even "Fort Dix 5" and find the other side of the story. There is plenty more than what the government portrayed about me being. A fact is that there are judges, lawyers, law professors, law students, human rights movements, family, friends, and complete strangers who have organized and are in my support. These people and some high officials in the legal field who support me cannot be ignored. Obviously they have seen something! I have received letters from all over the world from complete strangers stating that they believe in my innocence. So please, I urge you to do more research on my case and hear the other side. I am sure you will have a different opinion.

There is terrorism and extremism in all walks of life. Individuals, groups, politicians, and even governments perform acts of terrorism. They support their extremism on maybe their religious belief, their political view, or their objective. It is not only Islam and Muslims who are terrorists. Cite the man in Norway who killed over 70+ people.[9] He justified it upon his Christian belief. I also want you to ponder over and consider this: The United States—who is the only nation in the world to use an atomic weapon upon people—dropped one atomic bomb in the Japanese city of Hiroshima and another on the city of Nagasaki. Who was the intended target in the middle of these densely populated cities? Well over 100,000 civilians died instantly from the bomb and over 100,000 more civilians died from after effects. Til' this day, there are suffering Japanese civilians due to those blasts. Japan has yet to receive an apology from the U.S. This event has not been labeled as an act of terror, rather it was justified and celebrations erupted in the U.S.

because of the Japanese surrender from the result of these bombs.

So who is a terrorist? Who defines terrorism? And is terrorism ever justified??? These are questions I cannot answer. I will suggest a book for you to read which I have come across. It may help you with some of the questions that you posed to me. The book is titled "Nemesis: The Last Days of the American Republic" by Chalmers Johnson.

Once again, I was annoyed at first with your letter, but then encouraged by your courage in attempting to have these questions that may be troubling you for answers. I apologize that I am not the one to have the answers for you, but encourage you to research matters deeper before basing opinions. Please do dig deeper into my case your opinions or assumptions may change.

Respectfully,
Shain Duka

Most of the terrorists who responded to my inquiries admitted to what they were convicted of without reservation. The Duka brothers, however, maintained their innocence. While claiming innocence is common practice among inmates convicted of other crimes, it was less common with convicted terrorists. In later correspondence, Eljvir encouraged me to contact his younger brother, Burim; his mom, Lata; and his dad, Firik. He also urged me to watch a minidocumentary published by the *Intercept*, which, Eljvir explained, "gives a fair idea on what happened" to them.

The *Intercept* article was titled "Christie's Conspiracy: The Real Story Behind the Fort Dix Five Terror Plot," and the accompanying video was called "Entrapped."

The video opens with a clip from Chris Christie's news conference, the morning after the arrests, summarizing the allegations against the Duka brothers. That was the story disseminated in the public, but this video went on to shed insight into the brothers' home life and interactions with the informants before their arrest.

Their father, Firik, sipped coffee on the porch of his suburban home and smoked a cigarette, while birds chirped in the background. In a heavy Yugoslavian accent, he proclaimed, "Their judgment is God's judgment, whatever your deeds are, you're going to be judged for."

Burim, the youngest brother, who was not charged or convicted of any crime related to the Fort Dix plot, explained that the brothers owned and worked in a roofing company and in the winter, when they couldn't work because of the snow, would vacation in the Poconos.

Christie described their trip to the Poconos as being for training purposes in preparation for their attack on Fort Dix, but the video in the minidocumentary showed clips of the men snowboarding, commenting on the beautiful vistas, horseback riding, and at a shooting range—saying Allahu Akbar, God is great, while shooting at snowballs and targets. There was no mention of "jihad" and the video revealed what many would consider a typical "guys' trip."

After the Circuit City employee turned the video in to the authorities, two informants were paid to infiltrate the group: Besnik Bakalli, an undocumented migrant who was facing deportation after shooting a man in his home country of Albania, and Mahmoud Omar, an undocumented migrant from Egypt who was facing deportation after being convicted of bank fraud. Omar was paid $238,000 for his undercover work.

While under video surveillance, Bakali repeatedly attempted to convince the Duka brothers to join the "jihad," but they wouldn't take the bait and even stated that they didn't want to do anything to hurt anyone. They claimed it was *haram*, forbidden, to do so.

Burim explained that the other codefendant, Shnewer, wasn't like his brothers and said all kinds of crazy things, which were captured on camera. "If you want to do anything there is Fort Dix, and I assure you we can hit that easily," Shnewer explained to the informant—Omar.

However, during the more than 300 hours of conversation between the Duka brothers and their friends, the Dukas never mentioned any plot to attack Fort Dix. Moreover, the videos revealed the informant coercing Shnewer, who was described by family as being immature and impressionable, to download terrorist propaganda and concoct a plot to attack America. The evidence also uncovered that Serdar Tatar had reported the informant to a Philadelphia police sergeant for pressuring him to acquire maps of Fort Dix. Tatar expressed fear that it might be terrorist-related and attempted to alert the authorities, to no avail.

Mohamed Shnewer later wrote a letter to the judge stating that he believes the jury's decision to convict the Duka brothers was derived from the lies and the allegations that he said about the codefendants. The informant, Omar, stated Mohammed Shnewer wronged the Duka brothers and that he never heard anything about them planning an attack against Fort Dix. The informant said the Duka brothers were "good and kind people."

When the Duka brothers refused to engage in conversations about planning an attack, the government set up a sting operation to catch them attempting to illegally purchase guns. Given the below-market pricing on the weapons and their penchant for recreational shooting ranges, the Duka brothers admitted to attempting to illegally make the purchase but vehemently denied that the weapons were intended to harm any person. They repudiated having any awareness of the plot against Fort Dix.

Years after their convictions, some media outlets also began questioning the guilt of the Duka brothers.

"The outrageous, manufactured case against the 'Fort Dix Five,'" read one piece in the *Washington Post*.

"Fort Dix Five: Prosecuted by Christie, Muslim Brothers Get Rare Day in Court in FBI Entrapment Case," read another headline from *Democracy Now!*

The family, friends, and supporters of the Duka brothers were hopeful that they would have another chance to argue their innocence, but in 2016 the brothers lost their sole remaining claim for freedom.

Given the lack of evidence connecting the Duka brothers to the plot against Fort Dix, how did they end up convicted terrorists sentenced to life in federal prison?

The answer rests on the controversial policing tactics employed in America since 9/11. Counterterrorism informants have been known to target mentally ill, homeless, and other marginalized people, and coerce their involvement into fabricated terrorist plots with harassment, fraud, bribery, threats, and other radicalization tactics.

For example, the case of Matthew Llaneza, who, like many kids at risk of being recruited into extremism, was described as a "different child" who found it difficult to make friends. He was regularly bullied throughout elementary, middle, and high school.

As a young adult, Matthew was treated for schizophrenia, bipolar disorder, depression, and anxiety disorders. He believed that secret police were trying to follow him, was fearful of helicopters flying overhead, and entertained other delusions about work and romantic relationships.

While attending a Bay area community college, Matthew befriended a group of Muslim American students, which led to him converting to Islam. However, his psychological illnesses progressed, and during one paranoia episode, Matthew's father, Steve, sought mental health assistance for his son by calling 9-1-1. When the ambulance arrived, Matthew was shouting, "They're going to kill me! . . . Allahu Akbar! God is great!"[10]

While in the emergency room, Matthew told police that he suffered from mental illness and admitted to attempting suicide. He claimed that he knew how to assemble a gun from scratch, before banging his head against the wall and trying to choke himself.

Police later found an AK-47 in a safe in his Winnebago, which resulted in a gun charge conviction and a sentence of six months in jail. After his release, the FBI placed him under surveillance. First, they attempted to pressure him into violating his probation by visiting a shooting range to no avail, but the FBI didn't give up. They continued isolating Matthew and coercing him to pursue "jihad" in the United States. Matthew eventually acquiesced to their pressure and helped his undercover FBI agent "best friend" plan a bomb attack against a bank, which could have never been carried out on his own accord.

During Matthew's sentencing hearing, the judge acknowledged that his involvement in the bombing plot was part of an effort to "belong" and a by-product of his mental illness. Nevertheless, he was sentenced to fifteen years in federal prison.

When discussing preventive counterterrorism, more than one pundit has compared the practice to the Steven Spielberg's movie *Minority Report*. If you arrest a person before they commit a crime, they haven't broken the law. The movie's plot focused on the paradox of punishing someone for a crime that was prevented. Going a step further in regard to counterterrorism, the conspiracy of the crime may have never been set in motion, if it weren't for the coercive informant catalyzing a butterfly effect.

Since Muslims are more likely to be targeted for surveillance and undercover information gathering in counterterrorism actions, they are at greater risk of being entrapped in the same.

Simply thinking or talking about committing a crime shouldn't be an indictable offense, and for crimes other than terrorism, courts have treaded lightly on attempting to control freedom of thought and expression. Even conspiracy needs to involve an agreement to commit a crime and actions taken to actually complete it, not just hyperbole. For example, former New York police officer Gilberto Valle was charged and convicted for discussing with other online enthusiasts his intention to abduct, torture, cook, and eat women, including his wife.[11] He looked up women's information in a police database and researched chloroform recipes, but his attorneys claimed those discussions and actions were nothing more than a fetish, without any intent to commit an actual crime. While he was initially convicted of a conspiracy to kidnap and cannibalize, he was later acquitted on appeal because the court ruled it was just "fantasy" that was "protected by the US Constitution."

Since thinking and talking about crimes you have no intention of committing aren't indictable offenses, should discussions or actions that are initiated by undercover police officers or informants be criminalized? Young and impressionable people are at risk of being coerced, defrauded, and forced into all sorts of crime, including gangs, human trafficking, and terrorism. In order to combat these crimes, we shouldn't be facilitating radicalization in order to land preventive convictions. A more pragmatic approach would be to invest in support systems to prevent radicalization, such as education, risk assessments, counseling, mental healthcare, and social services.

In the aftermath of 9/11, the FBI should not be the organization responsible for planning the majority of terrorist plots in the United States.[12] Given the coercive and sometimes overbearing tactics used to induce terrorism conspiracies, it is questionable whether these crimes would have occurred in the absence of government intervention.

Although our counterterrorism investigation and policing tactics may be well intentioned, those intentions do not justify manipulating people into radicalization as a means to an end.

After all, *the road to hell is paved with good intentions.*

PART II

4

Sister of Terror

On March 30, 2015, the Islamic State of Iraq and Levant (ISIL) released Issue 8 of *Dabiq*—an online, English-language magazine used for radicalization and recruitment. While the mentions of women in the seven previous issues were scarce or nonexistent, the eighth issue contained a six-page feature addressed to women—"our sisters"—titled "The Twin Halves of the Muhajirin."*

The article, authored by a "jihadi bride"—Umm Sumayyah al-Muhajirah—stressed the importance of females embarking on *hijrah*.

In Islam, *hijrah* refers to the Prophet Muhammad's migration from Mecca—a place where he and his companions were aggressively persecuted for over a decade—to the predominately Jewish city of Medina, where Mohammed established a secular state with the Jews through the Constitution of Medina. Following the *hijrah*, Mohammed lived alongside pagan Arab tribes and Jewish people in peace.

This *Dabiq* article, however, described it as a migration from the places of disbelief and sin "to the land of Islam and obedience." Essentially, the article tried to convince women living in Western countries to migrate to Syria. According to the author, this is important because otherwise they will face tribulations and will be so affected by them, the disbelievers, and sin that they could experience a "death of the heart," which would make Islam, and its people "unrecognizable."

This claim illustrates ISIL's propensity for gaslighting—a form of manipulation that sows seeds of doubt in order to make the target question her or his own perception. The *Dabiq* article's argument is such that if you don't live with ISIL in their "Islamic State," you won't be able to recognize Islam, and therefore any critiques of their terrorist tactics and interpretations of Islam are invalid.

The author claimed that by joining men in *hijrah*, women would "strengthen their forces, and wage jihad against the enemies of Allah and their enemies," something she declared was obligatory for women, just as it was for men.

Al-Muhajirah went on to explain that she was the only Arab woman during her migration, suggesting the other women were mostly from outside the Middle East and North Africa. Although some assume these women are coming from marginalized places, facing unemployment, poverty, family problems, and psychological disorders, the author claimed she saw the opposite—women abandoning beautiful homes and luxurious cars to "depart for her Lord's cause."

According to al-Muhajirah, the first "obstacle" is family. She told the story of one woman who attempted to enter Syria with her husband, but soldiers stopped her at the airport because her parents notified the police.

If the woman bypasses what is described as the "obstacle of family," al-Muhajirah promised an exciting journey, full of memories, where she will leave darkness and caves for light and green land.

Al-Muhajirah gave more examples of women who migrated to Syria, two while expecting children. One traveled from Britain with her husband while six months pregnant. The other traveled by car with her husband through three countries, until she reached the Islamic State, where her son died during birth "due to pregnancy complications apparently caused by the difficulty of the trip." Yet al-Muhajirah rationalized this tragedy by claiming it was better for the newborn to die in the Islamic State than "die through the curriculum" of non-Muslim schools.

Last, the author described an elderly grandmother who traveled with her son, daughter, and grandchild. She claimed the woman told her, "My son was killed, so I came with my other son, my daughter, and my grandson!" To which al-Muhajirah replied, "Allah is the greatest! You've raised the bar for everyone after you!"

Al-Muhajirah concluded by pleading for women who performed what she described as *hijrah* to stay in the Islamic State and not ever return to their home country, even if their husband were to be killed, paralyzed, imprisoned, or have a limb amputated. She asked them to stay firm, "like the firmest of mountains." She claimed that "reward is in accordance with the degree of hardship"; just be patient. Patience is a theme reverberated across terrorist propaganda, given that their living conditions are often abysmal and inconsistent with the "paradise" that was promised.

The content included in this article of *Dabiq* demonstrates how the propaganda used to recruit women into terrorism is similar to tactics used to recruit and enmesh victims of sex trafficking.

Discussing family as an "obstacle" is the first red flag. Distancing a victim from her social support system is a tactic utilized to facilitate manipulation and exploitation.

Second, many of the women discussed in the feature were traveling with their husbands or in the pursuit of finding a husband. In the forthcoming chapters, it will become abundantly clear that romantic interests recruit the vast majority of women, especially from Western countries, into traveling to Syria and/or joining terrorist organizations. These women are manipulated into believing that the men coercing them to come to the Islamic State "love them," even though they are unwittingly being exploited. Convicted sex traffickers also often claim they were "in love" with their victims, despite exploiting and abusing them.[1]

Romantic love has been described by experts in the field as one of the most powerful sensations on earth, based in the reptilian core of the brain, below cognition and emotion.[2] From this area, feelings of love create and disperse dopamine in a way that drives desire, motivation, focus, and craving. The feeling can possess you and make you lose your sense of self to the point that you become willing to risk everything for it. For this reason, fabricated feelings of "love" are an effective tool for conscripting victims, as well as terrorists.

5

Jihad Jane

Colleen LaRose made headlines in 2010, after the US-born, blonde-haired, blue-eyed woman was charged with conspiracy to provide material support to terrorists, conspiracy to kill in a foreign country, giving a false statement to a government official, and attempted identity theft.

At the time, she was one of only a handful of women to be charged with terrorism in the United States,[1] and her appearance raised new fears about homegrown extremists who didn't fit the Arab male stereotype.[2] Although LaRose may not have fit the "terrorist profile," she absolutely exhibited the characteristics that elevate the risk of radicalization among Westerners, which bridge across socioeconomic and demographic groups—a need to fill the voids for love and belonging.

LaRose was raised near Detroit, Michigan, and had a tumultuous upbringing. Her parents were heavy drinkers and divorced when she was only three years old. Her biological father later began raping her repeatedly from age eight until age thirteen. LaRose was only in second grade when her father first appeared at her bedroom door, holding a bottle of lotion, signaling her to undress.[3] In order to escape the incest and sexual abuse, she dropped out of school, ran away, and began engaging in survival sex after seventh grade. For several years, LaRose lived on the streets, using heroin and cocaine and earning money in exchange for commercial sex acts.

At only sixteen, she married a man twice her age named Sheldon Barnum. A miscarriage left her unable to have children, and LaRose divorced her husband shortly thereafter. A year after getting married, she sought help from a teen runaway shelter in Memphis, Tennessee, which treated her for sexually transmitted diseases and had her committed to a psychiatric facility for several months.[4]

By age twenty-three, LaRose had made her way to Texas, where she married Rodolfo "Rudy" Cavazos in 1986. While married to Cavazos, LaRose was described as "good person" who went to church and carried a bible.[5] LaRose and Cavazos stayed together for ten years, but he eventually filed for divorce in 1997.

LaRose moved into a singlewide trailer with her mother, stepfather, and sister in an area south of Dallas, where she later met a new love interest—Kurt Gorman. Gorman had traveled from Pennsylvania to Texas for work to repair a radio tower in 2002. After hitting it off, LaRose quickly left her family and home in Texas and went to live with him in Pennsburg, Pennsylvania.

Gorman traveled often for work and didn't pay much attention to what LaRose did with her time when he was away. He never fathomed that she would be capable of joining a terrorist group and plotting a murder. In an interview with CNN, Gorman reacted to the news of LaRose's arrest, saying, "she wasn't no rocket scientist . . . she was limited in her capacity there, so . . . I don't know how much thought she could actually do on her own."[6]

While living with Gorman, LaRose didn't really have any friends or hobbies and was unemployed. For several years, she passed the time by caring for Gorman's elderly father, talking on the phone with her sister in Texas, watching music videos and movies, playing video games, and flirting with anonymous men in online chat rooms. She also suffered from depression.

Following the deaths of her brother and stepfather, LaRose attempted suicide on May 21, 2005, by ingesting as many as ten cyclobenzaprine pills—a muscle relaxant—and alcohol.[7] Fearing that she might attempt suicide, LaRose's sister in Texas called 9-1-1 to have police check on her in Pennsylvania. LaRose appeared to be under the influence of substances, but in response to questions from police, she declared that she didn't want to die.

Two years later, while on a vacation in Amsterdam in 2007, LaRose became intoxicated and started arguing with her boyfriend. In order to diffuse the situation, he left LaRose at the bar. She was alone, drinking, when a Muslim man approached and began flirting with her. To spite her boyfriend, LaRose left the bar to have sex with the man.

This one-night stand—what would be considered *haram* (a forbidden sin)—was what piqued her curiosity in Islam.

When she returned from Amsterdam to Pennsylvania, LaRose began secretly visiting websites about Islam and used her boyfriend's credit card to sign up for a Muslim dating website—Muslima.com. She met strangers who "mentored" her on the basics of the religion online and eventually helped her convert to Islam via instant messenger, taking the Muslim name Fatima LaRose. She later recalled that the conversion gave her a sense of belonging that had been largely absent throughout her life.[8]

Over the next two years, LaRose became fixated with YouTube videos of Israeli attacks on Palestinians and American attacks on Iraqis.[9] YouTube also provided the bulk of her religious instruction. She began actively posting comments and sending messages under the handle "JihadJane," without taking any measures to conceal her true identity:

> **Jihad Jane**: *I'm desperate to do something, somehow, to help the suffering Muslim people.*
> **Anonymous 1**: *I want to wage jihad and become a* shahed.*
> **Jihad Jane**: *I want to become a martyr too.*
> **Anonymous 2**: *I tried to enter martyrdom twice, but wasn't successful. I will try again until Allah will make it easy for me.*
> **Jihad Jane**: *Insha'Allah† I'll become a martyr too. You know, I have blonde hair and blue eyes. With my American citizenship, I could blend in with many people, which may help me achieve what is in my heart—martyrdom.*
> **Eagle Eye**: *I can deal in bombs and explosives effectively and you can certainly get access to many places due to your nationality. Marry me, so we can get inside Europe.*
> **Jihad Jane**: *Yes, I can obtain residence in a European country and we can get married to give you access.*
> **Eagle Eye**: *This is what I say to you—I want you to go to Sweden, find the location of Lars Vilks, and kill him to prove your loyalty.*
> **Jihad Jane**: *I will make this my goal till I achieve it or die trying.*
> **Eagle Eye**: *Kill him in a manner that the whole* Kufar‡ *world will be frightened.*
> **Jihad Jane**: *It is an honor and great pleasure to die or kill for the cause. Only death will stop me once I get close to the target.*[10]

The instructions to kill Swedish cartoonist Lars Vilks came from an anonymous al-Qaeda operative based in Pakistan, known only as "EagleEye." In

---

* Martyr.
† God-willing.
‡ Nonbeliever. Alternatively spelled kuffar.

2007, Vilks had sketched three drawings that depicted the head of the Prophet Muhammad on the body of a dog—which many considered blasphemous. Al-Qaeda responded by offering a $100,000 bounty for his assassination.

In response to the assignment, LaRose's heart quickened with adrenaline, as she felt a sense of purpose and belonging like never before and took multiple steps to carry out the attack. First, she sent an electronic communication to the Swedish Embassy, asking for instructions on how to acquire permanent residency status in Sweden. Next, she used other online contacts to post messages soliciting funds for the operation and other extremist endeavors. LaRose then performed online searches about Vilks and his location, joined an online community he hosted, and became a "citizen" of his artists enclave. Finally, after "EagleEye" connected LaRose with two European-based operatives—Ali Charaf Damache a.k.a. "Black Flag" and an alleged al-Qaeda operative known only as "Abdullah"—she packed up her belongings, stole her boyfriend's passport, removed the hard drive from her computer, and made arrangements to travel to Europe with the intent of living and training with terrorists to eventually assassinate Vilks.

Before she could even board a flight, the FBI was monitoring LaRose's online activity and visited her on two separate occasions. The first time she didn't answer the door, but, at the instruction of her al-Qaeda handler, LaRose later called the number on the business card left behind by the agent. During the conversation, she denied visiting extremist Islamic forums, claimed that she didn't know anyone who went by the online handle JihadJane, and told him that she never solicited money for terrorists—lies that later amounted to a federal offense.

During the second encounter with the FBI, LaRose admitted to converting to Islam and visiting Muslim websites but again denied any criminal activity. Two days later, she boarded a flight to Europe.

LaRose was elated with her arrival in Amsterdam. She felt significant and empowered. During the taxi ride to the mosque where she was scheduled to meet her al-Qaeda host, LaRose was singing the lyrics to *The Mary Tyler Moore Show* in her head.[11]

> *Who can turn the world on with her smile?*
> *Who can take a nothing day, and suddenly make it all seem worthwhile?*
> *Well it's you girl, and you should know it.*
> *With each glance and every little movement you show it.*

By this point, LaRose had survived a long history of sexual trauma, drug addiction, and failed relationships. She craved attention, belonging, and love and wanted to feel needed. The anonymous men whom she met online, claiming to be al-Qaeda operatives, made her feel valued.

It wasn't until she was away from her family that the façade began to fade.

LaRose arrived at the mosque to find no one waiting for her. She stood in the rain with her luggage for about an hour before a woman met her and took her to the home of her host—Abdullah—but he wasn't what she expected. There was no teaching, training, or missions. Their life amounted to the same mundane existence with daily struggles that she experienced previously—every day a repetitive exercise. LaRose no longer felt empowered or important, much less content.

Two weeks later, she packed her bags and traveled to the residence of "Black Flag" also known as Ali Charaf Damache. Damache was born in Algeria but raised in France before immigrating to Ireland. In addition to his online communications with LaRose, he had communicated with another blonde-haired American woman named Jamie Paulin Ramirez, whom the media dubbed "Jihad Jamie."

Ramirez was a single mom residing in a small mountain town in Colorado when she began researching Islam for a college paper. She had been divorced three times and was living with her mother to save money. After she converted to Islam, Ramirez met Damache online and through much convincing agreed to travel to Ireland, marry him, and join his "jihad."

Immediately upon her arrival in Ireland, Ramirez and Damache were wed. A few days later, LaRose came to live with them. Damache slept in the sole bedroom of the apartment, while Ramirez, her son, and LaRose slept in the living room. Damache had promised to teach Ramirez Arabic and the Qur'an, but instead she was ordered to stay home, cook, and clean.

In a typed diary, Ramirez lamented: "I wish I was never stupid enough to come here . . . I am just a sex slave to him . . . I cry because I always wanted a person in my life who could love me for who I am."[12]

It wasn't long before both women wanted to return to the United States.

Although LaRose had more freedoms than Ramirez—she was allowed to have a key to the apartment and leave to pray with other Muslim women at the local mosque—none of the plans from "EagleEye" materialized. Again, there was no training or planning, much less any "jihad," and her new host "Black Flag" was perpetually unemployed and appeared to use his interpretation of the Qur'an to gaslight the women in the house.

LaRose began to come to the realization that Damache and Abdullah projected themselves to be religious and romantic heroes on the Internet, but in reality they were tentative, manipulative, and chauvinistic pedestrians. More important, other Muslims didn't even share their beliefs. They weren't anything special, and, to them, neither was LaRose. Without an opportunity to self-actualize and become the terrorist version of Mary Tyler Moore, LaRose felt homesick and emailed her ex-boyfriend, Kurt Gorman.

Once Gorman got LaRose on the phone, he told her that her mother was ill, near death, and she needed to come home—a ruse concocted by federal police. LaRose alerted the FBI about her plan to repatriate to the United States, and Gorman paid for her return flight. LaRose was afraid to tell "Black Flag" about her desire to return home, unsure of whether she knew too much or if her life would be in danger. At first, "Black Flag" tried to talk LaRose out of leaving but eventually just let her go, even giving her a ride to the airport.

As soon as the flight landed in Philadelphia, FBI agents boarded the aircraft and arrested LaRose. Given her cooperation with police, Jihad Jane was sentenced to only ten years in federal prison. At one point, she was scheduled for release on July 8, 2018, but at the time of this writing, the Bureau of Prisons Federal Inmate Locator database listed LaRose's release date as "unknown."

* * *

I received a letter from Colleen LaRose in November 2014, nearly six months after I mailed my inquiry to her. I imagine the time lapse was due to her correspondence being under surveillance. The envelope from her letter had been sealed and subsequently opened, with a careful cut along the top. Whoever read and/or copied the contents then resealed the letter with Scotch Tape.

I also noticed that the postage was a stamp with the American flag and fireworks but was affixed to the envelope upside down—a symbol of distress (see Image 6). At the time of our correspondence, she had been incarcerated for more than four years, but her extremist views hadn't wavered.

(1) Why did you do what you are convicted of?
There's many reasons but the simplest reason is I did it for love. Love for my prophet, love for the Brother that gave me the assignment. Also, I think I did it for pride. Sisters are never given assignments

like the one I was given. I felt my Brother had enough confidence and trust in me that he honored me by giving me the assignment. I felt if he loved me that much, then I had to do what he told me needed to be done.

(2) If you could tell the world one thing, what would it be?

I would say that my Ummah* *is the most kind and loving people and please just leave them alone and quit invading their lands. Quit bombing them and stay out of their lands. I love my Brothers and Sisters in Islam and I just want for them what everyone wants for their loved ones. How hard is it to just give my* Ummah *peace and leave them lone.*

(3) Why do people commit acts of terrorism?

In my opinion, the Brothers and many other people "engage in terrorism" because they want to let it be known that the situation of their people is not good. People are quick to judge without knowing exactly why the so-called terrorist took the measures they resort to. People still don't understand why 9/11 happened. In many Muslim lands they are occupied by American troops. Osama bin Laden had several times said to get the troops out of their lands, but his requests fell on deaf ears. He had to take actions to make his point and to make people realize what is still going on in their lands. Just think of it like if America was invaded and occupied by many forces and these forces killed men, women, and children and caused many families to lose their homes. If this type of thing happens in America of course Americans would fight back and do what has to be done to end the occupation of their land.

(4) What, in your opinion, is the best way for the United States to prevent future acts of terrorism?

I go back to what I've already stated. Get the troops out of Iraq, Afghanistan, Somalia, Pakistan and all the other Muslim lands. And quit supporting the real terrorists—the Zionist in Palestine that are constantly killing men, women, and children so they can take over the Ummah's *land. The majority of Americans have no idea how hard life is for the Palestinians. I've witness the atrocity committed*

---

* Collective Muslim community.

against the Palestinians and yet America turns a blind eye on what is going on over there and the U.S. government supports the filthy Zionist. Look at what the U.S. has recently done in Iraq. Is it any wonder the Brothers from groups like ISIS take matters into their own hands? Someone has to defend our Ummah.

You may not like my answers, but I wrote what I feel and answered truthfully.

Best regards,
Fatima LaRose

My correspondence with Colleen LaRose suggested that she had latched onto an identity that she felt provided her with a sense of love and belonging. She clearly didn't have a robust understanding of Islam and interpreted conflicting information through the same gaslit lens with which the religion was introduced to her.

Religious leaders have said, unequivocally, that her actions and beliefs, as well as the actions and beliefs of other self-proclaimed "jihadists," do not represent Islam in any way, shape, or form. Instead, LaRose represents a population at high risk of manipulation, exploitation, and radicalization. Data on crime suggest that the same population that is at risk of victimization is at risk of criminalization.

For example, survivors of child sexual abuse, like LaRose, can often suffer from Child Sexual Abuse Accommodation Syndrome (CSAAS) or Rape Trauma Syndrome (RTS), which can lead them to reacting to victimizations with secrecy, helplessness, and/or feelings of entrapment or accommodation. These survivors may retract information, omit information, or make delayed or unconvincing disclosures, which can undermine their credibility as witnesses. This can also increase their risk of being victimized again and/or conscripted and exploited by criminal enterprises, including radicalization into terrorism.

LaRose has admitted that the men who recruited her online projected themselves as romantic heroes but in reality weren't who they claimed to be. This same disconnection between projected and true self-identity has been evidenced among convicted sex traffickers, who often use faux relationships and "love" to recruit and control victims.[13]

According to one pimp/sex trafficker:

> *Don't underestimate the power of love. Love was my most powerful tool. When a child is in a burning house, a parent will fight flames to save that child. Parents will run into a burning house for that child without thinking. That's the power of love. People kill for love and die for love. People spend their entire lives for a piece of something they can't touch.*[14]

Although sex trafficking is a very different crime from terrorism, both sex traffickers and terrorist recruiters utilize love as a tactic for conscripting women into exploitable situations. Similar to LaRose, her coconspirator Jamie Paulin Ramirez a.k.a. Jihad Jamie, was lured away from her family by false promises from a romantic interest. By the time she recognized the manipulation, it was too late. She was already in Ireland and felt trapped. Soon after Ramirez tried to rekindle the relationships with her estranged family and friends in the hope of returning to the United States, Damache impregnated her, leading to increased feelings of hopelessness.

Both of these women were manipulated into believing the men they met online loved them, but the reality is that they were just used as a means to an end by sacrilegious men in the pursuit of money and power. Manufactured feelings of "love" are used to manipulate women away from their family and social support systems and into exploitable positions, where they can be used as maids, sex slaves, coconspirators, and unexpected suicide bombers or combatants. The terrorist recruiter typically ingratiates the woman with compliments, builds up her self-esteem, makes her feel loved, and offers a "once-in-a-lifetime" opportunity at self-actualization. However, this all changes once the woman is under physical control of the terrorist, and she is left chasing an unobtainable dream that was promised to her, while fearing the repercussions of returning to the life she left behind.

Jihad Jane and Jihad Jamie aren't alone. Most radicalized women are lured this way, which is all the more reason why effective counterterrorism begins with identifying high-risk and at-risk populations and implementing interventions to prevent their recruitment, as opposed to solely relying on criminalization after the fact.

6

White Widow

Samantha Lewthwaite and I have several things in common. We were both born in 1983 and raised in bedroom communities—hers in Aylesbury, England, and mine in Reston, Virginia. Each of us has been described as a compassionate individual, with a strong inclination to social justice. And the two of us were tremendously affected by the separation of our parents, hers in 1995[1] and mine in 1996. But that is where our paths diverge.

She went on to become one of the most notorious international female terrorists, known as the "White Widow," while I became a criminologist. Why?

Some might erroneously attribute the differences in our respective trajectories to religion. Samantha was raised Christian but became withdrawn after the separation of her parents and sought solace from her Muslim neighbors,[2] eventually converting to Islam by the age of seventeen.[3] I, on the other hand, was raised Christian and Jewish, celebrating both holidays and learning about the two faiths from my Christian mother and Jewish father. As an adult, I do not necessarily adhere to any faith or denomination, but I consider myself a spiritual person.

Although there is a clear difference in the evolution of our respective ideologies, it would be incorrect to assume that Samantha's path into terrorism was a result of her Muslim faith. In life, so much of who we become is shaped by our experiences and by the people we interact with.

Samantha was no exception.

Much of her teaching on Islam began with Abdullah el-Faisal, a Christian-born, Muslim-convert cleric who was later sentenced to prison for "urging Muslims to fight and kill . . . Jews, Christians, Americans, Hindus and other unbelievers" and "using threatening, abusive, or insulting words or behavior with intent to stir up racial hatred."[4]

El-Faisal was born Trevor William Forrest and raised in an evangelical

Christian family before becoming a Muslim. During the 1980s, he studied Islam in Trinidad, Guyana, and Saudi Arabia and eventually traveled to the United Kingdom to become an imam at Salafi Brixton mosque in South London but was quickly ejected because of his radical preaching. That didn't stop el-Faisal from spreading his message, though, as he continued lecturing at mosques and community centers across the United Kingdom, including in London, Birmingham, Manchester, Scotland, and Wales.

In addition to el-Faisal's lectures, Samantha obtained her information on Islam from Germaine Lindsay also known as Abdullah Shaheed Jamal—a romantic interest whom she met through an Internet chat room.

Lindsay was originally from Jamaica and also had recently converted to Islam. He didn't have much of a relationship with his biological father and was raised by his mother, who partnered with one stepfather after another. Lindsay was described as a quiet, soft-spoken, and impressionable introvert who, like Lewthwaite, looked up to el-Faisal—the race-baiting, murder-soliciting, Muslim-convert cleric—as a father figure who imparted his knowledge of Islam.

Lewthwaite and Lindsay exchanged emails before meeting up at an anti-war protest in London in 2002. Only a few months had passed before they decided they would get married and Lewthwaite would drop out of classes at the University of London.

Lindsay felt abandoned by his mother, who had had moved out of their England home to live with a third stepfather in the United States. He also felt like a failure, after missing the opportunity for admission to Greenhead College and being unemployed. His marriage to Lewthwaite gave him something to look forward to, and he felt affirmed given her mirrored following of el-Faisal. Their relationship was symbiotic and cultivated their extremism, further ostracizing them from their former lives, family, and friends.

In April 2004, Lewthwaite and Lindsay became first-time parents to a baby boy, Abdullah. Even after the birth of their child, the couple continued connecting with other extremist followers of Abdullah el-Faisal, such as Mohammad Sidique Khan and his wife, Hasina Patel. They became fanatical about carrying out el-Faisal's violent message, in part because they felt they had so little going for themselves and lacked positive social controls—bouncing from residence to residence, unemployed, not enrolled in school, and guided predominately by an avowed terrorist recruiter.

In addition to following the extremist leanings of el-Faisal, Khan had traveled regularly to attend al-Qaeda training camps in Pakistan and Afghanistan, where he learned bomb-making skills.[5] Kahn, who was over ten years Lindsay's senior, conspired with him to become suicide bombers. Khan's publicized rationale read like every other propaganda script:

> . . . *democratically elected governments continuously perpetuate atrocities against my people all over the world and your support of them makes you directly responsible, just as I am directly responsible for protecting and avenging my Muslim brothers and sisters. Until we feel security, you will be our targets. And until you stop the bombing, gassing, imprisonment, and torture of my people, we will not stop this fight. We are at war and I am a soldier.*[6]

In other words, Kahn and Lindsay were brainwashed into believing that killing innocent men, women, and children—civilians—would somehow improve the plight of Muslims. To most, it is incredible how anyone could honestly believe that killing random people would be in accordance with any God or religion, much less that it would be an action that could catalyze peace or betterment for a group of people. Yet Khan and Lindsay were manipulated into believing this to such an extent that they pushed forward in becoming suicide bombers, leaving behind their young children in the wake of their terrorism.

On July 7, 2005, Samantha Lewthwaite was eight months pregnant with her second child, a baby girl, when her husband left in the dark hours of early dawn, arriving at Luton Railway Station at 5:07 a.m. Lindsay wandered around for more than two hours before meeting three other men, including Mohammad Sidique Khan, each carrying a large hiking backpack filled with peroxide-based explosives. All four men boarded a Piccadilly Line train to London.

At King's Cross station, they split up.

Lindsay continued on the Piccadilly Line, detonating his bomb at approximately 8:50 a.m., between King's Cross and Russell Square stations, killing himself and twenty other passengers. In rapid succession, the other three men detonated their bombs, as well. Mohammad Sidique Khan had boarded a westbound Circle Line train toward Paddington and detonated his bomb at Edgware Road, killing himself and six other people. The third bomber, Shehzad Tanweer, detonated his bomb on an eastbound Circle Line train, between Liverpool Street and Aldgate stations, killing himself along with seven people. And the fourth bomber, Hasib Hussain, had exited the King's Cross station and boarded a double-decker bus in Tavistock Square, where he detonated his bomb, killing himself and thirteen other people.

The 7/7 bombing tragedy killed fifty-two civilians in total and injured hundreds more; it is the single worst terrorist atrocity on British soil to date.[7]

Samantha Lewthwaite didn't contact the police until six days after the tragedy. She claimed that she had kicked Lindsay out of the house because she had suspected him of being unfaithful with another woman but reported him as missing when she hadn't heard from him and became worried. Lewthwaite portrayed herself to the police and the media as an innocent victim who had no idea that her husband had become radicalized:

> *The Jamal I met and married was a man of peace. We found that we were very much alike and kindred spirits. He wanted to qualify as a human rights lawyer and I was a member of an Amnesty International group at school.*

Lewthwaite claimed that Lindsay was a peaceful, innocent, naive, and simple man who must have had his mind poisoned by the men who had radicalized him.[8] She maintained that she had been completely unaware that he was planning the attack and began crying when she had learned what he had done:

> *Jamal is accountable for his actions one hundred percent and I condemn with all my heart what he has done. . . . I just hope people will understand I had nothing to do with this. We are victims as well.*

The police initially believed her when she told them that she abhorred the bombings, which kept her from being charged with any crime, but the public didn't necessarily agree. Days before giving birth to her second child, a daughter she named Ruqayyah, firebombs were thrown at her residence, prompting police protection and forcing her into hiding.

After Lindsay's funeral, Lewthwaite moved into a flat near her mom, and for a short while she began spending more time with family and friends, but that changed in 2007. She had been secretly visiting and speaking with el-Faisal while he was incarcerated. Despite having lost her husband in his terrorist attack, Lewthwaite was described as being "jovial and happy" during these visits. She appeared as if her husband's death and the murder of nearly five-dozen people were "business as usual."

As soon as el-Faisal was released and deported, Lewthwaite began traveling abroad more regularly. Despite not being employed, she traveled back and forth from England to different parts of Africa and refused to tell her loved ones where she was going or who she was with.

In 2008, el-Faisal called Lewthwaite to tell her that he had met a man named Fahmi Jamal Salim who was looking for a white, British, Muslim wife. After speaking for a few months over the phone and Internet, she traveled to Johannesburg, South Africa, to see him. The day after meeting in person, they were married, and soon after she was impregnated with her third child. She flew back to Alyesburn, England, in July 2009 to give birth to a boy but refused to write the father's name on the birth certificate.[9]

Afterward, she began distancing herself from family and traveling abroad more often and for longer periods of time, before leaving for good.

Authorities believe that Lewthwaite and her three children used forged documents to enter Kenya in August 2011. There, her new husband killed two police officers in Nairobi, while Lewthwaite worked in an al-Shabaab bomb lab in Mombasa. Following an anonymous tip from an informant about impending terrorist threats against tourist resorts in Kenya during Christmas, police raided the lab and used fingerprints and rental records to connect Lewthwaite to the bomb-making materials, as well as an apartment containing weapons, ammunition, and cash.[10]

Al-Shabaab, which means "the youth" in Arabic, is a Somali terrorist organization that carries out bombings, murders, and other acts of violence in the name of Islam. Similar to other terrorist organizations, al-Shabaab wasn't born from any altruistic religious cause, but rather poverty and conflict, which created an opportunity for criminals to exploit marginalized and disaffected young people into doing their bidding.

Lewthwaite began making a name for herself within al-Shabaab leadership. After more than a decade of being fed extremist propaganda, she felt that she had become an authority on the Muslim religion and could "incite" others to join her criminal endeavors. She wrote:

> All praises are for Allah alone. Him alone we worship and He alone
> we ask for help. May Allah's peace and blessings be upon the mes-
> senger of Allah and all his companions.

I have for many years now wanted to write something that would benefit my brothers and sisters. A message of hope, encouragement, and light in an era when many are still in darkness. But every time I wrote, I felt that lack of knowledge or not practicing completely the context led me to abandon these works. However, after reading the Woman's Role in Jihad, I realized that time had come for me to at least put forth what I have been blessed with and hope that this will incite others (Insha'Allah*).

Allah has blessed me with being married to a Mujahid *and meeting many wonderful, inspiring people along the way. I wanted to document the true reality of what it means to be a* Mujahid, *living as a* ghuraba† *and what it was that guided many of these amazing men and women to put forth all they have for Allah.*

By 2013, Lewthwaite had attempted to orchestrate the murders of hundreds of people[11] and was wanted by Interpol.[12] Authorities believed that she was implicated in various massacres, training of suicide bombers, and providing guidance on how to exploit the media. Lewthwaite became more involved with the radicalization of others by authoring her own propaganda and offering poverty-stricken families money to use their women and children as suicide bombers. Incredibly, like many women radicalized into terrorism, Lewthwaite even wanted the same fate for her own four children:

Recently, my beloved husband gave a talk to my eight-year-old son and five-year-old-daughter. He asked them, "What do you want to be when you are older?" Both had many answers, but both agreed to one of wanting to be a Mujahid.

Lewthwaite's manipulated interpretation of Islam was how she rationalized her criminality. She idolized false prophets, interpreting Islam only through the lenses of warmongers like el-Faisel and even Osama bin Laden. In a poem, she wrote:

Oh sheik Osama, my father, my brother
My love for you is like no other

---

* God-willing.
† Stranger.

Oh Sheik Osama, now that you are gone
The Muslims must wake up, they must be strong
I know that you are in a better place
That Allah has bestowed upon you grace.
Us, we are left to continue what you started.
To seek the victory until we are martyred.
To instill terror into kuffar.
Until the world is governed by la ilaha illa'llah.*
Oh sheik Osama, know this for true
My heart will not find peace until all Muslims do.
Everything you had, you gave for Allah
No surrender will take us all far.
Your life—an example of how we should be.
Oh Muslims, listen to our beloved sheik's words
Let not his struggle and efforts go unheard
Revive what he started and strive to success
Then maybe we can be raised with the best.
Oh sheik Osama, we are jealous of you, to be of those who the
*   promise is true*
The promise is truth, which is binding if only we knew
Verily Allah has purchased the lives of the believers that theirs shall
*   be paradise.*
They fight in Allah's cause, so they kill and are killed.
It is a promise binding on Allah in taurat,† injill‡ *and Qur'an*
And who is truer to his covenant than Allah?
As for our enemies our words will be less.
You picked the wrong army to contest.
Al-Qaeda are stronger and fiercer than ever.
Thinking in the end, you are stupid, it will NEVER
Be over until the day that we see our lands returned and governed
*   by He Allah the almighty, whose law is complete.*

---

* The one-and-only God.
† *Taurat* is the instruction that Allah gave to the Jews through the Prophet Musa. The Torah.
‡ *Injil* is the Arabic word for the Gospel of Jesus. The Bible.

So make your plans and He is the best of planners.
There was no victory for you Mr Obama, the honor is his on mar-
tyred Osama!!!!!!!!!!!!!!!!![13]

Samantha Lewthwaite had fully transformed from the girl next door to a violent terrorist. Although she believed her violence was justified by religion, all
true Muslims know that the Qur'an explicitly warns of people who manipulate
the interpretation of Islam.

Terrorist organizations clearly pursue disharmony by having an interpretation
of the Qur'an that is contrary to accepted standards and practice of Islam. For
example, after the Prophet Muhammad embarked on his *hijrah* from Mecca to
Medina, to escape violent torment, he returned to Mecca. The Qur'an documents
that although he had suffered brutal persecution and even his own children had
been murdered, Muhammad did not exact vengeance, nor did he force Islam
on the people. He forgave them. The religion of Islam does not permit violence
unless in direct self-defense.

In order to erroneously claim self-defense, al-Shabaab's propaganda presents
a perverse version of the Qur'an for the purpose of radicalization. According to
al-Shabaab's online English-language magazine, *Gaidi Mtaani*, which is Swahili
for "On Terrorism Street," democracy is an attack on Islam, "wherever [democ-
racy] is present, Islam does not exist, and wherever Islam is present there is no
place for [democracy]."[14] "*Hijrah*" is then defined as migrating "from the land of
disbelieve [*sic*] to the lands where sharia is fully implemented." Al-Shabaab wants
to turn Somalia into an Islamic State through "jihad," which according to them
includes "martyrdom, amputation, and orphanage" at the pleasure of Allah.

Al-Shabaab also claims that violence is the only tool at their disposal: "If our
words could have reached you by mouth, then they would not have been sent by
grenades."[15] They attempt to rationalize their terrorism by alleging that the "inva-
sion" and "occupation" of Muslim lands and deaths of Muslims were the catalyst.

However, even if their leaders honestly believed this and weren't simply war
profiteers and opportunists, experts contend that the Prophet Muhammad did
not act out of retaliation and refrained from forcing Islam on nonbelievers.
Moreover, according to religious leaders and Islamic scholars, jihad is not about
violence or war; it is about the struggle to live a good and pure life, rebuking sin.[16]
Although jihad was never intended to be used as a rationale for violence to force
people to convert to Islam, take occupation of land, or acquire money or power,

that is how terrorist organizations are using it, for their own selfish motives. In addition, it is considered sacrilegious to equate Muhammad's journey to escape persecution with that of people being deceived into leaving their families in order to be killed and/or kill civilians.

Terrorist recruiters manipulate at-risk people, like Samantha Lewthwaite, into becoming perverse—something the Qur'an explicitly warns against. This perversity is what facilitates their violent criminal behaviors, in spite of the consequences. Samantha Lewthwaite's radicalization, for example, had nothing to do with religion; Islam was simply used as a conduit for her recruitment by Abdullah el-Faisal—a criminal, not a true Muslim. He was simply a narcissist who used Samantha and her husband as a means to an end.

Ultimately, Samantha's descent into terrorism may ostensibly be linked to her religion, but it actually has more to do with risk factors and relationships.

For example, more than one person had described Samantha as lacking confidence and being a follower.[17] These characteristics are risk factors, because criminal enterprises need something to offer their target, be it physiological resources, money, safety, love, belonging, esteem, or self-actualization. In order to be a target, a woman must be in need of something that she is willing to sacrifice all to have.

A terrorist recruiter is skilled in making their target believe that ISIS, al-Shabaab, or al-Qaeda can or will fill the voids in life.

A high-risk target for radicalization has low self-esteem and is lost. She doesn't know where she wants to be, but she knows where she doesn't want to be; she may even know where she wants to be but doesn't know how to get there. The terrorist recruiter must appear to know the directions, but he never actually has to deliver, as long as the target is in an exploitable position before she comes to the realization of the façade.

In addition, Samantha had the misfortune of falling in with a bad crowd who didn't have her best interests in mind. She increasingly pushed away the people in her life who actually cared for her and her well-being and surrounded herself with acquaintances who reinforced the criminal and self-destructive path she had been set on.

If only she had heeded the warning that parents tell their children around the world, "You're only as good as the company you keep."

In the field of criminology, this idiom relates to social learning theory—an explanation for criminal behavior, which posits that crime motivation and skill come from the people we associate with. This is one reason why the family of the prospective recruit is referred to as an "obstacle" in terrorist propaganda; a good parent would not stand idly by while criminals—terrorists—attempted to exploit their child.

Terrorist recruiters lure young people with silver tongues that spout false promises. Parents should warn their children of wolves in sheeps' clothing who offer answers to all their problems and pretend to carry the message of their God but lie.

As a convicted sex trafficker once told me, "Don't believe what you hear and only half of what you see."[18] Although said regarding human traffickers, I believe this holds equally true in relation to terrorists, who often begin life just like you and me.

In the beginning of this chapter, I compared myself to Samantha Lewthwaite because I believe that, in many ways, she was not unlike me. We are about the same age and had comparable upbringings, including being the products of divorce. We both consider ourselves social justice advocates (albeit in completely different manners) and went on to become mothers of four children—two girls and two boys each.

Given what she has done, it is easy to dismiss someone like Samantha as an evil person, by nature or nurture. It is more difficult to consider that she was in the wrong place at the wrong time and was brainwashed into becoming a criminal.

When someone commits a heinous crime and is convicted, we lock them up in prison and vilify them in the media. Rarely do we reflect on what led to that person's criminality and whether it could have been prevented.

My first job out of undergraduate school was teaching high school equivalency,* adult basic education, and essential workplace skills classes to mostly medium- and maximum-security inmates at Prince William County Adult Detention Center. I taught rapists, gang members, and murderers. Going into the prison, I felt fearful, especially given the correctional facility's no-hostage policy.[19] But after working there for a few months, I realized that most of these men and women weren't evil people, despite having committed some malicious crimes. Most of them had been victims themselves at various points in their lives, especially as children. Others suffered from mental illness. In speaking with them, I

---

* General Education Development (GED).

could almost visualize how their existence could have turned out differently, if only a few things had changed—like a butterfly effect.

My best student was a murderer who killed two people—stabbing one over 100 times and slicing the other's throat and crushing his head with a weight. He was seventeen years old at the time of these offenses, and if it weren't for the Supreme Court decision in *Roper v. Simmons*, which abolished the death penalty for juveniles, he would have faced capital punishment. This man suffered from schizophrenia, and during the course of my class with him, I saw the changes in his behaviors from being untreated to receiving mental health care and medicine. It was like he became a completely different person. Although his illness didn't absolve the culpability of his crimes, it should be something to consider, especially when discussing methods for prevention.

Just like the criminals at that jail, terrorists are often the product of circumstance or mental illness. It is in our interest as a society not to simply dismiss them as evil people with psychotic penchants for violence, because there but for the grace of God go we.

7

Black Widow

Black widow spiders are best known for three distinctive characteristics—the red hourglass marking on their abdomens, fatal venom, and frequent practice of sexual cannibalism.

In Russia, female terrorists, especially suicide bombers, are known as чёрная вдова—black widows. The moniker is thought to have originated from the fact that radicalized women in the region are often widows of Chechen men who were killed in their struggle for independence from Russian occupation.[1] However, the term is certainly a double entendre—since men who become sexually involved with these dangerous women often meet untimely deaths thereafter.

For example, take the case of Naida "Black Widow" Asiyalova.

On October 21, 2013, at approximately 2:00 p.m. on a sunny afternoon in southwest Russia, Naida boarded the Number 29 bus through the city of Volgograd.

Volgograd, formerly known as Stalingrad, was the location of the largest and deadliest battle in World War II. Today, Volgograd is known for having the largest statue of a woman in the world—a monument of the Soviet victory and Germany's expulsion from the Caucasus called "Motherland Calls." The statue depicts a female, an embodiment of the Soviet Union, with her sword held high, encouraging her sons to protect their country from the enemy.

Through Naida's eyes, however, *Russia* was the enemy, and Volgograd was as good a place as any to fight. She had initially purchased a ticket from Makhachkala—the Daghestani capital—to Moscow but exited that bus early, took a brief walk, and boarded a second bus in Volgograd.

After paying her fare, Naida quickly navigated to the rear of the bus, hoping not to attract any attention. She kept her eyes lowered and didn't speak, but Naida could still feel the people watching as she walked by, taking notice of the light-green *hijab* she wore.[2] She didn't pay them any mind and took a seat near a window in the back.

Naida stared out from the bus, watching the fall trees sway in the wind, as she contemplated when to carry out her concluding act of terrorism. Suicide bombers often experience fear and doubt in the final moments before killing themselves in the name of "jihad." Although they won't be physically forced into carrying out the attack, suicide bombers have been manipulated to understand that they are at risk of losing the "respect" and "love" of their so-called "jihadist" community if they don't. If a suicide bomber refuses an assignment on multiple occasions, she or he could be expelled from their community or even unceremoniously murdered.

For Naida's final act of terrorism, coconspirators Ruslan Kazanbiyev and Kurban Omarov followed her, making sure she didn't act on any second thoughts.

Glaring from the large bus window, Naida's eyes appeared soulless, reflecting the blank slate in her mind. Her heart was filled with hate for the unaware and innocent people sitting next to her. She was on the precipice of committing a crime that she may have known deep down inside was wrong, but she was brainwashed into following through with it. Shortly after the second stop, Naida pulled the trigger and detonated her belt bomb, made from more than 500 grams of TNT, nails, and metal swarf.

A large blast of orange fire mushroomed out of the bus, which was traveling on the right side of a three-lane highway. The power of the explosion caused it to fishtail into the center lane, triggering a domino effect of vehicles swerving to avoid a collision. The large glass windows shattered, and metal pieces from the bus littered the road, which was shrouded in a thick fog of light-gray smoke. The cars behind could barely see as everyone rolled to a stop.

Naida had successfully killed herself, murdered six other passengers, and injured thirty-seven more, including a twenty-month-old toddler.[3] For those who didn't die, Naida made sure that the explosive would impale their bodies with shrapnel, sever their limbs, and severely burn their skin—scarring them for the rest of their lives. While catastrophic, the death toll certainly would have been larger if her two grenades had exploded alongside her. By some miracle, they didn't.

In the aftermath of Naida's attack, the public sought to better understand her path to radicalization. Like most female terrorists, Naida's extremism was tied to a "love story."[4] It only took a few days after her attack for details to emerge about Naida's husband—Dmitry Sokolov—and his involvement. According to the news coverage, he had built the deadly explosive used by Naida and even strapped the suicide belt onto his wife. Although the public was inclined to blame him, it was Naida who had radicalized her husband—a man ten years her junior.

Naida's path to radicalization had actually begun much earlier. She was born in Dagestan, which sits alongside Chechnya in the North Caucasus region of Russia—an area notorious for terrorism. In 2013, US intelligence estimated that as many as 17,000 foreigners were fighting on the side of rebels in Syria and 12 percent of ISIS were believed to be Chechens from the North Caucasus.[5]

Internationally notorious terrorists from Dagestan include Dzhokhar and Tamerlan Tsarnaev—the brothers responsible for the Boston Marathon bombings that killed three and injured 260[6]—as well as Mariam Sharipova, a schoolteacher whose suicide bomb killed herself and twenty-six others on a Moscow metro.[7]

In order to understand how Dagestan became "the most dangerous place in Europe,"[8] you must first recognize the protracted conflict in the region. For centuries, the North Caucasus have been ruled by either Persian or Russian empires and challenged by nationalists. Chechen and Dagestani residents became tired of imperial rule, associated taxes, and periodic expropriation of estates—catalyzing revolts in the early 1800s.

At first, the revolution was comprised of mostly secular nationalist groups, who desired independence. However, as time passed, a separate faction of extremist militants began co-opting the nationalist cause to push their own agenda. They described the conflict as a holy war and wanted to turn the region into an Islamic State.

Both groups were opportunistic in advancing their causes and often waited until Russian leadership was preoccupied before taking action. For example, in 1917, while the Russian monarchy was focused on mass demonstrations and violent clashes over food rationing and socialism, the people of Dagestan and Chechnya declared independence from Russia and formed a unified state known as the Mountainous Republic of the Northern Caucasus. It quickly gained de jure recognition from other empires and states but did not last for long.

As soon as the Russian Civil War started coming to an end, the military was directed to occupy Dagestan and Chechnya, and the regions were compelled to return to Russian control prior to the formation of the Soviet Union in 1922.

Nearly seventy years later, the Union of Soviet Socialist Republics collapsed, and leaders in Dagestan and Chechnya yet again saw an opportunity for independence. They attempted to negotiate with Russian leadership but failed. Russia sent tens of thousands of troops to invade and reclaim Chechnya resulting in the First Chechen War.[9] Russia was accused of killing thousands of people, including the deliberate execution of more than one hundred civilians.[10]

In response, the secular nationalists continued their fight for independence, but so-called "jihadi" extremists became more influential and powerful in the region, especially among the disaffected. Terrorist leaders had successfully latched onto the nationalist movement and catalyzed an incursion of Dagestan in 1999. The extremist militants declared Dagestan as an Islamic State and called for all "unbelievers" to be "driven out,"[11] resulting in the Second Chechen War, which lasted a decade.

The men and women who were recruited into fighting the Second Chechen War as a "jihad" were described by the nationalist Chechen resistance as "people who lacked a certain amount of attention at home, lacked love" and were "weak."[12] Extremist leaders were described as "good psychologists" who could read people and instruct them accordingly. Upon entering terrorist training camps, these men and women were provided with what they perceived as a sense of "love" and belonging. They were called brothers and sisters and were coddled by having their food prepared for them, prayers read with them, and receiving copious amounts of attention and conversation. The terrorist recruiters made the "pathetic" feel "powerful." They were given so much love, respect, attention, and affection that these people felt that they would rather die as a so-called "*mujahideen*" than leave or be exiled as a traitor or a coward.[13]

The continued conflicts between the Russian military and the Caucasus separatists have been described as avoidable and borne of "stupid pride and political opportunism on both sides."[14]

Terrorist leaders behave as parasites—organisms that live off of a host, often harming it. Without the host organism, a parasite can't survive, grow, or multiply. A terrorist uses religion or social movements to give them the façade of legitimacy, so they can survive, thrive, and recruit new terrorists,

If you separate a parasite from its host, it is less harmful and can be more easily exterminated. Similarly, removing terrorist criminals from the noble causes, religions, or hosts they latch onto will facilitate more effective counterterrorism interventions.

For example, ISIS misinterprets and uses Islam to conceal its interest in money, power, sex, and criminality. The Ku Klux Klan similarly uses Christianity to justify its racism, crime, and domestic terrorism. The extremist militants in Dagestan use the secular and nationalist quest for independence as an opportunity to gain money and power. However, each of these terrorist organizations has no genuine affinity or interest in the causes or religions they latch onto; they are simply used as a tool to rationalize and legitimize their criminality and self-interest.

People are often radicalized because they are manipulated into believing terrorists are going to fill some void in their life, but they are also led to believe their nefarious actions are part of a larger and nobler cause. Nadia Asiyalova was no different.

Although the details of her radicalization are sparse, we know that Naida was born and raised in a small mountain settlement of Gunib in Dagestan. Her hometown was the site of the final and deadliest battle fought by Imam Shamil, a Muslim leader in the 1800s for the Russian resistance in the Caucasian War.

We also know that Naida was raised mostly by her grandmother and was not particularly devoted to Islam in childhood.[15] She eventually left home as a young adult, in pursuit of a better life in Moscow.

There, she attended a university, worked multiple jobs to make ends meet, and began dating Dmitri Sokolov in 2010. Some media reports suggested that the pair had met on a dating website,[16] while others claimed the two got to know each other at their university.[17] Regardless, their relationship quickly progressed.

Naida was accused of radicalizing Sokolov, who was described as being "prone to outside influences."[18] She brought him to Dagestan, where he was trained in bomb-making skills, further indoctrinated into Wahhabism, and given the Islamic name Abdul Jabbar.[19] Naida married Sokolov before asking him to craft the suicide bomb belt that would ultimately be used in her terrorist attack.

Some media outlets also suggested that Naida had suffered from a painful and terminal bone disease, which could have influenced her decision to become a suicide bomber,[20] but the true catalyst is rooted much earlier in her life.

The people in Dagestan have undeniably suffered from massive human rights violations.[21] So-called "jihadi" leadership co-opted that cause, in conjunction with religion, as their veneer of legitimacy. Naida was likely manipulated by a boyfriend or love interest into believing that terrorism was the only path for self-actualization and obtaining justice for the Dagestani people. Naida then went on to recruit, radicalize, and manipulate Dmitri Sokolov in a similar fashion.

Naida's narrative is similar to that of other "Black Widows" in Russia. These women are manipulated by love interests into believing they are fighting for some altruistic cause but are simply being used as a means to an end to fulfill someone else's selfish, political, and financial aspirations.

For example, take the case of Alla Saprykina.

On August 28, 2012, Alla walked into the home of Dagestan's most influential Muslim leader[22]—Sheikh Said Afandi al-Chirkavi. After pretending to be a pregnant pilgrim interested in converting to Islam, she was able to circumvent a long line of people who were waiting to meet the Sheikh. He preached Sufi Islam, also called "traditional Islam,"[23] to tens of thousands of students. They described him as a man of peace who was patient, gentle, and altruistic.[24] Sheikh Said's influence and inclination for harmony among diverse people were what made him a target for the terrorists who preached Wahhabism.*

Wahhabism was founded in the eighteenth century by a man named Muhammad Ibn Abd al-Wahhab. His interpretation of Islam was considered extreme and was rejected and opposed by most notable Muslim scholars of the time. Al-Wahhab was accused of espousing violence against those who did not subscribe to his interpretation of Islam, including fellow Muslims. His extremist views ultimately resulted in his being exiled from his home village of Uyaynah, located in the Najd[25] region of the Arabian Peninsula.[26]

Despite his exile and related death threats, al-Wahhab continued preaching his strict interpretation of Islam and sought protection from Muhammad Ibn Saud, head of the Saud tribal family. He agreed to endorse al-Wahhab's austere form of Islam, providing protection, legitimacy, and power. In exchange, the Saud tribal family would receive regular tithes from al-Wahhab's followers.[27]

In other words, the Saud tribal family endorsed al-Wahhab not because they believed in what he was saying, but because he agreed to give them money. To the same effect, al-Wahhab partnered with the Saud tribal family, not because they believed in his interpretation of Islam, but because they provided a conduit to the power he coveted.

Today, practitioners of Wahhabism believe there is only one God and a singular interpretation of Islam, which some interpret as permitting terrorism against nonbelievers. This is the religious veneer that has rationalized the cold-blooded murder of countless people around the world, including Sheikh Said, simply

---

* Also known as Salafism.

because he exposed the terrorist criminals for what they were—wolves in sheeps' clothing and parasites. In his sermons, he preached,

> *Wahhabites are the people that convince those around them that their words are truthful, but in reality their acts are wrong. Beware of them, if you want to sincerely hold to the Islamic path! They may be good at lauding the followers of the Prophet, but they fail to follow him.*[28]

Alla—the woman sent to kill Sheikh Said—had converted to Wahhabism at the behest of her first husband. At the time of her suicide mission, she had been married four times and widowed three over the course of several years.[29] She had nothing to live for aside from the Wahhabism that she was brainwashed with, so she never questioned her orders to murder.

Alla took a taxi to Sheikh Said's home, which was filled with kneeling believers, and entered under the false pretense of converting to Islam. She walked toward him slowly, attempting not to draw any attention to herself, and when she was close enough to execute Sheikh Said, she detonated her bomb belt. The explosion instantly killed both of them, along with Sheikh Said's wife and five other people, including an eleven-year-old boy.[30]

In the wake of the attack, the media referred to Alla as a martyr, but Sheikh Said's followers refused to recognize her as such. Instead, they called her a suicide bomber.[31] Although it may seem like semantics, this is an important distinction.

Shahid, the Arabic word for martyr, refers to a person who dies while fulfilling a religious commandment. To that effect, supporters of Sheikh Said instead called *him* the martyr. This distinction was made because Sheikh Said was an Islamic leader who was revered in Dagestan and killed simply for teaching the truth and peace of Islam. Alla, on the other hand, was not a true Muslim. She murdered him and six other innocent Muslims, while committing suicide—crimes that, according to Sheikh Said's own sermons, were not in accordance with Islam.

Alla did not portray herself as a religious woman until she met her first husband. She earned a degree from Dagestan State University's drama school in Makhachkala[32] and worked in Gorky Theater as an actress and member of a breakdancing troupe, where she met Marat Kurbanov.

Marat was the younger brother of notorious Russian terrorist Renat Kurbanov. After Renat was killed in a special operation in the capital,[33] Marat decided to join the terrorist organization and brought Alla along with him as his wife, when she took the name Aminat Kurbanova after she converted.

Marat was eventually killed in antiterrorism operation as well, prompting his widowed wife to remarry again and again. The wives of Wahhabist insurgents are brainwashed to believe that they will obtain part of their husbands' rewards in paradise, which will be greater for each additional husband they live to see die in so-called "jihad."[34]

Counterterrorism experts often perceive the biographies of radicalized women as perplexing. Naida and Alla, for example, were not raised to become extremists. Their decision to suicide-bomb innocent civilians was not in retaliation for some direct harm they suffered. Moreover, these two women weren't living marginalized lives prior to radicalization. Both attended university, were gainfully employed, and were independent.

The perplexity of this type of terrorist recruitment is due to the fact that Naida's and Alla's conscription into terrorism were rooted in manipulation—similar to a Ponzi scheme.

In traditional Ponzi or pyramid schemes, targets are tricked into financially investing in a company that does not produce any goods or services. The business simply generates a return on investment when more defrauded victims invest. Similarly, the persons who are actually committing acts of terrorism and becoming suicide bombers are defrauded into believing they are contributing to an altruistic cause and will receive the benefit of salvation for their sacrifice. The scheme is that the people at the top would never go to the front lines of battle or kill themselves. Moreover, they have no interest in the salvation, safety, or betterment of the people at the bottom. The men leading terrorist organizations are simply guided by their selfish motives for money and power.

It is a well-known fact that traditional Ponzi schemes are discontinued when they can no longer attract new investors. To that end, terrorist Ponzi schemes, like those run by ISIS, al-Qaeda, al-Shabaab, and the Taliban will similarly cease when they can no longer attract new recruits. As such, instead of focusing counterterrorism interventions predominately on reactive punishments, it is imperative to identify persons at risk of radicalization and implement interventions to proactively prevent their recruitment.

Although this is certainly easier said than done, an important first step is to expose terrorist organizations for what they are: frauds, parasites, Ponzi schemers, criminals, manipulators, war profiteers, and selfish opportunists. No matter how you want to describe their evil deeds, it is critical to expose the fact that these men are not religious Muslims, they do not represent Islam, and they are not in pursuit of any nationalist quest for independence.

Separating the terrorist parasites from their hosts, removing their veneer, and exposing their façade will help prevent more young people from being radicalized. Although it will be difficult, we should remember:

An ounce of prevention is worth a pound of cure.
                                        —Benjamin Franklin

8

Terror Teens

Typical teenage behavior is often described as unpredictable, volatile, and driven by emotion. According to neuroscientists, this is due to a fundamental reorganization of the brain that occurs throughout adolescence.[1] During teenage years, the prefrontal cortex begins developing an adult-level capacity for personality expression, decision making, and moderating social behavior.

Until the brain is fully matured, adolescents can have an increased propensity for risk taking, criminality, and additional antisocial behaviors—in other words, they make bad choices. And like most red-blooded Americans, I did, too.

Beginning at age fifteen, as a sophomore in high school, I was sneaking out of my house at night, attending parties, and drinking with my peers on the weekends. During the summer, I got caught and released by the local police for skinny-dipping in a public pool and started using a fake ID to get into nightclubs and raves in Washington, DC. By sixteen, I was involved in multiple fistfights and came close to accidentally burning down a friend's house while intoxicated. At seventeen, I chose to get a tattoo of my nickname and my first boyfriend's name in the small of my back. By graduation, I had earned a reputation for my risk-taking behavior and even won the senior superlative for "Biggest Daredevil."

Looking back on my adolescence, I feel that I made incredibly bad decisions that I certainly would not make as an adult. However, as I matured and new social controls were introduced into my life, I began making exponentially better decisions and living a life that was in my best interests and within the confines of the law.

Despite the poor choices I made as a teenager, I went on to earn a PhD and now train law enforcement on how to recognize the red flags of human trafficking. As an adult, I now consider myself an overprotective mother of four children and a law-abiding, tax-paying, God-fearing American who works tirelessly in the pursuit of social justice.

While my poor teenage decision making is relatively tame compared to some, the timing of my delinquency is consistent with a critical risk window for terrorist recruitment.

Life course trajectory theory provides a framework to suggest that the maturity gap of adolescence encourages teens to mimic antisocial behavior in ways that are normative and adjustive.[2] Like me, most teens simply age out of these behaviors, which are limited to only a few formative years. According to theorists, teenagers rarely become life-course-persistent offenders. However, the decisions made as an adolescent can certainly result in irreparably life-altering and even life-ending consequences, especially when criminal enterprise recruiters, including terrorists, actively target teens.

* * *

Zahra and Salma Halane made headlines in 2014, when the sixteen-year-old twin girls left their home in Manchester to join ISIS in Syria. The sisters stole £840 from their father and left in the middle of the night to meet up with their traveling companions. Zahra and Salma pretended to be on holiday when they boarded a flight to Istanbul, Turkey, before crossing the border into Syria.[3]

Prior to being recruited into terrorism, the Somali twins were described as integrated, well liked, and highly intelligent. Their family was considered "conservative" and "religious," but not radical. This all changed when their older brother—Ahmed Ibrahim Mohammed Halane—left the United Kingdom to become a terrorist a year earlier.

As a teenager, Ahmed received international attention for his memorization of the Holy Qur'an, participating in contests around the world. After leading prayers in mosque and studying Islam with his father for years, Ahmed had become a skilled competitor. In 2012, he competed for the Dubai International Holy Quran Award, and in 2013 he won the Muslim Association of Britain National Annual Quran Competition, which examined memorization, rules of *tajweed*,[*] and presentation.[4] To most, Ahmed was considered a dedicated Muslim, but this

---

[*] Rules governing pronunciation during recitation of the Qur'an.

dedication evolved as he matured. Although he had memorized the Qur'an, his social network began maligning his interpretation of it.

Ahmed would shirk his responsibilities, like attending Arabic class,[5] and instead watched online videos of extremists like the notorious al-Qaeda recruiter Anwar al-Awlaki.

Al-Awlaki was a U.S.-born imam who fell under FBI scrutiny after it was discovered that he had ties as a "spiritual advisor" to 9/11 terrorists Nawaf al-Hazmi and Khalid al-Mihdhar. While under surveillance, al-Awlaki was caught regularly patronizing prostitutes—a clear violation of his faith.[6] When he discovered that the FBI had evidence of his commercial sex consumerism, which could threaten his career, success, and family, he decided to leave the United States and move to Yemen. His own immoral actions and subsequent expatriation led him to become increasingly resentful against America and non-Muslims.[7]

Al-Awlaki wanted money and power, and he conspired to get it by hook or by crook. While in the United States, he pursued a PhD; read Steven R. Covey's famous book *The 7 Habits of Highly Effective People*; networked with military, law enforcement, academics, and politicians; denounced terrorism; and engaged in philanthropy. After self-deporting to Yemen, he began training with al-Qaeda and made a name for himself by propagandizing their terrorism through videos and magazine articles.

As an educated and American-born mouthpiece, al-Awlaki became an effective conduit for recruitment. He would take his knowledge about the Qur'an and twist it to fit the narrative of al-Qaeda and their objective to profit from war.

For example, in the inaugural issue of *Inspire* magazine, which features al-Qaeda propaganda for the Arabian Peninsula, al-Awlaki wrote an article titled "May our Souls be Sacrificed for You!" It read, in part:

> *The hatred the West holds towards Islam and the Prophet of Islam is a smoldering fire only waiting for an opportunity, a chance, to vent itself through a "proper" channel within the boundaries set by Western laws and freedoms. Outrageous slander, blatant smearing of Muhammad, desecration of the Qur'an, and the insulting of over a billion Muslims worldwide are done under the pretext of "freedom of speech." They are never called what they really are: a deeply rooted historic hatred for Islam and Muslims. Yesterday it was in the name of Christianity; today it is in the name of Democracy.*

*Allah says: Hatred has already appeared from their mouths, and
what their breasts conceal is greater. For these reasons, for this combined effect of an escalating problem . . . We will fight for him, we
will instigate, we will bomb and we will assassinate, and may our
mothers be bereaved of us if we do not rise in his defense.*

Al-Awlaki's videos and magazine articles have been said to have inspired acts of
terrorism around the world. His propaganda has also led to the recruitment of
countless young people, most of whom were simply trying to fill a void in their
life and looking for a sense of belonging, including Ahmed Ibrahim Mohamed
Halane.

After being brainwashed by terrorist propaganda, Ahmed was manipulated
into believing that non-Muslims were infidel devils who needed to be defeated
with force; it was either "us or them" in a defining battle. Ahmed travelled to Syria
to meet up with extremists, before immigrating to Somalia to join al-Shabaab.[8]
He later regretted his decision and eventually returned to his birth country—
Denmark—but it was too late. Ahmed, was banned from Britain under an exclu-
sion order and was later charged with terrorism crimes.

Their brother had received international attention and awards for his memorization of the Qur'an, so after he left to join al-Shabaab, the twins became
curious. Salma started viewing ISIS propaganda in school, including images of a
suicide vest, a boy with a machine gun, and a British terrorist in Syria. When a
teacher caught her, Salma explained that she was trying to find her brother who
had gone to Syria.[9] The girls looked up to Ahmed, and his radicalization came at
a formative moment in their adolescence.

Salma and Zahra took steps to find love interests online to help them migrate
to Syria, but love was not the primary motivation for their conscription. Finding
a husband was discussed unemotionally as a transaction to facilitate their travel
to Syria and accommodations therein. Salma wrote, "It's best if you arrange
someone that you want to get married . . . through a *muhajir* sister . . . it's better
that way then staying at a *maqar** and waiting."[10]

Even following the deaths of their husbands, the twins failed to comprehend
the gravity of their situation, writing: "My twin sister's husband got killed too the

---

* An all-female dormitory, where ISIS fighters can go and select a bride.

same time as mine LOL. We both made the journey together, now both widows together too."

The twins were vocal on social media, consistently contributing to ISIS propaganda for Western females. The girls would evade attempts at online censorship by migrating Twitter handles, effectively using hashtags and networking to regain followers.[11] Although their posts often contained references to Islam or terrorism, the subtext across their communications consistently pointed to their lack of maturity. Their radicalization wasn't about religion, love, or a propensity for violence; these were teenage girls saying bad things and engaging in delinquency for attention.

Two months before traveling to Syria, on September 11, 2014, Zahra tweeted, "Happy #9/11 Happiest day of my life. Hopefully more to come InSha Allah #IS." While some counterterrorism experts claimed that this was an example of Zahra's contempt toward Western society,[12] I regarded it as a teenage girl saying something bad for attention. Considering that the twins were only three years old when the tragedies on September 11, 2001, occurred, the statement appeared to be more for shock value than an expression of genuine sentiment.

While communications from the twins would reference Islam and violence against Westerners, it would be done like a dart passing through a target. The true intent was to garner attention. For example, when attempting to recruit her younger brother, Zahra wrote:

> *Allah, the merciful, placed something in mine and Salma's hearts that we came to hate the infidels to such a degree we could not even bear to look at them. . . . We might seem evil to you, but we will all be happy in* Jannah* *. . . Are you coming to* Dawlah† *. . . ? They will train you up. You will meet boys from England, China, Ireland, Sweden, FROM EVERYWHERE. Want to see my* Kalash‡*?? Ha ha ha.*[13]

Although Zahra mentioned religion, the sales pitch to her brother for joining ISIS appeared to be more about traveling, meeting people from around the world, and being able to play with a big gun. Zahra and Salma were teenage

---

* Heaven or Paradise.
† "The State," a reference to ISIS territory.
‡ Kalashnikov or AK-47.

girls looking for a way to rebel and found it when their brother left home to join Islamic extremists.

Like any good parent, Salma and Zahra's mother—Khadra Jama—attempted to stop her twins from making the worst decision of their lives. "I have lost one son, so I don't want to lose the twins," Mrs. Jama said,[14] unafraid of risking her life to rescue her daughters.

Salma and Zahra's father, on the other hand, felt like giving up. When reporters asked Mr. Halane about his daughters, he said in a low, trembling voice, "I have nothing to say, except that if they want to come back, they can. If they don't . . ." Mr. Halane flicked his hand, as if to brush them away, and turned his back.[15]

Although his sentiments may seem callous, Mr. Halane certainly wasn't alone. On any given day, millions of parents are on the brink of giving up, searching in vain for solutions to how to deal with extreme teenager misconduct. In the United States, for example, parents are advised to seek out individual therapy, group therapy, family therapy, residential therapeutic placement, military school, boarding school, and/or psychotropic medication, to name a few. If these don't work, parents can be tempted to walk away, and many do so by pursuing a PINS[16] or CHINS[17] petition to have the recalcitrant teenager supervised by the juvenile justice system.

Although teenage delinquency can be incredibly frustrating and emotionally exhausting, psychologists universally caution parents not to give up on a child, because in the end, the child is longing for love and acceptance.

To that effect, although her husband had basically capitulated to their daughters' radicalization, Mrs. Jama couldn't give up on them. She followed the twins to Turkey and ventured into Syria after them. Nonprofit organizations helped locate the girls in Manbij, a popular city among European ISIS fighters, but Salma and Zahra were already married and refused to leave. Instead, their mother was arrested and detained by militants, accused of being a Western spy.

Mrs. Jama was eventually released after more than one month and returned to Britain dejected, without the girls. Their words, however, echoed in her ears. Before she left, Salma and Zahra told their mother that their choice to stay with ISIS was because their "hearts belonged to Islam."[18] Although many people would be inclined to believe the girls when they said that they stayed with ISIS because of their religion, as a faithful Muslim, Mrs. Jama knew better; this was not about Islam, Her twin daughters had been brainwashed and she was powerless to stop it.

* * *

The generic parent-teenager dynamic has remained consistent over time. Parents struggle in vain to prevent their children from making poor choices, while know-it-all teenagers contest that their parents just don't understand. For each generation, parents feel that kids these days are worse than the generation before and generally have no respect for their elders. Kids feel that parents are too controlling, old-fashioned, and risk-averse. What results is a power struggle between parents who want to protect their kids and kids who want the freedom to make their own mistakes.

Following the turn of the twenty-first century, technological advancements have made this already-difficult dynamic even more arduous. Increased access to people and information through the Internet has raised concerns over teenagers being more exposed to inappropriate content and predators. While some tech experts advise parents to closely monitor their kids on social media,[19] teens will often rebel to this type of supervision, citing feelings of invaded privacy and compromised autonomy. Alternatively, parents are encouraged to guide their teens in managing the hazards encountered on the Internet themselves, but this may be a Sisyphean task, especially given the clandestine and evolving tactics used by criminal enterprises.

A convicted human trafficker once told me: "A cunning individual is very capable of making another person believe that he or she is in control, concealing their intentions until they lead that person to the edge of the cliff."[20] I never realized how duplicitous certain criminals could be until I conducted interviews with human traffickers. Although I previously had a wealth of experience working with convicts—considering that I taught classes to medium- and maximum-security inmates at a local jail—human traffickers were very different.

It was easy to understand how most of the inmates I taught ended up incarcerated. These men and women were victims of childhood abuse; suffered from untreated psychological disorders; and experienced limited opportunities for social mobility, poverty, and stunted education—all correlates of crime. While some of these same issues may have equally impacted the human traffickers I interviewed ten years later, their projected self-identity concealed these issues, as well as their criminality. This is what made them such dangerous predators.

Warnings of bad people who are disguised as good can be found in Judaism, Christianity, and Islam. The Torah warns of false prophets, who will attempt to lead the Jewish people astray.[21] Similarly, Matthew 7:15 in the Bible cautions, "Beware of the false prophets, who come to you in sheep's clothing, but inwardly are ravenous wolves."

Islam warns of people who claim to be Muslim but simply use the religion as a means to an end—known as Kharijites.

After the murder of the third caliph, Uthman, on June 17, 656, Muhammad's son-in-law, Ali, became his successor. Since the persons implicated in Uthman's murder were supporters of Ali, he was disinclined to prosecute them. In response, Mu'awiyah, the governor of Syria, fought against Ali in the Battle of Siffin, which resulted in an agreement for arbitration by umpires. This concession undermined Ali's power, prompting a small number of families to withdraw from the caliphate.[22]

These people, who became known as Kharijites, were opposed to both the actions of Mu'awiyah and Ali. They repudiated existing caliphal candidates and engaged in campaigns of harassment and terror against all Muslims who did not accept their views.

Islamic *hadiths* contain multiple warnings of people like the Kharijites:

> *There will be division and sectarianism in my nation and a people will come with beautiful words and evil deeds. They will recite the Qur'an but it will not pass beyond their throats. They will leave the religion as an arrow leaves its target and they will not return to it as the arrow does not return to its bow. They are the worst of the creation. Blessed are those who fight them and are killed by them. They call to the Book of Allah but they have nothing to do with it. Whoever fights them is better to Allah than them.*[23]
>
> *If the [Kharijites] ever gained power, they would corrupt the entire earth, Iraq, and Syria. They would not leave alone a boy or a girl or a man or a woman, for in their view the people have become so corrupt that they cannot be reformed except by mass killing.*[24]
>
> *In the last days, there will be young people rebelling with foolish dreams. They will say the best of words but they will go out of Islam just as an arrow goes through its game. Their faith will not go beyond their throats. So if you meet them in battle, then fight them because whoever fights them will have a reward on the Day of Resurrection.*[25]

Many Muslims consider ISIS to be the modern-day Kharijites,[26] but this can be difficult for young people to understand. Good and evil is often discussed as a dichotomy, but the reality is that there are shades of gray.

In order to recruit and exploit people into terrorism, ISIS must rely heavily on fraud, coercion, and deception, hiding their crimes under the veneer of religion. In other words, ISIS recruits young people by pretending to be benevolent.

Experts believe that youth lack the psychosocial maturity to detect exploitative motives and withstand manipulation. ISIS recruiters are able to conceal their exploitative intentions through entrapment and enmeshment schemes, portraying themselves as boyfriends/lovers, faux family, or the voice of the Islamic *Ummah*. Since self-esteem can decline sharply during the transition from childhood to adolescence, and again from adolescence into young adulthood, ISIS recruiters may be more successful at conscripting and exploiting young people during these times in their lives.

In addition to the radicalization of Zahra and Salma Halane, ISIS has recruited a plethora of teenage girls using similar tactics, including Shannon Conley, Linda Wenzel, Jaelyn Young, and Leila Juma. Although the media can describe these teenage terrorists as "twisted"[27] or inherently bad, I do not believe these kids were evil, neither by nature nor nurture. Some of them, such as seventeen-year-old Samra Kesinovic and fifteen-year-old Sabina Selimovic, even live long enough to sincerely regret their decision.

Samra and Sabina were children of Bosnian refugees who were raised in Vienna, Austria. ISIS recruiters targeted the girls and made them feel empowered, prompting them to leave their comfortable existence in Europe for the "jihad" in Syria. Soon after they left, Samra and Sabina began sharing pictures of their new life in the so-called "caliphate." The girls donned black burqas in all of their selfies and initially tweeted about how happy they were to become terrorist brides to ISIS soldiers. Samra and Sabina were considered the "poster girls" for ISIS and attempted to facilitate the recruitment of other Europeans, specifically young "jihadi" brides. However, they were quickly disillusioned with the cause when the violence became too much for them to bear, but it was too late. Sabina was killed, and when Samra attempted to escape Raqqa, she was caught and forced to become a sex slave before being beaten to death.[28]

Based on my experience with criminals skilled in manipulation and exploitation, I believe these youths were susceptible to radicalization simply because they were going through the normal stages of maturation when they were targeted.

Terrorists recruit for their cause through fraud, coercion, and deception. Since teenagers are less able to detect exploitative motives, they are at higher risk than adults for radicalization into extremism.

As children grow into adulthood, most will inevitably make poor decisions, some worse than others. These choices are often inconsistent with who they become as adults but are nevertheless part of the process of maturing and learning. Friendships, romantic and familial relationships, education, and employment can all be impacted by the poor choices made during teenage years, but these mistakes aren't necessarily reflective of who we are as human beings or the potential of what we can become. Teenagers, in particular, are at high risk of being recruited by criminal enterprises, including terrorists. We must recognize this risk and implement preventive interventions accordingly. When youth experience voids in their lives, we must have social services in place to fill them with positivity.

In addition, for those teenagers who are radicalized and live to regret their decisions, we should strongly consider offering the opportunity for restoration and redemption.

After all,

Freedom is not worth having if it does not include the freedom to make mistakes.
—Mahatma Gandhi

9

Grandma Terror

When I hear the phrase "midlife crisis," I can't help but imagine a stereotype—a balding, middle-aged man, quitting his job for adventure, dumping his nagging wife for college-aged arm candy, and buying a red convertible for attention. I'm not alone. Americans generally associate this term with platitudes of male personality development; however, according to research, women are as likely as men to report experiencing a midlife crisis.[1] Precursors can include an emotional watershed of identity, lacking self-confidence, loneliness, feelings of emptiness and boredom, unhappiness in life, unclear direction, and yearning for adventure. Data on prevalence suggest that 20 to 30 percent of American men and women experience a midlife crisis in their lifetime.[2]

While the clichés of males in midlife crises include sports cars, hairpieces, and cradle robbing, women can engage in parallel behaviors with shopping sprees, plastic surgery, and self-exploration with younger men. Fear of aging, illness, and death; loss of attraction; stunted self-actualization; and empty nest syndrome can lead middle-aged adults into crisis, where they can make drastic and irrational decisions. Like adolescence, this period of biological and psychological change can also create an opportunity for radicalization.

Sally Jones, for example, exhibited multiple signs of a midlife crisis before leaving her home in England to join ISIS in Syria.

Jones was born on November 17, 1968, and raised near London. Her parents quickly divorced, and her father committed suicide when she was only ten years old. She was raised Catholic and participated in Christian youth groups as a teenager, before dropping out of school and looking for work at age sixteen. Although she held different blue-collar jobs to pay the bills, her passion was music, so she jumped at every opportunity to perform with her all-female punk rock band called Krunch.

Friends described her as an easily influenced fad follower who smoked weed and cigarettes, drank alcohol, and used heroin. To fund her party lifestyle, she allegedly engaged in prostitution and lived communally with her pagan friends.[3] For decades, she thought of herself as a free-spirited rock star and flew by the seat of her pants.

By age forty-five, the exhilarating performances and wild after-parties were long gone; Jones was plagued by boredom. Life had become a repetitive exercise for her, and she was tired of the monotony. She had two children with two separate partners but felt lonely and unattractive. Jones would spend copious amounts of time communicating with acquaintances on the Internet, soliciting attention that she no longer received in the real world, first in forums devoted to witchcraft and black magic and later with terrorist recruiters, like Junaid Hussain.

Although it may seem like there is a large gulf between persons engaging in virtual conversations about alternative lifestyles and those discussing terrorism, research suggests that people who spend too much time online can feel moodier, lonelier, and obsessed.[4] These types of people are at higher risk of being targeted by terrorists, regardless of their demographic or subject-matter interest.

Hussain was a hacktivist turned terrorist who had served time in jail for posting sensitive information about former Prime Minister Tony Blair.[5] He fled England to join ISIS in Syria after being released on bail while awaiting trial for a violent disorder charge. Hussain recruited Jones with romantic overtures, prompting her to convert to his version of Islam and leave England for Syria with her nine-year-old son, right before his tenth birthday.[6] Since she had nothing to show for herself and her midlife crisis compromised her judgment, Jones jumped at the opportunity to reinvent herself and get her adrenaline pumping again.

After traveling for twenty-four hours, she arrived in Syria and married twenty-year-old Hussain that same day. Their May–September romance was a whirlwind and offered Jones attention, excitement, and opportunity for what she thought was self-actualization.

While in Raqqa, she received attention like never before. Jones went from being virtually anonymous, talking about sex and witchcraft online, to having an international platform. She solicited attention by posting pictures of herself with weapons and social media messages about violence: "You Christians all need beheading with a nice blunt knife and stuck on the railings at Raqqa. . . . Come here I'll do it for you."[7]

The result was an outpouring of headlines and requests for interviews. Jones clearly followed the media coverage and engaged in reputation management when the narrative expanded beyond her newfound identity as a terrorist. For example, when one journalist accused her of abandoning her children, she was quick to clarify that her eldest son was eighteen and as an adult chose to stay in Britain, while her ten-year-old traveled to Syria with her. When her former neighbors claimed that she had lived off of welfare benefits for much of her life, she took offense and contended that she had been independent of the state, working as a saleswoman and makeup artist. She did admit to posting that Christians needed beheading with a blunt knife, but she rationalized it was only in response to cyberbullying.[8]

Shortly after Jones arrived in Syria, Abu Ahmad—an ISIS official in Raqqa—announced that it had established the all-female *al-Khansaa'* Brigade, named after a famous seventh-century female poet who was a Muslim convert and contemporary of the Prophet Muhammad. The group was formed to raise awareness and punish women who did not abide by ISIS law. The *al-Khansaa'* Brigade quickly began terrorizing local women, arresting, detaining, and whipping them if they wore veils that were too thin or walked in public without a male escort.[9] Of course, Jones became a member, adopting the noms de guerre Um Hussain al-Britani and Shakina Hussein. Membership in the al-Khansaa' Brigade gave her a newfound sense of purpose and sisterhood. As a former cog in the Western workforce, Jones reveled in her first-time position of authority.

She also began recruiting other women to come and join her in Syria. Jones portrayed her new life as "awesome," glamorous, and filled with meaning, as opposed to what she considered the frivolous and superficial existence that she had left behind in Britain. In one social media message, she claimed: "U will never want for money again u live a good life here. U need to get married to get a house . . . but there are loads of men.[10] My son and I love life with the beheaders."[11]

In addition to posts on recruitment, Jones frequently received attention for the violence she espoused: "Know that we have armies in Iraq and an army in Sham[12] of angry lions whose drink is blood and play is carnage." [13]

She publicly aspired to be the first female to behead a Westerner for propaganda[14] and was delighted when she was asked to star in a video of the *al-Khansaa'* Brigade.

Although her entire body was covered, including her face, hands, and distinctive blonde hair, a video emerged in Spring 2015 depicting a woman who experts believed was Sally Jones leading the *al-Khansaa'* Brigade in an automatic rifle training excursion. As she marched up a dirt road to the top of a hill in Syria, Jones shouted praise to Allah and ISIS, while carrying an AK-47 and hoisting it in the air. More than two dozen women in the brigade followed, each covered with an all-black *niqab*, raising their AK-47 rifles in unison with each chant.

At the summit of the hill, the women stood in a line to observe, while Jones shot her rifle in demonstration (see Image 7). The brigade yelled Allahu Akbar with every shot, before taking turns displaying their lethal armory skill for the ISIS propaganda videographer. The fabric from their veils fluttered in the wind.

Despite the fact that Jones clearly exhibited signs of a midlife crisis and had a family history of mental illness, the media described her radicalization as "perplexing."[15] Prior to leaving Britain, Jones had reached middle age, was neither gainfully employed nor able to retire, had one son "leave the nest" as an adult, didn't have a partner, and her youthful good looks had been replaced with signs of age. Although she vehemently denied being a recipient of welfare, there were multiple sources suggesting that she did accept repeated financial assistance, including receiving grocery parcels from a church-organized food bank only weeks before leaving for Syria.[16]

The fact that she was a blonde-haired, blue-eyed, Christian, former punk rocker had nothing to do with her risk for radicalization. In the West, terrorist recruitment has less to do with religion, socioeconomic status, and demographics and more to do with biological and psychological change (e.g., conscription during adolescence or midlife crisis), voids (e.g., lacking a sense of love or belonging, esteem, or self-actualization), and opportunistic targeting. This is perhaps the reason why 40 percent of terrorists arrested in the United States are described as converts to Islam[17]—they are looking for direction and a sense of belonging.

Upon arriving in Syria, Jones married a man twenty-five years her junior, became internationally known overnight, and received a position of authority, as well as a new lease in life. She began thriving off of attention, both positive and negative.

Case in point: almost one year after Jones left Britain to join the Islamic State in Syria, she became a grandmother. Her eldest son and his girlfriend had a baby boy, born on September 9, 2014. In the weeks that followed, Jones failed to publicly express joy in response to the birth of her first grandchild; instead, she posted a flurry of violent, attention-grabbing tweets:

> *When ur wounded & left on the Islamic State plains & the women come out to cut up what remains, just roll to your gun & blow out ur brains.*[18]

In addition to being a media maven, Jones and her young husband, Junaid Hussain, were effective recruiters for ISIS, luring young teens to Syria and catalyzing terrorist attacks abroad. For example, Hussain allegedly inspired the first ISIS terror attack on US soil—where Elton Simpson and Nadir Soofi attempted to attack a Muhammad cartoon contest but were shot and killed by security.[19] Following the incident, details emerged that Hussain had radicalized Elton Simpson via private messaging on social media.[20]

High-level involvement with radicalization and terror plots resulted in the couple becoming high priorities on the Pentagon's "kill list." Jones became known as the "world's most wanted female terrorist."[21] And Hussain was eventually ranked number three on the most wanted terrorist list behind Jihadi John, who gruesomely murdered multiple civilians on camera for ISIS propaganda, and ISIS leader Abu Bakr al-Baghdadi.[22]

On August 26, 2015, only a few months after the Garland, Texas, attack, Hussain was killed in an airstrike, prompting Jones's downward spiral to deepen. She claimed that she would never love again and threatened to become a suicide bomber but couldn't bring herself to follow through. Instead, she began calling for the assassination of others, such as Robert O'Neill—the US Navy Seal who claimed to fire the headshots that killed Osama bin Laden—and Dillard Johnson, an Army Sergeant who claimed the most kills in Iraq.[23]

On the one-year anniversary of Junaid Hussain's death, ISIS released a video of several children, including Jones's son—Joe "Jojo" Dixon—using handguns to brutally execute five Kurdish men.[24] Jojo was only eleven years old at the time and could face murder charges if he were to ever return to Britain.[25] His biological father and family in the UK were horrified to see the violence his mother had brainwashed him into committing, but it was too late.[26] Jones's midlife crisis and subsequent criminality had effectively corrupted her youngest son, from an "innocent schoolboy" to an "Islamic State executioner."

Internationally, Jones remained a high priority for law enforcement. It took three and a half years after she left Britain for reports to begin emerging that she was killed in a predator drone strike.[27] While some sources claimed that her son was killed alongside her, others contended that he was still alive, training with ISIS.[28] It remained unclear whether she was planning additional attacks at the time of her death or fleeing Raqqa to the Syria-Iraq border, in desperation to return to Britain.[29] If she were fleeing, however, it would align with the end-timing of an average midlife crisis, which some research suggests lasts only two to five years for women.[30]

Although the vast majority of people who experience a midlife crisis will never become terrorists, the potential of elevated risk should not be quickly dismissed. Think of it like a perfect storm. Psychological and biological changes create a crisis, and if that person happens to be targeted by a terrorist recruiter, an opportunity for radicalization will exist, regardless of the target's demographic or faith. Mental illness, combined with a history of marginalization and an easily impressionable personality, can further increase a person's susceptibility to influence from recruiters. The target is ultimately flooded with circular arguments, which are supported with cherry-picked evidence.

For example, in the first issue of al-Qaeda propaganda magazine *Inspire,* infamous terrorist recruiter Anwar al-Awlaki quoted the following passage from the Qur'an: "Hatred has already appeared from their mouths, and what their breasts conceal is greater, al-Imran: 118." Al-Awlaki interpreted this passage to mean that the West has a deeply rooted hatred for Islam and Muslims, which began with Christianity and continues with democracy.[31] He then rationalized this to mean that persons who draw cartoons of the Prophet Muhammad should be murdered: "So what is the proper solution to this growing campaign of defamation? The medicine prescribed by the Messenger of Allah is the execution of those involved."[32]

In the article, al-Awlaki specifically called for the assassination of Seattle-based cartoonist Molly Norris, for her role in the "Everybody Draw Mohammad Day" campaign.[33]

However, this type of one-sided violence in response to cartoons takes on an entirely different meaning when read in context. In Islam, Imran is the father of Mary, mother of Jesus. In fact, the earlier sections of this chapter in the Qur'an actually tell the story of Mary, who is the only woman named in the Qur'an:

- Verse 42 reads, "O Mary, indeed Allah has chosen you and purified you and chosen you above the women of the worlds."

- Verse 45 reads, "O Mary, indeed Allah gives you good tidings of a word from Him, whose name will be the Messiah, Jesus, the son of Mary - distinguished in this world and the Hereafter and among those brought near [to Allah]."

This same section of the Qur'an also speaks positively of Jesus:

- Verse 46 reads, "He [Jesus] will speak to the people in the cradle and in maturity and will be of the righteous."
- Verse 48 reads, "God will give [Jesus] wisdom and teach him the Book, the Torah, and the Gospel."
- Verse 49 reads, "He [Jesus] will be a Messenger of God to the Israelites to whom he will say, 'I have brought you a miracle from your Lord. I can create for you something from clay in the form of a bird. When I blow into it, it will become a real bird, by the permission of God. I can heal the blind and the lepers and bring the dead back to life, by the permission of God. I can tell you about what you eat and what you store in your homes. This is a miracle for you if you want to have faith.'

Given the information contained in the al-Imran chapter of the Qur'an, the verse quoted by al-Awlaki was unequivocally not about Christianity or democracy. Although not named in the specific passage, experts interpret the verse as referencing discord between Muslims and tribes from Mecca and their supporters.[34]

As mentioned in an earlier chapter of this book, Muhammad had faced persecution for over a decade while in Mecca, prompting him to migrate to Medina in 622. From Medina, Muhammad and his followers began raiding Meccan caravan routes, which resulted in Meccan tribes sending an army to confront the Muslims. Muhammad lured them to Badr, where he battled them and won, which was attributed to divine intervention.[35] However, upon returning home, he encountered local tribes violating the Constitution of Medina, catalyzing conflict there, as well.

Ultimately, it is believed the verse in question is advice not to trust the pagan tribes with whom the Muslims had quarreled. The entirety reads as follows:

> O you who have believed, do not take as intimates those other than
> yourselves, for they will not spare you [any] ruin. They wish you

would have hardship. Hatred has already appeared from their mouths, and what their breasts conceal is greater. We have certainly made clear to you the signs, if you will use reason.

Al-Awlaki's cherry picking and misinterpretation is a tactic used by all terrorist recruiters, yet explicitly prohibited in the Qur'an in Chapter 3, Verse 7:

It is He who has sent down to you, [O Muhammad], the Book; in it are verses [that are] precise—they are the foundation of the Book—and others unspecific. ***As for those in whose hearts is deviation [from truth], they will follow that of it which is unspecific, seeking discord and seeking an interpretation [suitable to them]. And no one knows its [true] interpretation except Allah.*** *But those firm in knowledge say, "We believe in it.* ***All [of it] is from our Lord."*** *And no one will be reminded except those of understanding.*

Terrorist recruiters clearly treat the Qur'an like an à la carte menu to support their perverse views, taking passages out of context and misinterpreting the intent of Allah.

When targeting people for radicalization, terrorist recruiters do not look for truly devout Muslims with conviction in their beliefs; they target easily influenced followers who are marginalized or suffer from mental illness and are at high risk of engaging in crime. It is no surprise, then, that the vast majority of ISIS recruits are teenagers or young adults—criminality peaks in adolescence, when psychological maturation is still underway.

Although adults don't have the same risk factors as adolescents, they can still become susceptible during times of psychological or biological change. While I discussed Sally Jones as an illustration, she certainly isn't the only middle-aged grandmother recruited into extremism. Kathie Smith was also forty-five years old when she left her home in Indiana to marry an ISIS supporter twenty years her junior. Although she didn't ultimately travel to Syria for combat, she and her husband did fly the ISIS flag from their apartment window, posted pictures of themselves with automatic rifles, and disseminated messages of extremist support from their home in Germany.[36] Similarly, although Colleen LaRose was not a grandmother, she was also radicalized at age forty-five and exhibited signs of a midlife crisis (such as having an affair) as well as mental illness, given her suicide attempt only a few years earlier.

While some readers may not find my examples compelling enough to believe that women experiencing a midlife crisis are at risk for radicalization, there are certainly enough anecdotal examples to warrant further exploration into the theory.

If it holds true and radicalized persons are found to share the common thread of experiencing voids, psychological and biological changes and crises, and mental illness, we must use this information to support interventions that prevent recruitment, as well as refine our response to radicalized women and men from Western countries.

At present, the West's reaction is to hate terrorists more than they hate us and retaliate with greater force. When stories emerged of Sally Jones's tearful pleas to return home, truthful or not, they were met with petitions to stop her from doing so and to remove her citizenship.[37] Certain members of her family and the media described Jones as evil and a "hate-filled psychopath," but this did absolutely nothing to change her disposition; it simply reinforced it.

Despite the fact that she had become a criminal, she was still a human being. In order to combat terrorists and their ability to radicalize recruits, we must go high when they go low. We have a duty to remain steadfast in our principles of humanity, freedom, and compassion. We should go to great lengths to prevent people from being conscripted and dismantle the veneer under which these criminals operate. This isn't about Islam. These terrorists are not practicing Muslims, despite what they profess. They are war profiteers using marginalized people to advance their access to money and power. This is about violent and criminal hedonism.

In response, we could certainly continue retaliating, but based on my research, I do not believe that will be effective. Instead, perhaps we should remember this:

> *Darkness cannot drive out darkness; only light can do that.*
> *Hate cannot drive out hate; only love can do that.*
> —Martin Luther King, Jr.

PART III

10

Brother of Terror

Counterterrorism experts agree that there is no single profile of an ISIS recruit.[1] While we know that radicalization generally happens on the Internet and the typical recruit falls between the ages of fifteen and twenty-five, persons conscripted into terrorism are remarkably diverse, including a growing number of radicalized females.[2]

Since *irjafi** ideologies have historically excluded women from armed conflict,[3] some experts are inclined to discuss the modern trend of radicalized women separately from that of men, although there is considerable overlap in tactics used across the two. According to largely qualitative research, females join terrorist organizations for multicausal reasons, including a broad range of push and pull factors, which are different in their influential weight for each individual.[4] Push factors can include: feelings of cultural and social isolation; inequality; belief that Muslims are being systematically oppressed; and anger, sadness, or frustration over the perceived inaction in response to this oppression.[5] While pull factors include: desire for romance and friendship or sisterhood, aspiration to live in an Islamic utopian "caliphate,"[6] and romanticism of the experience.[7,8]

Similarly, men recruited into ISIS and other terrorist organizations are believed to be pushed into extremism by feelings of prejudice and aversion to Western culture; and pulled by influence of recruiters, desire for brotherhood and adventure, and the male warrior hypothesis.[9]

The male warrior hypothesis argues that human tribalism and parochialism lead people to categorize individuals on the basis of their group membership.[10] In-group members are then treated benevolently, while out-group members are treated malevolently. According to the theory, men have psychologically evolved

---

* Arabic word for terrorist.

to initiate and display acts of intergroup aggression because it represents an opportunity to gain access to in-group friends, intimate partners, territory, and increased status.[11] Therefore, according to this theory, men may be drawn to ISIS as a result of their psychological proclivity to pursue intergroup conflict.

At present, there is not enough empirical data to measure the strength of correlation, much less draw causal inference, from these variables and theories, so it is impossible to know what is the greatest predictor of radicalization. However, this information does provide a foundation for future research and exploration into counterterrorism interventions that focus on recruitment prevention.

Through my research on terrorist radicalization, I have identified considerable overlap between the recruitment methods used by terrorists and other organized crime syndicates, such as human traffickers; specifically, the use of force, fraud, and coercion for the purpose of exploitation.

Similar to human traffickers, it is well documented that terrorist recruiters tailor their messaging to the individual being conscripted by mapping out and appealing to their social, psychological, and cultural landscape.[12] This is done so the recruiter can coerce and defraud the target into believing that the organized crime syndicate can fill the voids and provide direction in the individual's life.

Figure 10.1. Maslow's Hierarchy of Needs: ISIS Recruiter Targeting by Region

According to Abraham Maslow's *Theory of Human Motivation*, a hierarchy of needs influences individual choices (see Figure 10.1, with ISIS targeting modification). First, humans will seek to fulfill their basic physiological needs by seeking to obtain food, shelter, water, and sexual intercourse. Next, we are motivated to acquire physical and financial safety, followed by feelings of love and belonging. Once those first three levels of needs are met, people will seek self-esteem and respect from others, followed by self-actualization to realize their full potential and positively transform society.

Generally, terrorist recruiters and propaganda will coerce and deceive both male and female targets from around the world into believing that the criminal organization provides the only opportunity for self-actualization and betterment of the international Muslim *Ummah*. They falsely claim that this is in accordance with Islam, despite the fact that it is being used as a tactic to manipulate the target into an exploitable position and used in combination with the temporary fulfillment of at least one other self-interested need.

Men and women from Middle-Eastern countries are more likely to be *forced* into joining terrorist organizations like ISIS when compared to their Western counterparts. In ISIS-controlled territories, resources can be restricted, and recruits can feel compelled to join so that they can have access to food, shelter, employment opportunities, and other social and financial capital. When and if they decline to join, their safety and the safety of their families can be threatened.

On the other hand, men and women from Western countries are more likely to be *coerced* or *defrauded* into joining terrorist organizations like ISIS through false promises of love and belonging, romantic relationships, and in-group brotherhood or sisterhood. Additionally, men from Western countries are lured through overtures targeting their esteem and opportunities to gain respect from others.

Although some mistakenly believe that religious ideology is a significant predictor of terrorist recruitment, a growing body of data collected from radicalized individuals suggests otherwise. Persons recruited into ISIS from the West are often converts to Islam or weren't described as particularly religious prior to being targeted. Radicalization typically occurs during the peak of life course criminality, and male recruits often have histories of delinquency or drug use prior to conscription. Furthermore, ISIS recruits are often described as easily impressionable or socially isolated, and many exhibit signs of mental illness.

The following chapters continue to provide examples of how terrorist targeting and recruitment tactics are diametrically opposed to Islam, while focusing on men. ISIS leadership exploits marginalized communities and mental illness and engages in trafficking of child soldiers, for the sole purpose of acquiring money, power, and territory. I posit that men in the Middle East are recruited through threats to their safety and basic physiological needs of their family, while men from the West are radicalized through coercion, deception, and false promises of belonging, esteem, and self-actualization.

11

Tactics of a Desert Lion

Abu Wahib—also known as the "Desert Lion"—stood in the middle of an international highway in western Iraq, near the Syrian border, holding a semi-automatic weapon in his left hand and waving to three trucks, signaling them to stop with his right. He believed the drivers were going to bring supplies from Iraq to a minority sect of Shiite Muslims in Syria called Alawites.* To him, the Alawites were "dogs," and he wanted to send a message by cutting off supplies to the *rafidite*—those who had rejected ISIS and refused to support their plight.

Despite his signals, the first truck—a white flatbed—passed by him without immediately stopping. The trucker was in fear for his life and knew he could be murdered, so he initially ignored Wahib and kept driving. It wasn't until he spotted the additional gunmen ready for chase and fire that he realized it was a "damned if you do, damned if you don't" situation and accepted the futility of resistance. There was no doubt in his mind that he couldn't outrun them in his truck, so he pulled over to the side of the road as instructed.

A blue flatbed followed immediately behind him and then a red one. One of the gunmen who accompanied Wahib yelled to the men, "Pull over where you are!"

All three drivers complied.

Wahib walked up to the red truck first and gestured for the driver to open the door. He did.

"Your ID card," he demanded.

The man was not a soldier fighting against ISIS. He was simply a civilian working, trying to make a living for his family, but there he was, stopped on the

---

* The Alawites are an offshoot of Shia Islam who revere Prophet Mohammed; Ali, the Prophet Mohammed's cousin and son-in-law; and Salman the Persian, a companion of the Prophet Mohammed.

side of the road, surrounded by ISIS militants in combat boots, fatigues, and holding AK-47 rifles. The man didn't support their terrorism, but he was doing absolutely nothing to impede them, so he didn't understand why he, a fellow Muslim, was being stopped in such a menacing way.

Regardless, he knew that he was obligated to comply with their requests. The driver left his door open, while he reached inside the cabin for his identification. The man's fear was palpable and Wahib had no doubt that he would comply, so he left him searching and went on to the blue truck.

The driver had already hopped out of his cabin in order to gain a better vantage of the interactions and possibly figure out what was going on. Wahib approached him, casually swinging his arms, with his automatic weapon by his side, and demanded his identification, as well. The driver of the blue truck quickly retrieved and turned over his card for Wahib's inspection, before walking with him toward the white truck.

"Why didn't you stop?" Wahib angrily asked the man, who was also standing outside of the cabin.

The driver didn't have a good answer.

"You're both Shiite, right?" Wahib continued.

The men silently shook their head *no* in response.

The drivers knew that these were Sunni ISIS combatants who despised Shiites, so they attempted to lie. "We're both Sunnis from Homs," the driver of the blue truck implored, as his colleague nodded in affirmation.

"Both of you?" Wahib probed.

"Yes."

He didn't believe them and began reinspecting their identification documents, looking for some way to further scrutinize their answer and reveal that the men were in fact Shiites.

"You're Syrian?" he asked

"Yes," they replied in unison.

The men were frustrated and concerned with the fact that they were no threat to ISIS yet were being scrutinized about their faith, when all they aspired to do was work. The driver of the blue truck desperately wanted to be allowed to leave and tried to convince them that he was on their side, "Are you Sunni? May Allah give you victory," but his sentiments were clearly feigned.

As they spoke, the driver of the red truck approached with his identification card in hand. Wahib turned to him and asked, "Are *you* Sunni?"

"Yes," the driver of the red truck casually answered without pause.

"Are you sure?"

"Yes."

All three truck drivers stood facing Wahib, desperately trying in vain to convince him that they were in fact Sunni and were supporters of ISIS (see Image 8). However, the reality was that they were just blue-collar workers trying to make a living. The men were wearing collared shirts and belted pants, with business-style haircuts and minimal facial hair. They held their hands folded behind their backs as they stood in front of Wahib.

His appearance was drastically different. Wahib had long hair, wrapped in a black headscarf, and a long scraggly black beard with no mustache. He wore a tan uniform and military fatigue utility vest. During the course of their conversation, Wahib would switch from menacingly holding his large black rifle to casually using it to prop up his body weight as he stood.

It was obvious that he couldn't have been less fearful of these three men.

"Are you sure you're Sunni?" Wahib asked them again.

"Yes," they all three answered affirmatively, in fear for their lives. "We just want to live. We're here to earn a living," the driver of the red truck implored.

When Wahib didn't follow up immediately with a question, the men started to walk back to their trucks, but he quickly ordered them to stay right where they were.

"What proves to me that you're Sunnis?" Wahib asked in almost a whisper that could barely be heard over the hum of the idling trucks. The men leaned forward, and he repeated, "What *proves* to me that you're Sunnis?"

"By Allah the Great . . . and by the Prophet," the driver of the blue truck swore.

Wahib turned toward the driver of the red truck, "What about you?"

Without hesitation, he responded, "Allah is greater, there's no god but Allah. Allahu Akbar. I bear witness that there's no god but Allah, and that Muhammad is the messenger of Allah."

The driver of the blue truck chimed in, "Let's pray together!"

Although the men were trying their best to convince Wahib that they were Sunni and supporters of ISIS, he had already made up his mind that they were Shiites and he was going to kill them. However, with the ISIS cameraman videotaping the encounter for propaganda, Wahib wanted some fodder to rationalize their execution, so he continued interrogating them, giving them false hope of being let free and simply delaying what had become the inevitable.

"How many kneelings do you make at dawn prayer?" Wahib questioned.

"Four kneelings," the driver of the blue truck answered nervously.

"How many kneelings do you say?" Wahib asked the driver of the red truck.

"At dawn? Three kneelings," he replied.

"Three kneelings you say, the other says four. What about you?" Wahib pointed toward the driver of the white truck.

"Three," he sheepishly replied, hoping he had answered correctly.

Following their conflicting answers, Wahib instructed the three drivers, "Kneel down."

While two of the drivers squatted down and looked up hopefully, the driver of the red truck began to come to the realization of the peril he was facing. Unlike the other two, he sat down cross-legged, with the weight of each arm resting on a knee, and stared blankly at the pavement contemplating what he should do next. In a final moment of desperation, he asked to change his answer.

"Now he's saying at dawn its five kneelings," Wahib highlighted the man's uncertainty.

"At noon?"

"Three," the driver of the red truck answered.

"He says three," Wahib parroted the answer to his compatriots, "And in the evening?"

"Two kneelings."

"Two kneelings in the evening, at noon three, and five at dawn," Wahib again recapped the responses, mockingly. It was a trick question. The men had been repeatedly asked only about *three* daily prayer sessions at dawn, noon, and evening. While Shiites only pray three times per day, it is well known that Sunnis pray *five* times per day—a small but contentious difference between the two sects.

Before sunrise, Sunnis have the *Fajr* prayer to start the day with a remembrance of Allah. Shortly after noon, they break for the *Dhuhr* prayer to again remember Allah and seek guidance. In the late afternoon, they break for the *Asr* prayer to remember Allah a third time and contemplate the meaning of life. Soon after sunset, they have the *Maghrib* prayer to again remember Allah as the day comes to a close. And last, before going to bed, Sunnis will perform the *Isha* prayer to once more remember Allah and ask for guidance, mercy, and forgiveness.[1]

Shiites, on the other hand, will also perform the *Fajr* prayer in the morning, but they combine the *Dhuhr* and *Asr* prayers in the afternoon and combine the *Maghrib* and *Isha* prayers at night.[2]

Wahib knew that all three of the truck drivers were Shiite because a practicing Sunni would have corrected that there are five daily prayer sessions, but despite this confirmation that the truck drivers were from a different sect of Islam, he wasn't finished questioning them.

"What are the Alawites doing with the honor of the Muslims in Syria?" he continued.

The drivers of the red and white trucks had given up and didn't even attempt to answer, but the driver of the blue truck continued desperately trying to convince Wahib that they deserved to be let free, "By Allah, I don't know. We have nothing to do with this. They're raping women and killing Muslims. We've never been close to the Army or close to the Alawites." He was telling Wahib what he wanted to hear, but it was futile. Their fate was cemented before they had even pulled their vehicles over. If they weren't with ISIS, they were against them.

Wahib had heard enough and ominously interrupted the man's final plea for safety, "From your talking, you're a *mushrik.** Allah the Great says: 'Fight against all polytheists just as they fight against you.'"

Wahib was attempting to cherry-pick *Surat l-tawbah* 9:36 of the Qur'an to rationalize the impending violence he would exact against them, but, like every other ISIS terrorist, he had taken the quote completely out of context and misinterpreted it to rationalize his self-interested crimes. While it does read in part, "And fight against the disbelievers collectively as they fight against you," the historical context of the quote is that it was in reference to the idolaters of *Makkah*, who were not Muslim, Jewish, or Christian.[3] Moreover, it completely ignores countervailing instructions in the rest of the Qur'an. For example, *Surat l-baqarah* 2:190 reads, "Fight in the way of Allah those who fight you but do not transgress. Indeed. Allah does not like transgressors," which prohibits aggression. And *Surat l-tawbah* 9:6 reads, "And if any one of the polytheists seeks your protection, then grant him protection so that he may hear the words of Allah. Then deliver him to his place of safety. That is because they are a people who do not know."

Wahib's aggression toward these three men, who were simply doing their job as truck drivers and begging him for the protection to live, was clearly not in accordance with Islam. However, like all terrorism, this wasn't about religion, it

---

* Polytheist.

was simply a veneer for ISIS leadership's quest for money and power, as well as the control of land and resources in this particular region.

When the truck drivers were instructed to stand up, the last glimmer of hope in their eyes faded away. The three men were escorted from the highway to a piece of desert nearby, where they were forced to kneel with their hands resting on their laps.

Three ISIS combatants, holding semiautomatic rifles, stood behind each of the three truck drivers.

The militant to the far right waved his arm to people standing in front of the drivers, instructing them to move out of the line of fire and bear witness to the impending execution.

Wahib took aim from behind and began firing his rifle. He shot the driver of the white truck first. The bullet hit him in the back, causing him to lurch forward and grab his chest. Clouds of dust rose from the desert sand with each bullet fired, suggesting they had completely pierced through each victim's body and exited on the other side.

Wahib continued firing in rapid succession, while the propaganda cameramen filmed. Next, he hit the driver of the blue truck, causing his back to arch downward and forcing his arms to contract, wincing in pain. The man fell forward into the sand as Wahib continued shooting him in the back at point-blank range. His legs appeared to flinch with each subsequent shot, and his sandals jerked off of his feet into the desert sand. The spectators calmly cheered on the violent execution by saying, "Allahu Akbar," with every shot.

And Wahib kept shooting.

A bullet hit the driver of the red truck in the small of his back, making him grab his stomach as his body crumpled to the desert. Wahib advanced forward, shooting the driver of the blue truck again, but this time aiming for the man's head. At this moment, he noticed that the driver of the white truck, who had been wounded, was attempting to crawl away, prompting him to turn his gun against the man once more. In the concluding shots, he casually walked up the length of each man, shooting them repeatedly in the head while they lay there, helpless.

"Allahu Akbar," the cameraman repeated, again and again, as Wahib continued firing his weapon at point-blank range a total of thirteen times.

The cameraman captured their lifeless bodies, face down, seeping streams of blood into the desert sand, before a uniformed man with a black face cover relayed a message,

*Let Nuri al-Maliki [the Iraqi Prime Minister], his Shiite follow-
ers, and his demons see. Those who are bragging that they insured
the international highway among Baghdad, Amman, and Syria.
So here is the international highway in the hands of the Islamic
State . . . in the hands of the* mujahideen.

The camera lingered on the lifeless bodies of the truck drivers, as one of the ISIS
combatants began tying belts around their necks and another began checking
their pockets. "Allahu Akbar! . . . and glory be unto Allah and his messenger,"
the cameraman commented before the frame cut to a masked man throwing a
Molotov cocktail into the cabin of the blue truck. Pillars of smoke flooded out
of the windows as the arsonist ran back into the desert with his right hand held
high, pointing one finger to the heavens, yelling, "Allahu Akbar!"

ISIS had adopted the gesture as a symbol of *tawhid*. For most Muslims, *tawhid*
refers to the peaceful oneness of Allah, or monotheism. ISIS of course misinterprets this concept to mean that all other religions, as well as other interpretations
of Islam aside from theirs, are idolatry, which is deserving of death.

The end scene of this propaganda video included a voiceover from an extremist sermon, "Lo and behold the spark has been ignited in Iraq and its fire shall get
only bigger until it burns the armies of the cross in *Dabiq*."

Although ISIS propaganda portrays the group as religious and ideologically
driven, the reality is that many low-level fighters are forced to join out of fear for
their safety and the safety of their families. Not only has ISIS been indiscriminate
in their execution of anyone who is against their cause, but also those who fail to
join or actively support their terrorism. The execution described in this chapter is
only one example of the countless murders committed against civilian Muslims
by ISIS in Syria and Iraq.

Families who refuse to support them will, at a minimum, face restricted
resources to meet their physiological needs. In the most extreme circumstances,
they can be executed for their failure to support the plight of ISIS. The reality
is that many ISIS recruits are there, not out of their own free will and conscious
choice, but because they are forced into terrorism in fear for their safety.

Armed conflict amplifies the risks of being recruited into terrorism by weak-
ening rule of law and decreasing the availability of social services. Broken governments, judicial systems, and community support structures fail to protect
these populations from disasters and crime, including the internal threat of ISIS

recruiters. During armed conflicts, governments divert existing resources to respond to the imminent crisis with a resulting loss in facilities and personnel for peacetime governmental services, like law enforcement.[4] This exacerbates existing limitations and creates new gaps in government structures to protect its citizens. Armed conflict can break down government institutions and create a climate of impunity that encourages ISIS recruiters to prey on vulnerable populations.

The situation in Syria continues to deteriorate as the civil war endures. Sub-state armed groups of varying ideologies control wide swaths of the country's territory.[5] As a result, those who remain trapped in Syria, particularly in Raqqa and Dayr al-Zawr, can find themselves left with few to no options and forced into terrorism. Approximately half of Syria's prewar population has been displaced; nearly four million have fled to neighboring countries, and roughly 7.6 million are displaced internally.[6] Syrians, including those who remain in the country and refugees in neighboring countries, are considered to be highly vulnerable to ISIS recruiters.

Abu Wahib, for example, was a dangerous and cunning individual who made it abundantly clear that he would indiscriminately murder any human being who did not believe in his ideology and actively support ISIS.

Executing these noncombatant truck drivers on video, without covering his face, in broad daylight, on a major highway, was considered incredibly brazen, especially given that Wahib was a fugitive on the run from police after being sentenced to death and subsequently breaking out of jail a year earlier. In putting this violence on full display, his intent was to threaten and force people into joining his cause and adopt his manipulated interpretation of Islam. Two months following the truck driver execution, Wahib was blamed for kidnapping sixteen policemen along the Iraq-Jordan highway in Anbar, leaving twelve of them dead and four wounded.[7] By 2014, twenty-year-old Wahib was an internationally recognized leader and poster boy of ISIS, known as a "smiling chief executioner."[8] Countless beheadings, crucifixions, and amputations followed over the course of the next two years, which began occurring in front of observers and in central squares of major cities, as opposed to desolate deserts.[9] What choice does a person have when criminal militants have more money, power, and ability to protect than the government-sanctioned police?

Although Abu Wahib has since been killed in an airstrike,[10] civilians who remain in ISIS-controlled territories continue to be threatened with death if they refuse to join the extremist organization. They are also susceptible to being murdered if they attempt to flee. Notwithstanding the fact that they do not agree with ISIS ideology and violence, Middle-Eastern men and women in these war-torn areas are led to sincerely believe that they are safer with ISIS then against.

Yet, despite the undisputed peril faced by civilians in ISIS-controlled areas of the Middle East, opportunities for refugee resettlement continue to be contentiously restricted around the world. At the time of this writing, citizens from Iran, Syria, Yemen, Libya, Somalia, Chad, and North Korea are banned from entering the United States, and the number of refugees has fallen to the lowest level in decades.[11] Security concerns are cited as the chief justification for keeping borders closed and refusing to resettle refugees fleeing ISIS.[12]

For example, in 2016, Donald Trump Jr. analogized the "Syrian refugee problem" with a tweet: "If I had a bowl of skittles and I told you just three would kill you. Would you take a handful?" (see Image 9).

In response, I would first contend that people aren't the equivalent of Skittles, and analogizing them as such undermines the importance and inherent value of their lives. Second, the position assumes that some Syrian refugees will kill Americans, despite the fact that it is extremely unlikely. According to a September 2016 study by the Cato Institute titled "Terrorism and Immigration: A Risk Analysis," "not a single refugee, Syrian or otherwise, has been implicated in a terrorist attack since the Refugee Act of 1980 set up systematic procedures for accepting refugees into the United States."[13]

In fact, while the lifetime risk of being murdered in America is one in 229,[14] the odds of a fatal terror attack by a refugee are one in 3.6 billion.[15]

Instead of effectively protecting Americans and combating terrorism, the sentiment from Donald Trump Jr. and countless others is akin to propaganda for ISIS. This isn't about being politically correct. Criminal organizations like ISIS want Western countries to hate Muslim refugees and equate them with terrorism because it reinforces their veil of legitimacy.[16] Every Muslim refugee who is denied the opportunity to flee is a target for recruitment and a potential resource that can be exploited.

When Muslim refugees are afforded the opportunity to resettle in the West and are welcomed with open arms, however, it contradicts the Islamic State's message. Moreover, research suggests that Muslims make up the largest proportion of terror victims,[17] and, as a leader in the free world, we have a duty to protect them.

Syrian refugees who are risking their lives to flee ISIS are in desperate need of our help in resettlement. Before you dismiss their need out of self-interest and unwarranted fear, please remember:

> *If you are neutral in situations of injustice,*
> *you have chosen the side of the oppressor.*
>
> —Desmond Tutu

12

Terrorist for Hire

I've held a job ever since I was fifteen years old. My first was working as a bagger at a Fresh Fields grocery store, then as a retail employee at a bathing suit boutique, followed by a position as a hostess at Lone Star Steakhouse & Saloon. After graduating high school, I needed to make more money so that I could afford living independently, as well as college tuition, so I worked as a waitress, receptionist, and even, at one point, as a tow truck driver.

I stayed in a small apartment furnished with couches that I found on the side of the road and used my childhood bedroom set. Despite the fact that I worked full-time while going to school, my income still put me below the poverty line.

When I eventually graduated from my Bachelor's program with honors, I naively believed that I had "made it" and would soon land my dream job. Unfortunately, I quickly learned that opportunities for criminology graduates were limited and didn't provide the salary and benefits I had hoped for. My first job as a college graduate was paid hourly and, to my dismay, did not provide any health insurance or other benefits.

Considering that I had just spent four years of my life and tens of thousands of dollars for a degree that wasn't landing me gainful employment, I felt deflated. I was at a loss for what I should do, so I turned to my former professors for advice. They convinced me to take my Graduate Record Examination (GRE) and apply to a master's degree program.

I did.

In graduate school, many of my peers still had their parents subsidizing their bills so they could afford to only work twenty hours per week on a meager graduate assistant stipend. I, on the other hand, needed to work thirty to forty hours to make ends meet. I even took on additional odd jobs during the summers as a lifeguard manager at a pool and a day care provider at Gold's Gym. I earned my master's degree and then pursued my doctorate, because I figured the higher my education, the more opportunities I would have.

Even after finishing my PhD program, I have always held down multiple jobs simultaneously while also raising my four children. I think the most I ever had at one time was six: statistician, human trafficking expert witness, author, pundit, op-ed contributor, and adjunct professor.

I believe I take on so much because I have lived in poverty and I want to make sure my children do not have to experience the same struggles that I did. Luckily, I was afforded the opportunities to work and go to school, so I was able to eventually actualize my aspirations and live out my version of the "American Dream."

I now speak with teenagers in similar circumstances in Virginia. I talk about how I believe the greatest predictor of success is grit. By maintaining courage and resolve, strength of character, and perseverance under pressure, people can overcome seemingly insurmountable obstacles. However, there is more to that equation. Success cannot be achieved without opportunity, and, simply put, much of the world's population does not have the same opportunities as people in the United States.

Tunisia, for example, has been plagued by perpetually high rates of unemployment for decades, and in 2010 the poor living conditions in the country catalyzed an Arab Spring revolution. It began on December 17 after a twenty-six-year-old named Mohamed Bouazizi marched in front of a government building in Sidi Bouzid and set himself on fire.

Bouazizi was the sole breadwinner for his widowed mother and six siblings, and earlier that day he had been selling fruits and vegetables without a permit.[1] When police asked him to hand over his wooden cart, he refused, and a policewoman allegedly slapped him.[2]

The anger and humiliation from this incident was the last straw. Like many Tunisians at the time, he was so tired of living in poverty and being ruled by an autocratic regime that he had become desperate for change. The burns from his self-immolation killed him within a few short weeks, but his death created massive reverberations. People started protesting locally and posting videos on the Internet, which led to more protests cropping up around the country, and eventually in countries across the Middle East and North Africa, including Egypt, Libya, Syria, Yemen, Algeria, Iraq, Jordan, Kuwait, Morocco, and Oman.[3]

Not all of the protests were successful in effectuating change, but they were in Tunisia. After only a few weeks, Tunisia's President Zine al-Abidine Ben Ali stepped down from his position and fled the country to Saudi Arabia.[4] Six months later, he and his wife were convicted in absentia of corruption.[5] That same year, the Tunisian government began transitioning into a democracy by holding the country's first free elections.[6] However, the shift has been rife with challenges. Political assassinations, security threats from neighboring countries, and ballooning unemployment continue to destabilize Tunisian democracy.

Al-Qaeda was not involved with catalyzing the demonstrations but quickly began leeching off of the movement and co-opting it as their own. There were little to no mentions of Tunisia in al-Qaeda propaganda until Issue 5 of *Inspire* magazine, following the protests. The country was mentioned twenty times in that one issue, despite having only been mentioned once in the four previous issues. Al-Qaeda referred to the protests as their "Tsunami of Change" and erroneously suggested that the protesters were, like terrorists, demanding Sharia law, as opposed to basic freedoms and human rights.[7] Al-Qaeda further suggested that the protesters supported terrorism and were shouting "We are all Usama" as they marched, which couldn't have been further from the truth (see Image 10). Al-Qaeda was just using the movement in an attempt to recruit disaffected young people.

In November 2017, the International Labor Organization estimated that 35.8 percent of young people in Tunisia aged fifteen to twenty-four were unemployed compared to only 9.5 percent in the United States and 11.7 percent in the United Kingdom.[8] To put this figure in perspective even further, the unemployment rate during the Great Depression in the United States reached its highest peak in 1933 with 25 percent—more than 10 percent lower than the current unemployment rate for young people in Tunisia.[9]

This remarkably high rate of unemployment is one of the reasons why Tunisia has become a disproportionate source of terrorist recruits.[10] In 2015, experts estimated that 7,000 Tunisians had left the country to join ISIS—4,000 in Libya and another 3,000 in Syria or Iraq.[11] The Tunisian government further believes that at least an additional 12,000 have been stopped from leaving the country to join ISIS.[12]

Research on the profiles of Tunisian terrorist recruits suggests that these men typically experience long bouts of unemployment or underemployment prior to radicalization and became frustrated with the few opportunities to advance in their country.[13] They are often disillusioned with the new democratic government, having believed that the shift would have led to the creation of more employment opportunities for young people, only to find that the jobs still did not exist, even for those who graduated from college.

Strain theory provides a conceptual foundation for understanding the pathway to this "sudden-onset extremism."[14] The theory states that every person aspires to attain certain goals and individuals who lack the means to achieve those goals can experience strain.[15] This strain can result in crime because the individual aspires to something that they have no legal opportunity to actualize. As a result, they may feel a financial, social, or cultural pressure to resort to illicit means.

Young men in Tunisia, like young people around the world, want gainful employment and opportunities for self-actualization. If they are not able to secure jobs that utilize their full potential, they may be left economically stagnant and struggling, which can result in strain. This strain is what an ISIS recruiter will seek out and exploit.

Take the case of Walid Ismail, whose story of conscription represents how ISIS draws disaffected young people from troubled countries with promises of financial opportunity.

The twenty-year-old looked like the stereotypical ISIS militant, with long scraggly hair, a full beard, and a shaved mustache. He also dressed the part, wearing an army fatigue t-shirt and khaki cargo pants, with desert military boots.

Ismail was once a law-abiding citizen who worked in a bakery but now found himself hiding inside a dilapidated building in the town of Bashiqa, near Mosul, Iraq. He stared at the blood and debris on the dirt-covered floor and contemplated his next course of action. His most immediate concern was the conditions of his surrender to the two dozen Kurdish Peshmerga soldiers outside.

Ismail had taken cover inside the building with about a dozen other ISIS militants. A Tunisian among them had just detonated a suicide bomb that was intended to massacre the Kurdish military but backfired, killing himself and five of his fellow terrorists instead. The soldiers responded to the attempted attack on their lives by taking turns blindly firing their semiautomatic weapons inside the building, simply hoping to hit something affiliated with ISIS and then dipping down behind a short brick divider wall for protection.

"You're going to kill me," Ismail shouted.

"We won't kill you. Come out," one of the soldiers yelled back.

The only route of escape had been blocked, so they were confidant Ismail wouldn't get away. The only question was whether he would be captured dead or alive and with or without any Kurdish causalities.

"Come, your friends are with us. They've surrendered," the officer coaxed.
Ismail listened but didn't believe him. "Which friends?"

"His name is Hazim Minuh. Abus Mustafa is also with us."

Ismail furrowed his brow in disbelief. Those men had already been killed.

Following the botched suicide bomb explosion, several of the remaining ISIS militants debated on whether they should make another attempt at exiting the hideout, each holding a grenade to his neck, before pulling the pin. Surely at least one of them would be successful in killing some of the soldiers who had surrounded them, while committing suicide in the process. Most of the men felt there was nothing to live for, aside from the existence that ISIS had manipulated them into, so they didn't give much thought into the prospect of ending their lives.

Ismail, on the other hand, was trying to convince the men not to go forward with their grenade-to-the-neck suicide bomb plot, because he didn't want to die and frankly didn't want to kill anyone, either. He was lured for about two years before joining ISIS simply in exchange for money and the ability to provide for his family. He soon realized it wasn't worth it but had no opportunity for escape until now. By his lights, being captured and jailed as an ISIS militant was the first and only chance he had of being rescued from them.

"Come, we won't kill you," the officer coaxed again.

Ismail knew there was a strong possibility that he could be shot and killed, but at this point he felt he had nothing left to lose. He was already disillusioned by the cause and found himself at a crossroad—either escape from them or die with them.

"Okay, I'll come out," Ismail surrendered, repeatedly yelling that he didn't have a bomb, before emerging with his hands high in the air, hoping they would refrain from firing their weapons.

"Slowly, *slowly*," the soldiers ordered, as they adjusted the aim of their rifles, preparing to make a kill shot if necessary. "Turn around!" they shouted, inspecting him to see if he had any weapons or bombs strapped to his body before he got any closer. Ismail lifted his camouflage shirt to show that he was not armed.

The fear on both sides was palpable.

"Please don't kill me, I don't have anything!" he begged, as he walked toward the group of soldiers. The bottom half of his tan pants were soaked in rust-colored stains of war.

"Stop! Stop! Don't move!" they ordered with more intensity as he advanced forward, cautioning him not to come any closer.

"*Please*, I don't have anything, see?" he begged, lifting his shirt up higher. "Don't kill me!"

"Turn around!" they yelled again. "We won't kill you."

Ismail turned his back toward the officers so they could pin his hands behind his head, and to his relief they did. Several men kept vigilant aim on the building, while others grabbed Ismail's neck and shoulders, whisking him away from the line of fire. "Don't be afraid, I won't blow myself up," he assured them (see Image 11).

Once he was a safe distance from the hideout, a commander began questioning Ismail for intel. "How many are with you?" he asked. "Five," Ismail admitted without hesitation. "Three or maybe four are still alive. They don't want to surrender." The commander believed him and, more important, sensed that Ismail was willing to provide more inside information about ISIS, so he strategically treated him like an asset and ordered his soldiers to take Ismail to a secure location.

"What's going to happen to me?" Ismail asked, worried that he would be beaten or killed once out of public view.

"You have nothing to worry about," the commander assured. But just as soon as he finished his sentence, a junior officer, angry from the near-death shootouts that had just transpired, shoved Ismail and yanked him by the top of his hair.

Now even more afraid of his fate, Ismail reminded the soldiers, "I listened to you! You said surrender, and I did."

After the commander reprimanded his recalcitrant officer for deliberately disobeying his order, he turned toward Ismail and reiterated, "Don't be afraid!" To further ensure his protection and give him peace of mind, the commander personally escorted him to the transportation nearby.

The commander's intuition paid off. After being detained at a security compound in the city of Erbil, Ismail cooperated with every single one of the military's requests for information. When asked about his impetus for joining ISIS, he claimed that he was formally an employee at a bakery, but it was forced to close.[16] Facing poverty and unemployment, Ismail went to listen to Islamic State leader Abu Bakr al-Baghdadi speak at a local mosque and, at the time, Ismail felt he was charismatic. "Whoever goes to the mosque is safe," al-Baghdadi promised Ismail's Sunni community, "We are your Muslim Brothers. We aim to rid you of the Shiites and no one will oppress you. We will give you food and money. Whatever you want."[17]

Ismail became intrigued in the prospect of joining ISIS when he learned that he could earn 500,000 *dinars** per month holding a machine gun and standing guard on the street. Although ISIS had been the direct cause of his unemployment, considering they had cut off the gas supplies that forced the bakery he worked at to close in the first place, Ismail felt that he had no other option but to join ISIS in order to support himself and his six younger siblings.

He wasn't alone. Other militants captured alongside Ismail concurred that ISIS caused the lack of work and poverty in their respective communities, which was also the primary motivation for local recruitment. For these men, Joining ISIS had nothing to do with religion. Their recruitment was the result of the fact that any man who wasn't sufficiently enticed by salary would face an escalation of threats and force if they didn't join the terrorist group. If they even thought about voicing dissent or if they attempted to leave, these "radicalized" militants would have risked being jailed, whipped, or killed.

Given the horrifically violent crimes committed by ISIS, it is difficult to imagine any person making a rational choice to join them. They brag about keeping young Yazidi girls as sex slaves and repeatedly raping them.[18] The group has filmed themselves gruesomely decapitating civilians, burning men alive, and drowning people in cages. And they are responsible for indiscriminately murdering tens of thousands of innocent men, women, and children with their acts of terrorism. Yet these extremist criminals are still able to recruit seemingly average young people from around the world. How?

If you look past the religious veneer, you will find clear and secular manipulation tactics used by ISIS to radicalize exploitable people. Although these schemes have some common threads, they are adaptable to different target populations. For example, persons who live in destabilized countries can be recruited with opportunities to meet physiological needs—such as food, housing, and employment.

Individuals experiencing voids in meeting basic needs are clearly in desperate situations. Some risk their lives to emigrate elsewhere, while others go to inordinate lengths to effectuate change to their living circumstances at home. When human beings are urgently struggling to meet their most basic needs, they can be more easily defrauded, coerced, and/or deceived into believing that joining a criminal enterprise is their best or only option to survive.

---

* More than $400.

Terrorists are not the only criminals who employ these tactics. For example, in my work as a human trafficking expert, I have encountered multiple cases where victims of sex trafficking were manipulated into believing that entering the commercial sex industry would facilitate an improvement of their lives, only to find themselves exploited.

I've seen cases where teen girls testified that they considered being sex trafficked by "the most dangerous gang in America"—MS-13—*preferable* to returning home. One trial transcript makes this point particularly well:

> *[Q:] Is it fair to say that you didn't want to go home?*
> *[A:] Basically, yes.*
> *[Q:] Despite the fact that you were being prostituted by MS-13, you
> didn't want to go home?*
> *[A:] Yes.*[19]

I've met victims who were manipulated into staying with their traffickers, despite being repeatedly beaten, raped, and even shot at. Although they had ample opportunity to physically escape, it was the mental manipulation, deception, and coercion that kept these girls and women compliant in their own exploitation—a mental tether, as opposed to a physical chain.

In the anti-human-trafficking field, we discuss this phenomenon as "trauma bonding." Sex traffickers form trauma bonds with their victims through abusive control dynamics, exploitation of power imbalances, and intermittent positive and negative behavior.[20] This makes the victim lose her sense of self, adopt the worldview of the abuser, and take responsibility for the abuse.

A human trafficking victim once confessed to me, "Even if I'm being exploited and getting my ass beat every day, at least I have a roof over my head."[21] The unfortunate reality is that this problem is larger than one crime.

ISIS marginalizes people living in destabilized regions by effectively limiting economic opportunities, controlling resources, and wantonly exercising unbridled power. Then, ISIS leaders will offer these communities the opportunities to meet basic physiological needs by way of joining the same terrorist organization that deprived them of resources in the first place. Although presented as a "choice," it is predetermined and socially engineered; individuals who don't join or support the organization face consequences of extortion and violence for not complying. Law-abiding citizens have no power, and ISIS militants can be perceived as exercising greater authority than local government and police.

Most people living in destabilized countries are not making the rational choice to become terrorists. In fact, criminality is rarely a rational choice, which is one of the reasons why capital punishment is not a general deterrent. ISIS recruits, like other criminals, typically don't weigh the costs and benefits of a criminal act before committing it. Psychological and sociological explanations of crime are more empirically supported, hence why these are more accurate explanations of ISIS radicalization.

While people in the West can be recruited through promises of love and belonging, esteem, and self-actualization, individuals radicalized from the Middle East are often recruited through the deprivation and subsequent provision of more basic needs such as employment, food, shelter, and safety. In the face of limited alternatives and absence of local resources to fight ISIS, people join out of survival necessity. They figure, "if you can't beat 'em, join 'em."

Armed conflict results in even greater destabilization of job markets and increased economic desperation. Without legitimate options to maintain their livelihoods, people are more likely to resort to illicit activities or risky, informal means to survive. These are the circumstances where ISIS recruiters thrive. The national and civil disorder caused by such conflict makes certain recruitment tactics—including job offers and shelter—more enticing to vulnerable populations. Especially when local business owners are forced to pay heavy taxes or have their utilities and resources cut off, if they don't "choose" to join or support the terrorist organization. It is clear that many people in Iraq and Syria are influenced into joining ISIS because in some places it can be one of the few options available to provide for their families, not necessarily because they believe in their extremist cause.

Ultimately, when we think of ISIS, there should be absolutely no association with religion, because that is nothing more than the façade they want everyone to believe in. The reality is the plight of ISIS is driven by its leadership's quest for money and power and achieved through the manipulation of exploitable populations.

In order to combat ISIS's ability to radicalize, we must continue dismantling the lies under which their criminal organization operates and address the underlying push and pull factors that make people susceptible to their cunning recruitment tactics. No person should ever believe that joining a terrorist organization is their best or only option to provide for their family. However, that is a perceived reality for some.

Moreover, human beings should have the inalienable "right to work, to free choice of employment, to just and favorable conditions of work and to protection against unemployment."[22] But that is simply not the reality for much of the world. Instead of simply consigning people to society's margins, we must globally prioritize efforts to combat poverty because, after all:

> *Poverty is the mother of crime.*
> —Marcus Aurelius

13

Ginger Jihadi

In 2014, conservative provocateur Milo Yiannopoulos was the rising star at Breitbart. The far-right syndicated news website was known for its controversial stances, especially on social justice issues such as racism. Yiannopoulos and his colleagues polemicized that racism against black people in America no longer existed and any discussion of it was the equivalent of "race-baiting" against white people by "spoilt brats of color."[1] Despite the overwhelming research on disproportionate contact with[2] and disparate treatment by[3] the criminal justice system, the possibility that black people continue to be unfairly treated was entirely dismissed as a "myth." Moreover, anecdotes of black men, such as Michael Brown, killed by police were defended as justified uses of force against so-called "criminals."[4]

Yiannopoulos contended that anyone advocating for black lives was doing so to incite a race war and force "white people to sit at the back of the bus."[5] To combat this modern civil rights movement, he went as far as advocating for the criminalization of Black Lives Matter activists, writing:

> Black Lives Matter is a racist black supremacy group that achieves nothing for black people. Its only achievement is black neighborhoods in ruins. Huge numbers of alt-righters describe themselves as "woken up" by the lies the media told in the Trayvon Martin and Michael Brown cases.[6]

While Yiannopoulos wholly dismissed the idea of institutionalized racism, arguing that America demonstrably overcame the legacy with the election of our first black president, Barack Obama,[7] he did believe that certain types of bias exist today, for example, "gingerism":

gin·ger·ism[*]

ˈjinjerizəm

noun

> 1. prejudice, discrimination, or antagonism directed against someone with red hair based on the belief that blonde, black, or brown hair color is superior.

In his writing and speeches, Yiannopoulos would assert that persons with red hair are marginalized, especially in Britain, because they are less attractive.[8] Although the small body of research on the effect of hair color on social evaluation and behavior has revealed discrepant results,[9] Yiannopoulos based this concrete conclusion on a couple of studies that found when confederates wore a red-haired wig or dyed their hair red, females were approached less often and males were rejected more.[10]

Incidentally, Yiannopoulos completely ignored the much larger body of research supporting the fact that colorism has historically lead to African Americans with lighter skin hues being perceived as more attractive and treated more favorably in regard to income, education, and housing.[11] There is no mention of the "brown paper bag test" on Breitbart, where persons with skin as light as or lighter than a brown paper bag were granted admission to colleges, fraternities, sororities, churches, and nightclubs over persons with darker skin.[12] Milo also failed to acknowledge the hair-texture hierarchy that has historically resulted in black women who chemically straighten their hair to conform to Anglicized aesthetics being perceived as more worthy, valuable, and beautiful than women with curly, kinky, or natural hair.[13] Instead of accepting what should be the indisputable existence of pervasive racism in colonized parts of the world, he decided to focus his journalistic coverage of prejudice on the "othering of whiteness" and the less favorable treatment of so-called "gingers."

In 2014, Yiannopoulos published an article in Breitbart titled "Ginger Jihadis: Why Redheads are Attracted to Radical Islam" in which he argued that the marginalization from "gingerism" is why redheads are more likely to be radicalized than brunettes and blondes.[14]

---

[*] Aside from a couple of references in graduate student thesis and dissertation papers, as well as in the media, this term is not accepted among the larger academic community.

Although there were no reliable data on the descriptions of radicalized British, Yiannopoulos based his assertion on a content analysis that he supposedly conducted of national newspaper stories published from August 5, 2013, to August 4, 2014.[15] Yiannopoulos claimed that 76 percent of on white British converts to "radical Islam" reported in news stories had red hair—approximately 70 percent in the *Daily Mail*, *Telegraph*, and *Mirror* archives and 100 percent in the *Guardian*.

From these data, he concluded that since the average incidence of red hair in the general population is 5 percent, "Islamic extremists reported on by the media are fifteen times more likely than the general population to have red hair."[16]

In his story, Yiannopoulos named eight radicalized redheads for reference. However, publicly available data on the nature of their crimes and path to radicalization made no mention of their hair color, much less any discrimination thereof, as the impetus for their extremism.

Redheaded convert Jordan Horner, for example, was arrested after posting a video on YouTube of him and his non-"ginger" friends—Royal Barnes and Richardo MacFarlane—enforcing "sharia law." The three young men called themselves the "Muslim patrol" and walked around London with a megaphone, stopping people from holding hands and drinking alcohol, as well as warning women they would be punished in "hellfire" for their non-Muslim style of dress. When asked about his radicalization, Horner made no mention of being targeted by any recruiter because of his red hair, but rather claimed he was radicalized primarily through the Internet.[17]

Former cocaine dealer and redhead Abdullah Deen adopted a radicalized interpretation of Islam after his eighteen-year-old sister died of a cocaine overdose.[18] Samantha Lewthwaite was radicalized by a love interest, and Richard Dart was attracted to the sense of belonging and empowerment offered by extremist recruiter Anjem Choudary, who was alleged to have encouraged 850 people to fight for ISIS in Syria and 110 Britons to commit terrorist acts locally—the overwhelming majority of whom did not have red hair.[19]

Since Milo's story, there have been a half dozen people nicknamed the "ginger jihadi" by mainstream media, all with similar stories of radicalization to their brunette, blonde, and nonwhite counterparts.

For example, in June of 2014, Australian teenager Abdullah Elmir told his parents that he was going fishing with a classmate but never returned.[20] A few months later, he began appearing in internationally disseminated ISIS propaganda, flanked by militants in Syria (see Image 12).

In the first video, Elmir was wearing a black uniform, tan utility vest, and holding a machine gun. A black-and-white-checkered *shemagh* scarf draped down around his neck and covered his red hair.

With dozens of more experienced militants behind him, Elmir felt like a badass. As their selected spokesman, he conveyed the group's message with confidence—his head held high in propagated pride. Despite the fact that he had only been there for a few months, he dared world leaders to come after him and his newfound friends:

> *To the leaders, to Obama, to Tony Abbott, I say this: these weapons that we have, these soldiers, we will not stop fighting. We will not put down our weapons until we reach your lands, until we take the head of every tyrant and until the black flag is flying high in every single land, until we put the black flag on top of Buckingham Palace, until we put the black flag on top of The White House, we will not stop and we will keep on fighting.*

Although Elmir was described by family and friends as a "good" and "smart" kid, he had become an ISIS poster boy by the age of seventeen. Terrorism experts likened his recruitment to how a pedophile grooms a victim.[21] Not more than a year after his disappearance, the media reported that he had been killed in a bombing raid.[22]

Even before Elmir's death, the title of "ginger jihadi" had already been given to someone else—Tarhan Batirashvili, also known as "Omar the Chechen." After high school, Batirashvili joined the Georgian army and made good money as a sergeant in the fight against Russia.[23] However, it all began to unravel in 2010, when he contracted tuberculosis and was discharged from the military. His mother died from cancer, and he struggled to find employment in short order, causing him to become disillusioned.

Batirashvili was recruited as a rebel in the second Chechen war but was arrested for illegally harboring weapons and sentenced to three years in prison, where he was fully radicalized. After being released early in 2012 for good behavior, Batirashvili immediately left the country and traveled to Turkey with the hope of crossing the border into Syria.

At first he joined a group called Jaish al-Muhajireen wal-Ansar or "Army of Emigrants and Helpers" but eventually was recruited into ISIS and rose to the position of senior commander in Syria (see Image 13).[24]

When asked about Batirashvili's path to radicalization, his father made no mention of his son's red hair. He lamented, "My son was a man with no job, no prospects. So he took the wrong path."

Before Batirashvili was killed in an airstrike in 2016,[25] the "Ginger Jihadi" nickname had already prematurely passed on to the next redheaded Caucasian recruit. A video emerged of light-skinned man with an almost neon orange beard in a rural town square of Yarmouk, Syria (see Image 14). In the video, the man is seen sentencing a prisoner to death by decapitation for allegedly being a "sorcerer" and practicing "magic." At the time, the media didn't have a name for the executioner, so "Ginger Jihadi" it was.[26]

Ibrahim Anderson also was dubbed the "Ginger Jihadi" in 2016 and sentenced to three years in prison for attempting to recruit for ISIS outside of a Topshop store in the United Kingdom.[27] Nathan Saunders earned the nickname next in 2017 for, as the media claims, "radicalizing himself" by downloading propaganda on how to carry out "lone wolf" attacks and make homemade bombs.[28] Most recently, Lewis Ludlow was called the "Ginger Jihadi" in 2018, after he was charged with plotting a "multiple casualty vehicle-borne assault" in London.[29]

A total of fifteen "Ginger Jihadis" over the course of six years is what Yiannopoulos considered a factual trend worthy of perpetuation.

In his "10 Things I Hate About Islam" talk at the University of Central Florida in 2016, Yiannopoulos claimed that "Islam preys on the most vulnerable people in society," and his case in point was that "gingers convert to Islam at such high rates."[30] Although his earlier article had erroneously concluded that "Islamic extremists reported on by the media are fifteen times more likely than the general population to have red hair," Yiannopoulos further misinterpreted this already invalid "statistic" by telling a redhead in the audience that he was five times more likely than a brunette to wake up one day and join ISIS solely because of his hair color. This is preposterous and reminds us that there are lies, damned lies, and statistics.[31]

Yiannopoulos's conclusions were ill-conceived and unsupported by the data he collected. He certainly didn't perform any type of empirical test to calculate the odds ratio of radicalization between redheads and brunettes, much less any significance testing—there wasn't even a large enough sample size to have the statistical power to do so. More important, he cited two studies to support his theory of so-called "gingerism" and accepted those findings as fact yet dismissed the hundreds of academic articles supporting the continued legacy of racism in America.

While bullying against people with red hair might very well be an issue, it is nowhere near being equivalent to the social, financial, and political marginalization that comes with racism.

The reality is that there is no evidence that terrorist recruiters disproportionately radicalize redheads. However, there is a wealth of propaganda that suggests African Americans are in fact targeted. Groups like al-Qaeda and ISIS focus their recruitment efforts on disaffected young people of color by leeching their criminal organizations onto legitimate civil rights movements.

For example, following the shooting of Trayvon Martin in 2012, terrorist propaganda began increasingly focusing on racial injustice. The articles would pose questions for readers to ask themselves, such as: "Why are Americans afraid of racial profiling? Is it because the false sentiment of racism being vanquished is beginning to collapse?" and "If American policemen kill their own people for just being young black men, imagine what they have done with Muslims in Afghanistan and Iraq?"

The propaganda also began reviving quotes from black Muslim civil rights activists, such as Malcolm X (see Image 15): "I am not an American, you are not American. You're one of the 22 million black people . . . who are victims of America. . . . Ain't no democracy there. We've never seen democracy. All we've seen is hypocrisy. We don't see any American dream. We've experienced only the American nightmare."

As the Black Lives Matter movement gained momentum, terrorist recruiters began more actively targeting persons of color. For example, Issue 14 of al-Qaeda's *Inspire* magazine included a six-page feature titled "The Blacks in America." The article opened by commenting on the same officer-involved incident that Yiannopoulos and his Breitbart colleagues flippantly dismissed:

> *The killing of Michael Brown, American of African descent, incited wide demonstrations all over the United States. As news resonated across the global media, in America the media was contradicting and having different point of views regarding this tragedy. At first many channels portrayed the incident as it was, but later on presented the event to the viewer as a mere daily criminal incident. And that the victim was a person who deserved to be stopped and imprisoned. And that the crime of the officer was nothing but a general mistake that had nothing to do with racism or religion.*

The article went on to discuss other incidents, attaching their terrorist organization to the Black Lives Matter civil rights movement,

> *Within a short period, a similar incident occurred, the brutal killing of Freddy Gray. . . . The killing of Gray shocked the Afro-American community. This is mainly because, it occurred while they were still mourning Michael Brown's death, and the manner in which Gray was killed. The incident was shocking. How do five police officers attack an unarmed person in such a manner? Hitting and strangling him to death. How can they say that the killing was not intentional, when the place and manner indicated clear intent? The Baltimore community was shocked; widespread demonstrations began across the city, alerting state security organs. They began by announcing a state of emergency, followed by deploying 5000 National Guard soldiers across the city in order to protect it, as they claim. Demonstrations sprawl to other states echoing the call for America to stop racism. The attempt by American leaders, top of them President Obama, in their addresses indicated sympathy and solidarity towards the black community. Maybe as an attempt to desensitize them from their anger.*

To this effect, Yiannopoulos and his colleagues at Breitbart did publish articles suggesting "Gray was 'trying to injure himself'"[32] and dismissed the civil rights protesters as "anarchists and other professional grievance organizations."[33] These sentiments were used by al-Qaeda to argue that their terrorist organization had been dismissed as criminals, in the same vein as Black Lives Matter civil rights advocates:

> *Many might be surprised as to why we are discussing about this subject matter, and ask why does a* Mujahid *write about an internal American affair? We answer by saying: Many among the masses fall victim to the western media, which is persistent in portraying a negative image of Islam, with regards to Mujahideen. In contrast, racism has always been among the core issues in Islam. . . . Islam does not allow even the smallest kind of injustice; be it by words or having contempt for a particular race. We the Mujahideen are a portion of the Muslim Ummah, we do not accept any type of oppression*

against our Muslim brothers among the Afro-Americans, or even the non-Muslims. And the opposite of oppression is Justice, and this is what we have been commanded by our religion.

After substantiating the Black Lives Matter concerns and aligning themselves with the civil rights movement, the Islamic State's propaganda then juxtaposed the American legacy of racism toward persons of color with the romanticized narrative of their self-proclaimed "caliphate,"* which is described as a place with no inequality, discrimination, or racism. For example, the first issue of *Dabiq* reads:

> *It is a state where the Arab and non-Arab, the white man and black man, the easterner and westerner are all brothers. It is a* Khilafah *that gathered the Caucasian, Indian, Chinese, Chami, Iraqi, Yemeni, Egyptian, Maghribi, American, French, German, and Australian. Allah brought their hearts together, and thus, they became brothers by His grace, loving each other for the sake of Allah, standing in a single trench, defending and guarding each other, and sacrificing themselves for one another.*[34]

Although the Islamic State is an entirely criminal organization, designed to further the leadership's pursuit of money and power, its sustainability rests on its capacity to radicalize exploitable young people. Recruiters shapeshift in order to align themselves with disaffected persons of color, using propaganda to send messages of support and advice:

> *Qaidatul Jihad and the entire Muslim* Ummah *are against the oppression and injustices directed towards you. . . . We want to hear your voices against the crimes committed by your government. We encourage you to form political groups in order to pressurize your government to lift the general oppression against you and to stop aggression towards Muslims. And condemn the support your government gives to Israel. From there we will take practical steps to*

---

* A caliphate is a state ruled by a caliph, or the elected religious successor to the Prophet Mohammad, who serves as the leader of the *Ummah*.

avoid targeting you in our operations. . . . We advise you to move out of big cities that represent the economy, politics or military strength of America like New York and Washington. . . . Rights cannot be earned except by force, your own history is a witness to this. With that, we advise you to confront this issue in two directions. The first is a civil open approach, not military. Demanding your total rights, by pressuring your government using a soft approach like; demonstrations, stage sit-in and civil disobedience. The second approach is by forming small groups that will be responsible for assassinating, targeting these racist politicians.

While Yiannopoulos and Breitbart cite back-of-the-envelope calculations as "truth" to support the unfounded correlation between so-called "gingerism" and radicalization, terrorist propaganda tells a different story—extremist organizations clearly and consistently recognize the marginalization of people of color and target black men and women accordingly.

Data suggest that a growing number of young black people are converting to Islam. In 2001, 9 percent of the black population in Britain identified as Muslim, and ten years later, the proportion rose to 14.5 percent.[35] In the United States, 67 percent of US-born black Muslims were converts, compared to 35 percent of non-black Muslims.[36] Some believe this is because Islam is the "natural religion of black people and provides the means for full spiritual, mental, and physical liberation from an oppressive system designed to subjugate them."[37] Others agree that young people's embrace of Islam is partly symptomatic of widespread rejection from society, in which "many black people continue to experience discrimination and marginalization on a daily basis, and in which young black men are being criminalized and jailed in ever greater numbers."[38] Islam's ability to empower was described as a magnet to black British youth.[39]

While the overwhelming majority of black converts to Islam adopt a traditional and peaceful interpretation, they can be susceptible to targeting by extremist preachers. According to Lee Jasper, a race relations activist in the UK, "Black rage against institutional racism has massively increased and it provides a willing group of vulnerable young people who are susceptible to this kind of radical Islam."[40]

Race scholars contend that the overcriminalization of persons of color is the new Jim Crow[41]—a means of perpetuating disenfranchisement. According to the Sentencing Project, "one of every three black American males born today can expect to go to prison in his lifetime, as can one of every six Latino males—compared to one of every seventeen white males."[42] Similarly, in the UK, "black youths were six times more likely than white youths to be stopped and searched by police. If convicted, they were 20 percent more likely to be sent to prison and would typically serve a sentence seven months longer than the equivalent punishment for a white offender." By ignoring the wealth of scholarly research on the realities of racism and wholly dismissing the legitimacy of civil rights organizations such as Black Lives Matter, conservative provocateurs like Yiannopoulos and his colleagues at Breitbart provide fodder for terrorist propaganda.

If we want to combat terrorism, we must discontinue this legacy of disenfranchisement and empower the disaffected. We can start by acknowledging that racism still exists and black lives matter, without exception. Muslims are not terrorists, and no country is a "shithole."* All human beings deserve to be treated with dignity and respect no matter their race, religion, national origin, citizenship status, gender, or sexuality.

Ultimately, in order to combat terrorism, we must perpetuate the unified message that threats to justice will not be tolerated anywhere, under any circumstance, to any human being. *What affects one of us directly affects all of us indirectly.*[†]

---

* In reference to President Donald J. Trump's January 2018 statement in which he referred to Haiti and African nations as "shithole countries."
† Adapted from Martin Luther King Jr.'s quote: "Injustice anywhere is a threat to justice everywhere. We are caught in an inescapable network of mutuality, tied in a single garment of destiny. Whatever affects one directly, affects all indirectly."

14

Orphans of ISIS

At 11:30 a.m. on January 7, 2015, brothers Cherif and Said Kouachi entered the Paris headquarters of satirical weekly newspaper *Charlie Hebdo*. The brothers were armed with assault rifles, submachine guns, a pump-action shotgun, and pistols. Upon entering the building, Cherif and Said sprayed the lobby with a hail of bullets, killing a maintenance worker who was sitting at the reception desk. After making their way to the second-floor conference room, the brothers found fifteen key staff members, meeting together for the first time in the new year.

"Charb?!" one of the hooded gunmen asked with angst in his voice.

He was looking for editor-in-chief and cartoonist Stéphane "Charb" Charbonnier. Two years earlier, al-Qaeda had placed him on a most wanted list, published in their propaganda magazine *Inspire*—a response to *Charlie Hebdo*'s depictions of the Prophet Muhammad. The militants felt the satirical cartoons were blasphemous and responsible parties were deserving of death.

The Kouachi brothers obliged that day by murdering Stéphane Charbonnier along with ten other reporters and cartoonists, while injuring twelve others and killing one police officer. They left the crime scene yelling, "Allahu Akbar! Allahu Akbar! We have avenged the Prophet Muhammad. We have killed *Charlie Hebdo*!"[1]

In the following edition of *Inspire*, al-Qaeda described the massacre as a special intelligence operation, categorized under assassinations. The terrorist organization praised the Kouachi brothers for accomplishing their mission "with high precision and excellence" on "an exceptional level." In hope of inspiring future executions, the article reviewed the stages of planning.[2]

Al-Qaeda claimed it began when central leadership selected the targets—caricature artists who they believed had defamed the religion and the Prophet

Muhammad. The selections were published in the form of a most wanted list featured in Issue 10 of *Inspire* (see Image 16).[3] *Charlie Hebdo*'s editor-in-chief was listed as number six, misspelled "Stéphane Charbonnie."

The text accompanying the list suggested that the terrorist group published it because they were upset about the *Innocence of Muslims* video that had been uploaded to YouTube several months earlier. The amateur video catalyzed international protests for its blasphemous depiction of Prophet Muhammad as a "bastard," buffoon, womanizer, homosexual, child molester, and greedy, bloodthirsty thug.[4] The low-budget video gained international attention after a Florida pastor named Terry Jones began promoting the film along with his proclamation that September 11 should be known as "International Judge Muhammad Day."[5] Jones had a reputation for his hatred of Islam—burning a Qur'an in his church and publicly threatening to burn more. He described the video as an American production that reveals "the destructive ideology of Islam" and depicts "the life of Muhammad" in satirical fashion.[6] When asked about the video, the pastor— Sam Bacile—was quoted as saying, "Islam is a cancer."[7]

Transnational protests began after the Egyptian media covered the video's release, and it eventually came center stage with the Benghazi scandal. On September 11, 2012, four Americans were killed after the United States diplomatic compound in Benghazi was attacked. Then-Secretary of State Hillary Rodham Clinton infamously made public statements suggesting that the attack was part of the international demonstrations against the YouTube video, likening it to a less deadly attack on the US Embassy in Egypt. It was later discovered that the Benghazi incident had been a planned and coordinated terrorist attack that was not catalyzed by the video.[8]

In response to the *Innocence of Muslims* video, al-Qaeda publicly reaffirmed its position against satirical and blasphemous depictions of the Prophet Muhammad in a feature titled "Defending the Prophet":

> *America has allowed the production of a film which commits blasphemy against the Prophet, under the pretext of freedom of expression. But this freedom declamation did not stop Americans from torturing Muslim prisoners in Bagram, Abu Ghuraib, Guantanamo, and other secret prisons. May the blessings of Allah be upon those, enthusiastic Muslims, who torched the American Embassy in Benghazi, those who protested in front of the US*

Embassy in Cairo, those who replaced the American flag with the flag of Islam and Jihad. I call upon them to continue to confront the Zio-American crusade on Islam and Muslims. And I call upon all Muslims to follow their example.

Although Hillary Rodham Clinton was publicly condemned for allegedly lying to the American people about Benghazi by blaming the attack on the video instead of al-Qaeda,[9] the reality was that al-Qaeda propaganda also attributed the Benghazi attack to the video.

In fact, al-Qaeda has prioritized deadly attacks against satirical and blasphemous depictions of Muhammad for over a decade.

For example, in September 2005, Flemming Rose, the cultural editor of *Jyllands-Posten*—a Danish daily broadsheet newspaper—invited forty-two Danish cartoonists and illustrators to draw cartoons of Muhammad "as they see him." Twelve were published by the end of the month under the title "The Face of Muhammad."[10]

The cartoons included one drawing of Muhammad as a crazed, knife-wielding Bedouin, another of him at the gates of heaven telling suicide bombers, "Stop. Stop. We have run out of virgins!" and a third in which he was portrayed as an apparent terrorist with a bomb in his turban.[11]

The Danish Muslim community generally felt the drawings were a symptom of the lack of respect for Muslim culture and religion in Denmark, but the response was split—some wanted to stage boycotts and protests, while others felt it was best to ignore the blasphemous cartoons. Within a week, a third, smaller group of extremists began making serious threats to the illustrators, which led police to advise the latter to go underground.[12]

Once again, extremists had latched their criminal organization onto a legitimate social rights movement, the consequence of which was the continued confounding of the two completely separate populations. On one hand, law-abiding Muslims who wanted to advocate for their civil rights; and on the other, criminal terrorist extremists who were exploiting the marginalized for their own selfish motives.

Muslim leaders, such as Egyptian ambassador Mona Omar Attia, diplomatically conveyed the community's discontentment with the drawings. In a letter to Danish Prime Minister Anders Fogh Rasmussen, Attia and nine other ambassadors lamented that the cartoons were part of an "ongoing smear campaign" against Islam and Muslims in Denmark, and they asked him to take legal "action against the responsible parties" and "necessary steps" to avoid defamation of Islam.[13] Saudi Arabia, Iran, and Syria recalled ambassadors and initiated boycotts of Danish goods. However, the international media largely ignored the peaceful demonstrations and predominately focused attention on the violent response.

Protestors outside the Danish Embassy in London called for the execution of those who insult Islam[14] with signs that read, "Whoever Insults a Prophet, Kill Him," "Slay Those Who Insult Islam," and "Europe, You Will Pay, Your 9/11 is on Its Way!"[15] Extremist group al-Ghurabaa also published an article titled "Kill those who insult the Prophet Muhammad," which read, in part:

> *The* kuffar* *in their sustained crusade against Islam and Muslims have yet again displayed their hatred towards us this time by attacking the honor of our beloved Messenger Muhammad. . . . The* kuffar *will never have respect for our* deen,† *they will never honor it and will always seek to ridicule and disparage it. At every opportunity they will try to attack and belittle it whilst concealing the greater hatred they have for it in their hearts. . . . The insulting of the Messenger Muhammad is something that the Muslims cannot and will not tolerate and the punishment in Islam for the one who does so is death . . . the* kuffar *are attacking our Messenger and are allowed to get away with it whilst the Muslims have no power to do anything about it. The leaders of the Muslim world have no care for the* deen *of Islam as they are busy cementing their seats content with their power and wealth.*

Demonstrations spread across Europe, the Middle East, and North Africa. The Danish Embassy in Beirut was set on fire, a protester was killed,[16] and gunmen raided European Union offices in Gaza, demanding an apology.[17] Following the international republication of the cartoons, mobs in Damascus attacked Norwegian, Danish, Swedish, and French embassies.

Still, media organizations were defiant and continued exercising their freedom of speech by further disseminating the controversial cartoons. In France, *Charlie*

---

* A non-Muslim person, unbeliever, or infidel.
† Religion.

Hebdo printed the images along with an additional cover cartoon of Muhammad that read, "It's hard to be loved by imbeciles."[18] A year later, Muslim groups sued the satirical magazine for publicly insulting Islam, but the court ruled in favor of *Charlie Hebdo*.

Two years after the initial publication, the mass demonstrations had diminished, but the extremist threats subsisted. Osama bin Laden recorded and published a video propagandizing the need for violent consequences. The following year, twenty-eight-year-old Mohamed Geele was shot and arrested after entering the home of Kurt Westergaard—the cartoonist who drew the image of Muhammad with a bomb in his turban—with an axe and knife. A year later, five more men were arrested for allegedly plotting a massacre of *Jyllands-Posten* employees at their headquarters.

By 2010, al-Qaeda had given a name to the continued depictions of the Prophet Muhammad by the West, calling it "The Cartoon Crusade," while their terrorist response was dubbed "The Dust Will Never Settle Down Campaign."[19] The first issue of *Inspire* refocused attention on blasphemy and quoted Osama bin Laden's related video: "If there is no check on the freedom of your words, then let your hearts be open to the freedom of our actions." The ominous statement was published alongside al-Qaeda's first official hit list (see Image 17), which named nine people.

Kurt Westergaard, Carsten Juste, and Flemming Rose were targeted for their role in publishing the Muhammad cartoons featured in *Jyllands-Posten*. Lars Vilks was also on the list. He had gained the ire of al-Qaeda for drawing the head of the Prophet Muhammad on the body of a dog the following year. Despite the previous failed attempts on his life, including one by "Jihad Jane," al-Qaeda continued listing him as a high priority. Ulf Johansson, editor-in-chief of the *Nerikes Allehanda* newspaper, was also listed for publishing Vilks's caricature of Muhammad.

Right-wing Dutch politician Geert Wilders was targeted for making an anti-Qur'an movie that incidentally opened with a reproduction Westergaard's cartoon of Prophet Muhammad with a bomb in his turban.[20] Molly Norris was included for her role in the 2010 "Everybody Draw Muhammad Day." And Dutch Member of Parliament Ayaan Hirsi Ali was listed for her support of *Jyllands-Posten*, as well as her role in writing the script for *Submission*—a film that criticized the treatment of women in Islam.[21] The filmmaker, Theo van Gogh, had already been shot and stabbed three months after the release of the video. His body was left with a note containing a death threat toward Hirsi Ali.

The final target on the list—Salman Rushdie—had the most enduring death threat. The first demand for his assassination was in 1989 for the publication of his novel *The Satanic Verses*. The book was considered blasphemous for its discussion of the history of Islam. Iran's first Supreme Leader, Ayatollah Khomeini, called for Rushdie's death in a *fatwa*:*

> *I inform the proud Muslim people of the world that the author of*
> The Satanic Verses *book, which is against Islam, the Prophet and*
> *the Qur'an, and all those involved in its publication who are aware*
> *of its content are sentenced to death."*[22]

Rushdie subsequently went into hiding with police protection.

The Japanese translator of *The Satanic Verses* was stabbed to death, while the Italian translator and Norwegian publisher survived assassination attempts.

The threats against persons who depict the Prophet Muhammad in satirical or blasphemous fashion have persisted for decades. Each terrorist leader has echoed the violent responses of the last. The *Charlie Hebdo* massacre was set in motion when al-Awlaki reiterated the message from Osama bin Laden's video in a three-page article published in the first issue of *Inspire*, excerpted below:

> *If you have the right to slander the Messenger of Allah, we have*
> *the right to defend him. If it is part of your freedom of speech to*
> *defame Muhammad, it is part of our religion to fight you. . . .*
> *Outrageous slander, blatant smearing of Muhammad, desecration*
> *of the Qur'an, and the insulting of over a billion Muslims world-*
> *wide are done under the pretext of "freedom of speech." They are*
> *never called what they really are: a deeply rooted historic hatred for*
> *Islam and Muslims. Yesterday it was in the name of Christianity;*
> *today it is in the name of Democracy. . . . For these reasons, for*
> *this combined effect of an escalating problem, I gave my lecture the*
> *title, The dust will never settle down. Today, two years later, the*
> *dust still hasn't settled down. In fact the dust cloud is only getting*
> *bigger.*
>
> *Whenever the affair calms down, someone somewhere in the*

---

* Ruling.

Western world is sure to flare it up again. From 2005 onwards the cycle of offense is unabated.

What the West is failing to realize is that these attacks are also serving as a mobilizing factor for the Muslims and are bringing more and more Muslims to the realization that jihad against the West is the only realistic solution for this problem along with a host of other problems that cannot be cured without fighting in the path of Allah.

Muslims do love Muhammad and do want to defend his honor and their methods of doing so are varying. Muslims protested and demonstrated worldwide. They burned flags and struck effigies. They boycotted products manufactured by some of the countries involved. All of these acts of good were a manifestation of the solidarity of Muslims in defense of the Messenger of Allah. On the other hand, there were some completely misguided efforts such as those of some of the callers to Islam who paid a visit to Denmark along with young Muslim boys and girls to start a dialogue in order to build bridges of understanding between the Muslims and the people of Denmark!

It is not enough to have the intention of doing good. One must do good in the proper way. So what is the proper solution to this growing campaign of defamation?

The medicine prescribed by the Messenger of Allah is the execution of those involved. A soul that is so debased, as to enjoy the ridicule of the Messenger of Allah, the mercy to mankind; a soul that is so ungrateful towards its Lord that it defames the Prophet of the religion Allah has chosen for his creation does not deserve life, does not deserve to breathe the air created by Allah and enjoy a life provided for by Allah. Their proper abode is Hellfire.

Despite the threats, media outlets continued exercising their freedom of speech by circulating drawings of Muhammad.* On November 2, 2011, *Charlie Hebdo* produced an issue with Mohammad as "editor-in-chief" and a speech bubble

---

* It should be noted that freedom of speech is not absolute. For example, words that incite violence and obscenities can be enjoined.

that said, "100 lashes if you don't die of laughter." The following day, extremists burned their Paris offices in an apparent arson attack. The next year, *Charlie Hebdo* published two cartoons of Muhammad: one in which he appears on the cover in a wheelchair, saying, "You musn't mock," and another inside the magazine, with the Prophet Muhammad depicted in the nude. The following day, extremists rioted around *Charlie Hebdo*'s offices in Paris and viturally attacked their website. A few months later, two Muslim organizations again sued the magazine, this time for inciting racial hatred.

However, the editors were undeterred. Again, the very next year, *Charlie Hebdo* released a sixty-five-page special edition illustrated biography of the Prophet Muhammad. Two years later, Cherif and Said Kouachi brutally murdered the magazine's editor-in-chief and ten other staff members.

The *Inspire* issue published in the wake of the *Charlie Hebdo* attack included an eighteen-page "Military Analysis" of the assassination. After placing Stéphane Charbonnier on a "wanted list" to "guide" and "inspire" lone wolf terrorists, al-Qaeda claimed to have prepared Said Kouachi for the attack with "military" and "psychological" training, both in person and remotely. He was instructed to conduct surveillance of the *Charlie Hebdo* building and collect information on the optimal day and time for execution, before carrying out the terrorist attack. Al-Qaeda polemicized that the brothers had given "victory to the honor of the prophet and silenced the abusive mouths," before delivering a warning: "And to Charlie Hebdo . . . If you return, We too shall return."

In the end, the brothers were killed in a gunfight with police and reduced to nothing more than manipulated and exploited pawns—a talking point for propaganda (see Image 18).

Al-Shabaab also responded to the *Charlie Hebdo* shooting with praise and recognition of the brothers as heroes:

> *We extend our congratulations and blessings to our beloved Muslim* Ummah *regarding the heroic operations carried out against the lair of evil and center of disbelief, the offices of "Charlie Hebdo"—the magazine that insulted the Seal of all Messengers and the Leader of the Prophets, Muhammad. For too long, their filthy hands and vile fingers have characterized the Prophet Muhammad in drawings that vilify his honor, insult his nobility and belittle his high rank, assuming that they will get away with their evil actions.*[23]

ISIS responded by using the *Charlie Hebdo* tragedy as a platform to ostracize Muslim leaders who decried the tragedy, calling them apostates. In issue seven of *Dabiq* magazine, titled "From Hypocrisy to Apostasy: The Extinction of the Grayzone," ISIS leadership wrote:

> *The grayzone is critically endangered, rather on the brink of extinction. As Shaykh Usāmah Ibn Lādin said, "The world today is divided into two camps. Bush spoke the truth when he said, 'Either you are with us or you are with the terrorists.' Meaning, either you are with the crusade or you are with Islam".* . . . *Some apostates, who abandoned the grayzone, claimed that the operations in Paris contradicted the teachings of Islam! They then gathered the masses in rallies under the banner "Je Suis Charlie," leading them on towards the gates of Hellfire designated for the* murtaddin. . . . *If merely sitting silently with the* kuffār *during a gathering of* kufr *is* kufr, *how much more so is it to rally on behalf of a newspaper mocking the Messenger? Or give verdicts in defense of the newspaper, against the* mujahidin *who killed those who mocked the Messenger? Or raise banners and slogans with the words "Je Suis Charlie" on them? There is no doubt that such deeds are apostasy, that those who publicly call to such deeds in the name of Islam and scholarship are from the* du'at *(callers) to apostasy, and that there is great reward awaiting the Muslim in the Hereafter if he kills these apostate imams.*[24]

While terrorist organizations used the *Charlie Hebdo* tragedy as an opportunity to propagandize the need for more violence and criticize Muslim leaders who condemned the tragedy, one thing they omitted were the details of the assassins' path to radicalization.

Cherif and Said Kouachi were French citizens, born in Paris to Algerian immigrant parents. They lost their father when they were young, prompting their mother to send the boys off to a state school for children with social difficulties and special needs.[25] After their mother's apparent suicide, they were placed in a foster home and later moved to an orphanage.[26] The boys were described as having "low intellect" and suffering from emotional trauma.

It wasn't until the Kouachi brothers met Farid Benyettou that they felt a sense

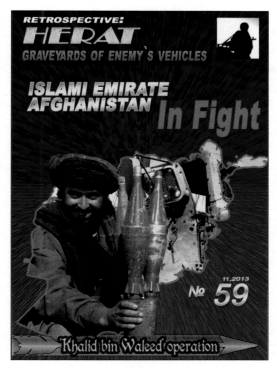

1. *In Fight*, a propaganda magazine published by the Afghan Taliban.

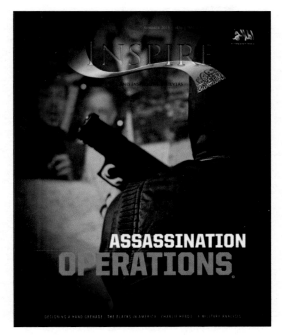

2. *Inspire*, published by al-Qaeda.

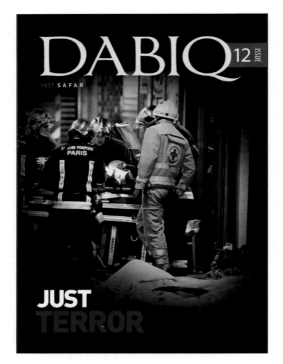

3. *Dabiq* magazine, published by ISIS.

4. *Rumiyah* magazine, published by ISIS.

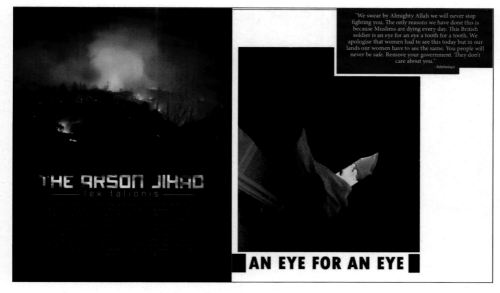

5. *Lex talionis* in Issues 11 and 12 of *Inspire* magazine.

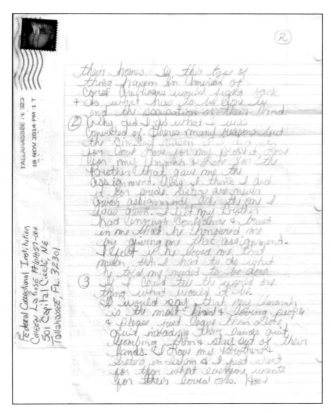

6. Letter from Jihad Jane.

7. Sally Jones shoots rifle in ISIS propaganda video of *al-Khansaa'* Brigade.

8. Screenshot of the exchange between Abu Wahib and his victims.

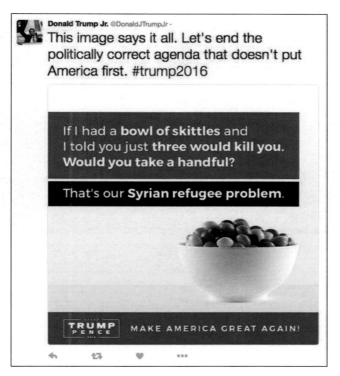

9. Tweet from Donald Trump Jr., about Syrian refugees.

10. Al-Qaeda leeching off of the Arab Spring in Issue 10 of *Inspire*.

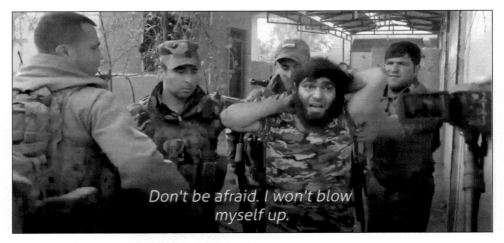

11. Screenshot of Walid Ismail's capture in Iraq.

12. "Ginger Jihadi" Abdullah Elmir.

13. "Ginger Jihadi" Tarhan Batirashvili.

14. Unnamed "Ginger Jihadi" reads an execution sentence for "sorcery."

15. ISIS targeting black men and women for recruitment in Issue 10 of *Inspire*.

16. Al-Qaeda's second hit list, published in Issue 10 of *Inspire*.

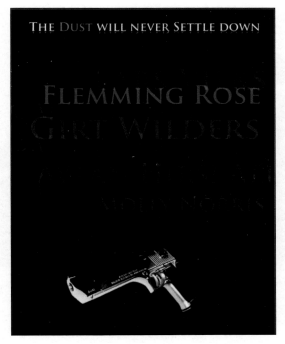

17. Al-Qaeda's first hit list, published in Issue 1 of *Inspire*.

18. Al-Shabaab feature on the *Charlie Hebdo* massacre in Issue 7 of *Gaidi Mtaani*.

19. Screenshot of ISIS's orphan army.

20. Sally Jones's son, Jojo, executing for ISIS in propaganda execution video.

21. Toddler used by ISIS as child soldier in propaganda execution video.

وبفضل الله هما الآن في قبضة أشبال الخلافة

By Allah's grace, they are now in the custody of the lion cubs of the Khilafah.

22. Child solider featured in ISIS propaganda video killing alleged Russian spies.

They only fight the Muslims because they believe in Allah

THE CRUSADERS' INDISCRIMINATE BOMBING SHOWS NO MERCY TO THE YOUNG, NOR TO THE ELDERLY

23. ISIS's *Dabiq* and *Rumiyah* magazines illustrating children injured from alleged American airstrikes.

24. Issues 2 and 4 of ISIS's *Dabiq* magazine, illustrating services from the Islamic State.

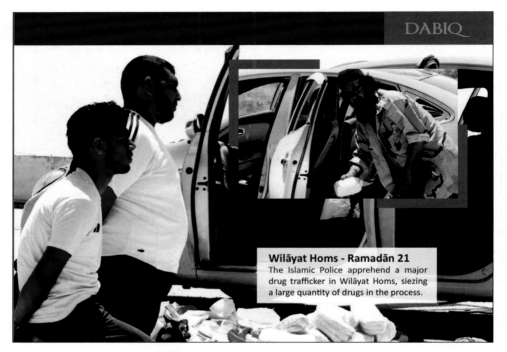

Wilāyat Homs - Ramadān 21
The Islamic Police apprehend a major drug trafficker in Wilāyat Homs, siezing a large quantity of drugs in the process.

25. ISIS claims to fight drug trafficking in Issue 2 of *Dabiq*.

26. Image of Alan Kurdi from Issue 11 of *Dabiq*, used to threaten people from leaving the Islamic State.

27. ISIS administered punishment for apostasy, according to Issue 14 of *Dabiq*.

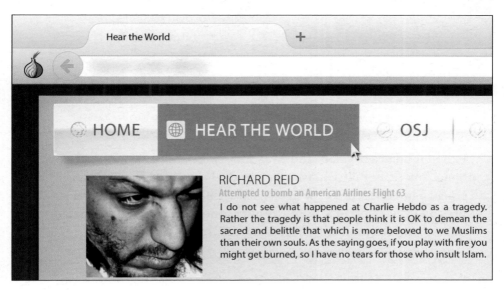

28. Issue 14 of Al-Qaeda propaganda magazine *Inspire* features a quote from my Richard Reid letter.

When it comes to Islam and Muslims, there are no hawks and doves among American politicians. In terms of their enmity for Islam, they are all equal. The difference that does exist is that some are open and frank in expressing their hostility, while others conceal and deceive ... Democrats and Republicans, are serpents carrying lethal venom,

29. Terrorist perceptions of American presidents, discussed in Issue 17 of *Inspire*.

of belonging. Benyettou "mentored" many disenfranchised youth by guiding them to adopt his brand of religious extremism.[27]

Belonging to the extremist group made surviving poverty and working menial jobs easier for them. The orphaned brothers absorbed the information like sponges. They felt that for the first time in their lives, they had a purpose and were prepared to die for it.

Benyettou and Cherif attempted to travel to Iraq through Damascus in 2005, leading to their arrest for "criminal association in relation to a terrorist enterprise."[28] After admitting to convincing ten other people to go to Iraq and teaching others about jihad and suicide attacks, Benyettou was convicted and sentenced to six years in prison, while Cherif was punished with three years.[29]

While incarcerated, Cherif was further mentored by Islamic extremists, such as Djamel Beghal, who was serving time for his 2001 plot to bomb the US embassy in Paris.[30] After being released from prison, Cherif secured employment and got married but continued receiving radical guidance. Said, who was two years younger than Cherif, looked up to his brother and followed his direction into extremism.

Over the course of several years, the brothers were brainwashed and radicalized. Although being disenfranchised youths didn't make the Kouachi brothers become terrorists, their childhood did make them more susceptible to extremist recruitment strategies. ISIS targets their propaganda and recruitment toward orphaned and disenfranchised youth because they are more easily coerced and defrauded into terrorism through appeals to their needs for belonging and love. Also, because they don't have the "obstacle" of parents reinforcing positive social development.

For example, in April 2016, ISIS released a video of what they called a "child orphan army." The video depicted dozens of children wearing fatigues and carrying assault rifles. On the soundtrack, a child sang a cappella in French, as messages directed toward the West flashed on the screen: "Your blood will flow for your heinous crimes. Beware, we have what we need to defend ourselves" and "Beware, our orphans are growing. They feed their thirst for revenge in rage" (see Image 19).

Orphans and children who lack familial love and belonging are easy targets for organized crime groups in general, not only terrorist organizations. Gangs and human trafficking syndicates have been known to target recruitment efforts at shelters and group homes. Homeless and fostered kids are targeted by sex traffickers because they are more likely to feel compelled to engage in survival sex, which is generally described as prostitution in exchange for resources to meet basic physiological needs (i.e., food, water, shelter).

Similarly, these kids are also at risk of being radicalized into terrorism. More than one ISIS propaganda video has claimed that they are building an army of orphans who lost their parents in the war in Syria and are "thirsty for revenge."

Given the risks of being targeted for recruitment into criminal organizations, child welfare agencies are uniquely positioned to intervene by disrupting cycles of marginalization and exploitation. Youth who come in contact with child welfare systems typically have a multitude of unmet needs. Specifically, available data suggest that these populations are more likely to be food insecure; experience unstable living situations; become victims of emotional, physical, or sexual abuse; suffer from depression or other forms of mental illness; experience hampered opportunities for social mobility; and have lower levels of self-worth. Evidence-based screening tools, training protocols, and service delivery models can facilitate the identification and provision of services to these children, who are at risk of being victimized as well as recruited into crime, including terrorism (for example, see Appendix A). Ultimately, it is important to remember that:

No one is born hating another person because of the color of his skin or his background or his religion. People must learn to hate, and if they can learn to hate, they can be taught to love, for love comes more naturally to the human heart than its opposite.

—Nelson Mandela

15

Cubs of the Caliphate

Here before you are the Sharia institutions, training camps, and even the kindergarten . . . preparing the lion cubs of the Khilafah . . . first comes knowledge, then the weapon.
— ISIS propaganda magazine *Dabiq*[1]

Five Kurdish men were forced to kneel in the ISIS-controlled desert of Syria. Each man was dressed in an orange jumpsuit, designed to convey his prisoner status: hands bound with zip ties, head shaved, and facial hair cut down to a five o'clock shadow.

Behind each prisoner stood a preteen child, dressed in a camouflage uniform, with black fingerless gloves and shoulder holsters for their guns (see Image 20). The kids had black caps covering their heads and wore military-style boots. They were dressed like soldiers but had not yet reached puberty.

The eldest child stood in the center and recited the propagandist message that he was taught:

Here, before you, are these Kurds. Fueling a contamination and a war. With them are America, France, Britain, and Germany. A group of Satans, who are killing and imprisoning our community. We are more than ready for them.

As he spoke, the other children to his left and right stared blankly at the camera filming them. Their eyes glazed over as if their souls had been drained by the violence they were forced to witness and experience at such tender ages.

At the end of the boy's speech, he slapped his prisoner on the back of his head, shoved him forward and proclaimed:

These guys are awaiting their destiny. The same destiny we will
bring to you.

The boy shouted praise to Allah, prompting all five children to unholster their handguns and point them straight in the air while yelling in unison. Each kid then took aim at the back of his prisoner's head. The boys held their guns in trained stance, with their right hand firmly wrapped around the gun's grip and their pointer finger on the trigger. Each child used his left hand to steady his aim by holding the base of the gun's magazine.

The prisoners bowed their heads, attempting to brace themselves for the impact from the bullets, before the first child fired his gun. The shot went into the back of his prisoner's head and exited the front, jolting his body to the ground. Despite the child's repeated training, he still hadn't gotten used to taking a life and grimaced at the sight.

One after the other, the boys kept firing until all five men were lying face down in the dirt, with blood pouring out from their head wounds. The guns were fired at such a close range that some of the victims had pieces of soft tissue exiting the bullet holes.

The boys hailed from around the world—Tunisia, Egypt, Turkey, Uzbekistan, and Britain. They were child soldiers, trafficked to the war in Syria by their parents, and radicalized before they were cognitively developed enough to fully understand the consequences of their actions.

Becoming a terrorist was never a choice for these kids.

The eleven-year-old British boy—known to family and friends as Jojo—was the child of Sally Jones. Two years before executing this Kurdish soldier for ISIS propaganda, Jojo had been forced to leave Britain with his mother so she could marry a man twenty-five years her junior in Syria. Jojo's brother was eighteen years old at the time and as such was afforded the choice to stay home in Britain. Jojo, on the other hand, was only nine and had no other option but to leave his childhood under the guidance of his mother.

Following the video of Jojo and his friends executing the five Kurdish prisoners in 2016, ISIS began increasingly filming and disseminating propaganda using child soldiers; each video featured younger kids and was more gruesome than the last.

For example, in 2017, ISIS released a video titled *He Made Me Alive With His Blood*, which featured three children executing prisoners from Deir ez-Zor in Syria.[2] After a little over ten minutes of routine propaganda, the execution sequence began, with a young boy—possibly eight or nine years of age—climbing the stairs of a discolored and antiquated Gravitron ride at an abandoned fun fair.

A thin man in a white t-shirt and blue shorts was at the apex, with his hands bound to the ride's lifted, lap-bar seatbelt. The man's head lay in the seat of the ride with his entire neck exposed. His body seemed relaxed, despite his knowledge of impending death. There was a good possibility that he had been drugged.

The child solider, clad in pint-sized green and tan military fatigues and a black cap, looked at the camera, curling his lip in disgust. He stood over his victim, with his left knee kneeling on the seat and right foot planted on the base of the ride. The boy placed his left hand over the man's mouth and gripped a twelve-inch hunting knife with his right.

The camera cut to an adult at the entrance of the ride wearing an all-black uniform and black leather fingerless gloves, with MMA-style knuckle padding. The video didn't show the ISIS combatant's face but instead focused on his hands making a single-slice, chopping motion—ordering the child to decapitate the man.

As soon as the boy saw the directive, he turned his face to the prisoner's head and began vigorously sawing at his neck. The knife cut through the man's flesh like butter, blood pouring out onto the seat and down the cracks of the ride. Notwithstanding the unimaginable pain this would have caused, the man didn't move much, likely from the drugs. Only a straightening of his legs in Lazarus reflex.

Despite his best effort, the child didn't have enough strength to fully decapitate the man, stopping after he was only three-fourths of the way finished to wipe the blood off of his knife onto the chest of the victim's white shirt. The boy continued watching, as pints of blood poured from the man's neck and his lungs labored for air. The sounds of his dying gasps were muted postproduction with a dubbed *nasheed,** but this child heard, felt, saw, and experienced every horrific moment.

Off camera, the adult finished the job and sawed until the man's head was fully amputated from his body, which remained at the apex of the ride. It was placed several feet in front of him on the floor, at the opposite side of the ride, and filmed as the Gravitron spun slowly, for added terroristic effect.

---

* "Chanting" music that is either sung a cappella or accompanied only by percussion instruments.

The propaganda video then cut to different scenes at the abandoned amusement park—miniature train tracks, enveloped by patches of long dried grass and an outdated Ferris wheel covered in faded colors of peeling paint from rusted metal. The location looked like scene from a postapocalyptic horror movie, but this was real life.

Next, the videographer filmed a panoramic of a man with his hands bound to a fence like a crucifix, before taking an aerial shot of a three- or four-year-old toddler in an all-black uniform and black cap, walking through a pit of crushed and sun-bleached plastic balls. The boy was so small, he labored at times to walk over the crushed pieces, which weren't more than a few inches above the ground.

The same adult man who had overseen the earlier execution stood catty-corner to the boy and the prisoner, with his face off camera once more. The video again focused on his hands, as the ISIS militant cocked a chrome, pearl-handled, semiautomatic twenty-two-caliber pistol and handed it by the barrel to the toddler.

The boy wrinkled his nose and squinted his eyes, preparing almost immediately for the weapon's kickback—something he had clearly felt before. The child's tiny fingers could barely wrap around the width of the gun's handle. He was so small that he had to grip it with his thumbs interlocked and two fingers on the trigger. Absolutely all of his strength was used to hold the gun, pointed at the prisoner, with his arms fully extended (see Image 21).

The boy's face strained as he aimed the weapon.

Although the target was physically present in the abandoned ball pit, facing down a toddler with a gun and hanging from the fence by his wrists, mentally, he was somewhere else.

The boy closed his eyes and fired the gun three times in rapid succession.

The bullets caused the man's body to jump, but his drugged facial expression didn't change. For a brief moment, it looked like he was unharmed, until blood began to spill from the top of his head and his eyes rolled back.

The boy fired once more, hitting the man in the face, making his head jerk. And again, striking the prisoner in the right temple, producing a river of blood that spilled down, soaking his shirt and dripping onto the cracked plastic balls that lay next to him.

Once the man had breathed his last breath, the boy turned toward one of the cameras filming him, raising the small gun with his right hand high in the air, and screamed to the top of his lungs, "Allahu Akbar! Allahu Akbar!"

The video cut back to the train track ride, where the children from the first two executions joined a third boy, dressed in all black, roughly ten years of age. He held a prisoner on his knees, with his hands bound in rope behind his back. The boy kicked the man to the ground for the camera, grabbed him by the back of the hair, and lifted. The toddler watched on and signaled the decapitation as he was taught, by using his right hand to make a slitting motion across his neck.

Following the cue, the ten-year-old straddled the man, who was lying on his stomach, and began using a knife to saw at the front of his neck. The man clenched his jaw and grunted in pain as his blood smeared onto the boy's gloves, soaked into the sand, and coated the dried grass beneath him. Although a *nasheed* again muted the sounds of the gore in the video postproduction, all three boys heard each snap from the cut ligaments and every gurgle for air.

The man's eyes widened the closer his head came to decapitation. The drugs only sedated him so much. His lip snarled and feet kicked with each cut deeper, until his head was completely ripped from his body.

Blood soaked the soil and grass beneath him, as flies buzzed around.

The director ordered the child executioner to stab his knife into the back of the man's lifeless body, as if it were their black flag, making claim on territory.

These boys had committed gruesomely horrific crimes. Watching them would make any person with a regard for humanity feel physically ill. My heart sunk into my stomach, and I had to repeatedly look away from the videos of these child murderers, but the fact of the matter is—they were victims, as well.

* * *

On February 12, 2002, the United Nations adopted the Optional Protocol on the Involvement of Children in Armed Conflict. At the time of this writing, 167 countries had ratified the commitment, which agrees that:

> *States will not recruit children under the age of eighteen to send them to the battlefield; should take all possible measures to prevent such recruitment; and will demobilize any child soldier and help their social reintegration by providing physical and psychological recovery services.*[3]

Congress reaffirmed this commitment in 2008 by passing the Child Soldiers Prevention Act, mandating that the United States government should:

> *(1) condemn the conscription, forced recruitment, or use of children by governments, paramilitaries, or other organizations;*
> *(2) expand ongoing services to rehabilitate and reintegrate recovered child soldiers by offering ongoing psychological, educational, and vocational assistance; and*
> *(3) work with the international community to bring to justice rebel and paramilitary forces that kidnap children for use as child soldiers.*[4]

The Child Soldier Prevention Act also required the US Department of State to include in the annual Trafficking in Persons (TIP) Report a list of foreign governments identified during the previous year as having governmental armed forces or government-supported armed groups that recruit and use child soldiers. The 2018 report included eleven countries: Burma, Democratic Republic of the Congo, Iran, Iraq, Mali, Niger, Nigeria, Somalia, South Sudan, Yemen, and Syria.[5] It also opened with a message from Secretary of State Mike Pompeo highlighting the gravity of the child soldier trafficking problem in Syria:

> *The use of human trafficking by terrorist groups, such as ISIS and Boko Haram, not only reflects the brutality of these groups, but also acts as a means by which terrorist organizations recruit adherents and finance their operations. Combating human trafficking is not merely a moral issue or one that affects the interests of the American people; it is also an issue that threatens international peace and security.*[6]

Syrian government forces, proregime militias, and armed nonstate actors have all forcibly recruited child soldiers, some as young as three years old, into combat in Syria. This includes ISIS, Jabhat al-Nusra (the al-Qaeda affiliate in Syria), the Free Syrian Army (FSA), Hezbollah, National Defense Forces (NDF), and Kurdish forces.[7] Jabhat al-Nusra and ISIS are especially brutal, routinely using children as human shields, suicide bombers, snipers, and executioners.

Although there is no way of knowing exactly how many child soldiers have been trafficked into conflict by ISIS, estimates combined with the increase in related propaganda are certainly a cause for great concern. In the first six months of 2015, ISIS was believed to have recruited more than 1,100 child soldiers, and fifty-two of them were estimated to have been killed during that same time-frame—all under the age of sixteen.[8]

ISIS propaganda magazine *Dabiq* attempted to justify their trafficking of child soldiers in an article titled "The Lions of Tomorrow":

> As the mujahidin *of the Islamic State continue their march against the forces of* kufr* *there is a new generation waiting in the wings, eagerly anticipating the day that it is called upon to take up the banner of* iman.† *These are the children of the* Ummah‡ *of jihad,§ a generation raised in the lands of* malahim** *and nurtured under the shade of Sharia,†† just a stone's throw from the frontlines.*
>
> *The Islamic State has taken it upon itself to fulfill the* Ummah's *duty towards this generation in preparing it to face the crusaders and their allies in defense of Islam and to raise high the word of Allah in every land. It has established institutes for these* ashbal‡‡ *to train and hone their military skills, and to teach them the book of Allah and the* Sunnah§§ *of His Messenger.*

The article was specifically addressing criticism following the release of two ISIS propaganda videos that showed a ten-year-old Russian boy speaking of his ambitions to grow up and "kill infidels" before shooting two alleged Russian spies repeatedly in the head (see Image 22).

> *It is these young lions to whom the Islamic State recently handed over two agents caught spying for Russian Intelligence and an agent caught spying for the Israeli Mossad, to be executed and displayed as*

---

* Disbelief.
† Faith in metaphysical aspects of Islam.
‡ Community.
§ Struggle against sin and/or the enemies of Islam.
** Bloody battles.
†† Islamic law.
‡‡ Lion cubs.
§§ Legal custom and practice.

*an example to anyone else thinking of infiltrating the mujahidin.
As expected, the kuffar were up in arms about the Khilafah's use of
"child soldiers."*[9]

ISIS claimed the use of child soldiers was religiously permissible because it
believed a polytheist pagan critic of Muhammad named Abu Jahl was killed
by two children, brothers, in the Battle of Badr. Although Abu Jahl isn't mentioned by name in any translation of the Qur'an, some impose his name in four
verses, which incidentally say nothing about the manner in which he died.

While the Qur'an doesn't discuss the death of Abu Jahl by name, it does mention children around eight dozen times, none of which have anything to do with
manipulating them into being soldiers. Instead, the Qur'an focuses on how they
are a blessing and worthy of protection:

> *Your riches and your children may be but a trial: but in the Presence
> of Allah, is the highest, Reward. (64:15)*
>
> *Kill not your children for fear of want: We shall provide sus-
> tenance for them as well as for you. Verily the killing of them is a
> great sin. (17:31)*
>
> *Lost are those who slay their children, from folly, without
> knowledge, and forbid food which Allah hath provided for them,
> inventing (lies) against Allah. They have indeed gone astray and
> heeded no guidance. (6:140)*

However, it didn't matter how diverged they were from the true interpretation
of Islam, because this was about money and power, not religion. They needed
more marginalized people to radicalize, and children were easier to exploit.
This message was again reiterated in the ninth issue of their latest propaganda
magazine, *Rumiyah*, with an article titled "Raising Them to Love Fighting for
the Cause of Allah":

> *From among the greatest of Allah's blessings upon the lion cubs in
> the Khilafah . . . they grow up with their eyes becoming accustomed
> to seeing weapons and equipment, including rifles, tactical vests,
> bullets, grenades, and explosive belts. Likewise, watching the muja-
> hidin's video releases and following their written and recorded news*

nurtures within the lion cub the love of jihad and the mujahidin
and hatred towards their enemies.

The mother may hear criticism from some people who would ar-
gue that the manner in which she raises her children might kill their
childhood and destroy their innocence," but she should ignore.[10]

By 2017, ISIS was operating at least three child-training camps in which they
coerced children to attend radicalization seminars in exchange for promised
salaries, mobile phones, weapons, a "martyr's" place in paradise, and the "gift"
of a wife. After being successfully indoctrinated, the children were deployed
into hostilities as combatants or informants, exposing them to retaliation and
extreme punishment. ISIS deliberately targeted children for indoctrination due
to manpower shortages, as well as facility and longevity of radicalization.

These kids were undoubtedly trafficked into terrorism but were denied
opportunity for rescue, much less education, vocational training, trauma-in-
formed therapy, or opportunities for reintegration. Instead, they found themselves arrested, detained, severely abused, or killed as a result of being radicalized into ISIS, even if they were able to eventually escape. At present, the
Syrian government does not investigate or punish trafficking offenders, nor
does it identify or protect any trafficking victims. Ultimately, these kids who
are trafficked into ISIS as child soldiers are denied relief and indefinitely lose
their victim status once they turn eighteen, so there is little hope for their rescue and rehabilitation.

For example, in 2016, as the rates of child soldier recruitment started to rise,
a video was released, allegedly depicting an "ISIS Child Soldier" who had been
captured by Iraqi forces in the Kurdistan region of Erbil. The grainy cellphone
video featured a frightened teenager, no more than fourteen or fifteen years of
age, lying on the sand, as several soldiers tauntingly stood around him.

The men wore tan uniforms and appeared to have been riding in a convoy of
tanks. Each soldier had the stereotypical military haircut—high and tight with
no facial hair. Although it was difficult to confirm from the video, a patch with
the Iraqi flag appeared on at least one of the officers' utility vests. They didn't
look like militants; these men looked like government-funded soldiers.

As the boy lay on the ground, cowering in fear, one of the men grabbed the
neck of his jacket and began dragging him. He didn't appear to have any weapon
and wasn't wearing a uniform, although his pants were soaked in blood from the

knee down. The boy was so light that the soldier dragging him was able to toss his body like a rag doll in front of one of the tanks.

"Please, release me, I did nothing," he begged.

"How is it, *Daesh?*" the soldier replied.

The boy's head was forced at the base of the tank's track, and his heart was pounding out of his chest with fear. He desperately wanted to run away but couldn't because of the injuries he sustained to his legs. So he lay there, face in the sand, with his body as straight as an arrow—in the path of a sixty-two-metric-ton tank.

The cameraman ordered the driver to run the boy over. But before he could, one of the soldiers shot the boy several times, perhaps in the hope of killing him with some sense of mercy before he was excruciatingly flattened to death. Only a few seconds passed before the tank then drove over his lifeless body, as the soldiers danced, cheered, and waved their arms in celebration.

In response to the video, the Iraqi government claimed the individuals weren't military officers, but actually ISIS in disguise.[11] In support of their defense, they pointed to the color of the uniforms, which were allegedly different from those worn by the Iraqi military, as well as the style of guns, which they claimed were more common among ISIS militants.

Regardless of whether the heinous act was truly perpetrated by the Iraqi military or ISIS, the reaction to it is perhaps what was most concerning. While some were horrified at the treatment of this child, others had a complete disregard for the extralegal form of punishment and the child's age. Commenters on the video posted:

> **Tripp1001:** *Good, fuck that kid.*
>
> **ParkourPerson:** *At first I thought it was a little savage to execute a child, but then I wondered how many lives were saved in the process.*
>
> **THOMMO:** *That little fucker won't be playing soldiers again.*
>
> **Dargis49:** *Very possible this little cocksucker took out a few of their guys.*
>
> **Mld5504:** *No news here, shit happens during war.*
>
> **RoudyDog44:** *LOL. Now, how does that work for ya, ISIS goat fuckers.* ☺
>
> **Tomira09:** *I would run over him legs first…slowly.* ☺
>
> **WmsTwo02:** *Child Soldier = Combatant.*

LongLiveIraq99: *Sure, it's a kid, but it doesn't matter anymore. Once you fight, you'll be treated like the rest of soldiers.*
Speel Obmam: *They solved an inevitable future problem in the "here and now." Kudos! Well-done! All such ISIS vermin should be handled in a similar fashion. All of 'em.*[12]

In reading these responses, I felt disgusted and at a loss for words. This was a young boy, not a man. Regardless of what he had done, he was a child soldier and therefore a victim. While he may have deserved a humane punishment that was within the confines of the law, this boy, according to international law, was also deserving of the opportunity to be rehabilitated.

Most of the people who advocate for this type of harsh response to child soldiers and ISIS in general are doing so out of teleological ethics—the outcome determines the justness of an act. These people would rather demobilize a child soldier with death than live with the possibility of him killing others, and, by their lights, a violent death was warranted in retribution for the havoc ISIS wreaks.

On the opposite end of the moral spectrum, there are people who believe that this type of behavior should never be justified. They base this determination on deontological ethics—the justness of an act should be judged in and of itself, regardless of the outcome. *These* people would rather treat this child humanely, regardless of his risk of recidivating because violent deaths are not permissible, no matter the executioner or executed.

Ultimately, irrespective of where you fall on the spectrum of normative ethical theories, I thoroughly believe that:

There can be no keener revelation of a society's soul than the way in which it treats its children.

—Nelson Mandela

PART IV

16

Counterterrorism

When I was a child, one of my favorite stories was about my mom standing up to a bully.

She was in fifth grade when she overheard a boy taunting a developmentally disabled student in her class. She did not feel this was right and told the bully to leave the boy alone. When he tried to get physical, she swung him around by his arm and knocked him down four or five stairs.

When she told the story, I remember feeling proud. I suppose I liked the idea of my tiny mom defending an innocent kid from a big, bad oppressor.

It might sound childish, but I used to look at the United States of America in the same light. When we were in conflict, I wholeheartedly believed we were always in the right, making the world a better place and defending innocent people and countries against the evil criminals and dictators of the world. I believed what I was taught—that our country was number one, the best, the heroes, just like my mom.

I had no reason to doubt the concept of American exceptionalism until I realized that many of our interventions, domestic and abroad, would simply replace one problem with another, and the situation sometimes became worse after we intervened.

For example, look at how ISIS came to be in the first place.

In 1979, Soviet troops invaded Afghanistan, prompting Saudi Arabia-born Osama bin Laden to join the resistance.[1] He had been influenced by an extremist named Abdullah Azzam to rise up against Western influence on Middle-Eastern life and engage in so-called "jihad" to create a single Islamic state.[2] Bin Laden was wealthy and privileged, so he of course did not become a fighter himself but instead used his extensive connections to win financial and moral support for the so-called "*mujahideen*"—the Afghan rebels who were fighting against the USSR.[3]

At the time, the CIA perceived bin Laden and his small group of Islamic militants from Egypt, Pakistan, Lebanon, Syria, and Palestinian refugee camps all over the Middle East as "reliable" partners of the United States in its war against Moscow.[4] In the context of the Cold War, these militants were given access to a fortune in covert funding and top-level combat weaponry to aid in the downfall of the Soviet Union.[5]

Bin Laden went on to form al-Qaeda in 1988 and soon after began aggressively committing acts of terrorism: the World Trade Center bombing in 1993; the US National Guard bombing in Riyadh in 1995; US Embassy bombings in Nairobi, Kenya and Dar-es-Salaam, Tanzania, in 1998; an attack on the USS *Cole*, an American naval destroyer off the coast of Yemen in 2000; and, most notoriously, the attacks on the World Trade Center and Pentagon on September 11, 2001.[6]

It took another ten years for bin Laden to be brought to justice, with his assassination on May 2, 2011, but his ideas didn't die with him. From al-Qaeda, ISIS was born and continues to terrorize the world.

ISIS's belief system originated with bin Laden and was built upon by Jordanian leader of al-Qaeda in Iraq (AQI) Abu Musab al-Zarqawi.[7] Zarqawi was killed on June 7, 2006, and Abu Bakr al-Baghdadi eventually took command of AQI, changing the name to Islamic State of Iraq (ISI), which later became known as Islamic State of Iraq and al-Sham or Islamic State of Iraq and Syria (ISIS) and Islamic State of Iraq and the Levant (ISIL). This is why I often refer to ISIS as a monolith in this book—the Taliban, al-Qaeda, Boko Haram, al-Shabaab, and ISIS are all criminal organizations run by men governed by the same ideology, using the veneer of religion to selfishly pursue money and power.

The CIA calls this "blowback," and, unfortunately, it isn't the only time it has happened, even here in the United States.[8]

For example, look at the case of La Mara Salavatrucha—MS-13—one of the most dangerous gangs in the world.

Although people assume the criminal organization began in El Salvador, it actually started in California when refugees from the Salvadoran Civil War sought protection in the United States. However, many settled in lower socio-economic neighborhoods of California where established gangs, like the Mexican Mafia, began victimizing the Salvadoran refugees.

MS-13 was originally formed by a group of teenagers, largely in response to the abuse and social marginalization they faced.[9]

Members of the gang were arrested and incarcerated for their crimes in

California and faced deportation after the end of the civil war. Since El Salvador didn't have the infrastructure to deal with the organized crime group, the gang began to spread.

MS-13 eventually became the first transcontinental gang and effectively went from being a one-state problem to a fifty-state and multinational catastrophe. Some attribute this proliferation to the collateral consequence of mass deportation.[10]

Ultimately, hindsight is 20/20 and perhaps we wouldn't have done anything differently in these situations, but there were undoubtedly unintended consequences to these interventions that replaced one problem with another or made a situation worse. It is important to acknowledge that our democracy is not perfect, and we shouldn't expect it to be. We have made mistakes, and it is important for us to recognize them, so that we can learn and grow as a nation.

For many Americans like myself, I think it is in our culture to aspire for heroism, but in order to do that, we need to practice what we preach and protect the marginalized, at home and abroad. Before intervening, we must question our intentions, identify root causes, evaluate alternatives, and project collateral consequences. It isn't in our best interest to blindly ride in like cowboys when we see a threat to our national ethos of democracy, liberty, opportunity, or equality. In fact, we still need to take action to fully implement these tenets at home, before we can adequately project them abroad.

We will undoubtedly still fight for justice and stand up against criminal organizations like ISIS—after all, it *is* the American way—but in doing so, we should remember:

Every battle is won or lost before it's ever fought.

—Sun Tzu

17

Rumiyah

Over the last four years, I have downloaded so much terrorist propaganda in research for this book—countless execution videos and sermons; thirteen issues of *Rumiyah** magazine and fifteen issues of *Dabiq* from ISIS; seventeen editions of al-Qaeda's *Inspire* magazine and thirty issues of *In Fight* from the Afghan Taliban; and nine editions of *Gaidi Mtaani,* published by al-Shabaab—that I would be surprised if I wasn't on a watch list somewhere.

I was able to find and access much of it through simple Google searches, but for other content I needed to use a virtual privacy network (VPN) with end point encryption, just as actual members of ISIS do. Encrypted privacy networks facilitate access to terrorist propaganda in two ways.

First, they allow Internet users to circumvent government restrictions to blocked and filtered content on the Internet. Both democratic nations and authoritarian governments can restrict access to online content for users who reside within their borders. They do this by obstructing or tampering with domain names, filtering specific keywords, blocking IP addresses, and simply urging online providers to remove certain search results.[1] Online content can be blocked for a number of reasons, including shielding children from obscenities, preventing access to copyright-infringing material or confusingly named domains, or protecting national security.[2] At present, certain types of terrorist propaganda, namely, recruitment sermons and execution videos are typically blocked to users in the United States.

Second, encrypted privacy networks preserve online anonymity. Theoretically, an Internet user's IP address serves as their virtual identification. Some websites collect this information for tracking purposes, and law enforcement can use it

---

* *Rumiyah* is Arabic for *Rome*.

in surveillance of criminals on the World Wide Web. In a perfect world for law enforcement, anything an Internet user did or said online could be traced back to their real identity and location using their IP address. However, encrypted privacy networks facilitate anonymity by constantly bouncing the IP addresses between users across the world and periodically erasing the trace memory. Technically, information accessed or distributed through an encrypted privacy network travels through encoded layers of the network and Internet Exchange Points (IXPs) or autonomous systems (ASes) that control multiple routers, such as ISPs (Internet Service Providers).[3] Thousands of relays are randomly used to encrypt the identity of users within the network.

The first issue of al-Qaeda's propaganda magazine *Inspire* provided details on how aspiring terrorists could send and receive encrypted messages with software called Asrar al-Mujahideen 2.0.[*4] Essentially, the software allowed the sender and recipient to each create a private key, which they would share with each other, in order to encrypt and decrypt text messages and files, while ensuring that contents couldn't be easily viewed during transmission.

However, I was not inclined to install or use any software developed by or for al-Qaeda and providentially didn't need to. In the mid-1990s, the United States Naval Research Laboratory developed an encrypted privacy network called The Onion Router (Tor) in order to protect United States intelligence communications online. By 2002, Tor became available to the general public in order to defend average citizens against traffic analysis—something the Tor website explains is a form of network surveillance that threatens personal freedom and privacy, confidential business activities and relationships, and state security.[5] One of the many uses of Tor is to facilitate communications between journalists and whistleblowers or dissidents,[6] but it is also used to gain access to terrorist propaganda and for other criminal exchanges.

Using Tor, I was able to watch more than three dozen execution videos and listen to over one hundred recordings of extremist lectures in English as part of my research. I had access to the same things that terrorist recruits are exposed to prior to their conscription, and from this content, I could understand why they, as well as counterterrorism advocates, believe that Islam is the root of these ideologies, but they are wrong.

My opinion may not carry a lot of weight, considering that I am not a

---

* Mujahideen Secrets.

counterterrorism scholar—the overwhelming majority of whom are men, parenthetically. However, I am tangentially informed through my background as a human trafficking expert and PhD-educated criminologist. I have conducted thousands of interviews with convicted human traffickers and have researched hundreds of human trafficking cases. Perhaps it is because of my education and experiential knowledge that when I watch, read, and listen to extremist propaganda, I do not take away any truth about Islam or Muslim people. By my lights, the content of terrorist propaganda is closer to tactics used by a human trafficker than a sermon of a true religious leader.

Human traffickers are incredibly skilled in manipulation and are capable of feeding their targets whatever they want to hear. One man, serving a life sentence for sex trafficking a twelve-year-old girl, once told me:

> *Why does a prostitute need a pimp? To guide her, to love her, to protect her. The pimp is her father that she never had. He is that big brother that she misses, or the boyfriend from back in the day. The pimp is that husband that she fantasized about over and over. He is the popular guy in school that never paid her attention in class. To her, he is what Christ is to a Christian. . . . The blood that pumps in her heart and keeps her legs moving. Without him, there's no her. You must understand, a ho was put on earth to be pimped by her pimp. . . . Not all pimps, players, or macks possess the same characteristics. But, what we all have in common is a unique way of life and love for women and how they are able to use what they have to get them, and us what we need (notice I said NEED); we all need money to survive![7]*

Like human traffickers, terrorist recruiters speak in analogies and tell intricate stories to help make their points resonate with wide audiences of disenfranchised people. For example, in a lecture entitled "Stop Police Terror," notorious terrorist recruiter Anwar al-Awlaki didn't speak of murdering or pillaging. Instead, he told a fable about four cows:

> *Once upon a time, there were four cows—one of them was white and the other three were black. They lived in a dangerous area surrounded by wolves, but protected themselves by sticking together*

and watching out for one another. Everyone was keeping an attentive eye and they survived, even though wild beasts surrounded the area.

One day the three black cows had a meeting. They said, "This white cow is giving us away. When we hide at night no one can see us because we are black, but the enemy is able to see the white cow, so why don't we just let him go? The three of us will be together and let's just get rid of the white cow because he is just too much trouble."

From that day on, the three black cows would be on one side and the poor white cow was left all alone.

Now, the wolf was very intelligent. He was able to detect the disunity amongst these cows. So he made his move and attacked the white cow first.

While the wolf was devouring his flesh, the three black cows did nothing. They watched while their brother was being torn into pieces!

The following night, the wolf attacked the three black cows. Why? Because they were one cow short and not as strong as they were the day before. Since they had let their brother white cow down, the wolf attacked them and was able to snatch away one of the black cows. And then there were two.

The next night, it was an even easier task for the wolf to eat one of the two remaining cows.

And on the final night the last cow was frantically trying to run away from the wolf, but he was all-alone, without any support or help. The wolf pursued the cow with confidence, knowing he would get tired and fall down. There was nothing the cow could do, nobody to help him. When the wolf finally pounced on the cow and grabbed him by the neck, the cow pronounced his last words while he was dying—a statement that is a great lesson that we can learn from: "I died the day the white cow was eaten!"

Al-Awlaki went on to analogize this story to the Muslim community. He professed that these were the consequences of having disunity. He argued that the white cow was the representation of someone who is outspoken, causing a lot of trouble, or accused of being a terrorist—like him. The wolves, he proclaimed, were communities of disbelievers. He cautioned law-abiding Muslims that if they allow a fellow Muslim to go to jail for terrorism, they would be next in line:

> *Don't think by ducking down and being quiet you will be safe, you will not, you'll be next. . . . If you don't stop it now, it could happen to you, it could happen to your wife, it could happen to your own daughter. You need to stop it in its tracks before it grows.*

Ostensibly, the lecture advocated for the unity and protection of the Muslim community from criminalization of their religion. But this was simply a tactic of misdirection, meant to distract the listeners from the fact that he was radicalizing them into criminal exploitation. Osama bin Laden used the same tactics decades before him, saying, "The survival of Islam and the Muslim world is, God willing, in the hands of every Muslim, and is the responsibility of each."

While Muslims in various parts of the world are certainly suffering and are in desperate need for humanitarian aid, al-Awlaki was not radicalizing others for their salvation. Like every other terrorist leader, he could not have cared less about the religion of Islam or the Muslim people he was radicalizing. He coveted money and power, as well as obedience and respect. He wanted to be revered as a religious leader, which is why he referred to his *fable* of the four cows as "parable," like those told by the Prophet Muhammad and Jesus.

Ultimately, no matter the platform or terrorist organization, there is one common thread across all extremist propaganda—the veneer of religion is used to coerce, defraud, and force already marginalized people into exploitation.

In my review of countless terrorist recruitment materials, I have found there are six consistent themes of misinformation used in radicalization.

First, terrorist organizations want the world to believe that the word *terrorist*, in application to extremist organizations such as ISIS or al-Qaeda, is a misnomer for "religious Muslim." In each lecture and propaganda publication, the words *Muslim* and *Islam* are mentioned at least one hundred times, while *terrorist* is mentioned less than a handful. They want Muslims to believe that

> *To Americans, your belongingness to Islam is enough to classify you as an enemy. As a matter of fact, they look at us as Muslim youth*

*regardless of our appearance and education. They do not consider
our citizenship and the childhood we spent in their neighborhoods.
. . . Our enemies treat us as Muslims only, nothing more.*[8]

Second, extremists recruit by repeatedly asserting that their cause seeks to protect the children who are being killed in war. Graphic images of the horrific
injuries and deaths sustained by children are prominent throughout their propaganda (see Image 23). They assert that these injuries are the direct result of
American actions, such as airstrikes, without regard for civilian safety. Injured
children are not only used as a recruitment tactic to coerce people into joining the war in their defense, but also in order to dissuade adversaries from
attacking.

For example, Anwar al-Awlaki was considered a high-priority target in
American counterterrorism efforts. In 2011, al-Awlaki was killed in an airstrike,
and shortly after, his sixteen-year-old American-born son—Abdulrahman bin
Anwar al-Awlaki—was hit by an airstrike as well, even though he was not on any
"kill list."[9] Seven years later, his eight-year-old daughter, Nawar Anwar al-Awlaki,
was also killed.[10] Terrorist combatants often reside and travel with women and
children, so they can use them as human shields and talking points in propaganda. For example, Issue 9 of *Inspire* included the following feature titled "They
Killed Father, They Killed Son":

> [The] *American administration led by Obama proved yet again
> it is without any moral code of warfare. It is not the first time
> U.S. drones are killing children all over the Muslims lands. But
> it is the first time that a child was killed intentionally. The reason
> why [Abdulrahman bin Anwar al-Awlaki] was "guilty" was the
> fact he was a son of Shaykh Anwar al-Awlaki. But can we blame
> somebody because of being somebody's son? What will next America
> do, will they kill Shaykh's Anwar parents only because they are his
> parents? Will they kill all Shaykh's children only because they are his
> children? America showed again its hypocrisy accusing Muslims for
> killing women and children in "suicide attacks" but in reality who
> is the one who targets children?*
>
> *One should wonder what Obama will do, what Obama would
> feel if Muslims kill his daughters only for being his daughters?*

We are sure that not only the Americans, but the whole world
would condemn such murder. But Muslims would never intention-
ally kill children no matter who their parents are. No matter if they
are the worst enemy of Islam, if they are children it is prohibited to
target them intentionally.

We are asking Obama, even if Shaykh Anwar is guilty accord-
ing to your man-made laws, even if he was on you capture or kill list
without any trial, we are asking you what guilt does his son have?
How can you allow yourself to be judge without jury, to make de-
cision not respecting any moral code and International laws, while
in the same time you accuse Muslims who are defending themselves
of being terrorists? We really fail to understand how defending our-
selves from your occupation can be terrorism. We do not see al-
Qaeda planes above the U.S. but we see U.S. drones killing women
and children of Yemen.

This horrible act of murder showed us again how much respect-
ing human rights and justice are not something that America's ad-
ministration takes into consideration when Muslim individuals are
targeted. They will find millions of lame excuses to justify themselves
and the world will swallow it. Only the believers, only the followers
of the Book which brings light, justice and truth will open one's eyes
to know how much innocent blood America has on its hands, the
blood of the children whose guilt was only being Muslims.[11]

The deaths of children and women from airstrikes are used as the primary
justification for ISIS's brutal assassinations—*lex talionis*—law of retaliation.
For example, both James Wright Foley and Steven Sotloff—American journalists—were decapitated in ISIS propaganda videos. The accompanying explanation claimed that they were "executed in retaliation for the numerous Muslims
killed in Iraq by the U.S. American airstrikes." Similarly, when ISIS killed
a Royal Jordanian Air Force pilot by burning him to death in a cage, they
asserted it was in retaliation for airstrikes. Issue 7 of *Dabiq* includes images
from his murder and an accompanying explanation, which reads:

This week, the Islamic State released a video depicting the execution
of the Jordanian crusader pilot, Mu'adh Safi Yusuf al-Kasasibah. As

displayed in the video, the Islamic State had resolved to burn him alive
as retribution for his crimes against Islam and the Muslims, including
his active involvement in crusader airstrikes against Muslim lands.[12]

Third, despite these mass casualties from an increasingly brutal war, terrorist recruiters also want marginalized people to believe that the Islamic State is Utopia. They publish images of hospitals treating children, giving charity to orphans, and providing services for the elderly (see Image 24). They share pictures of ISIS fighting crime (see Image 25) and regularly discuss the equality, belonging, and brotherhood among recruits. Prospective extremists are led to believe that they will have a home and everything they need to live will be provided to them upon arrival, which can be an attractive possibility, especially for persons who are barely surviving. In the first issue of ISIS's *Dabiq* magazine, the listed benefits and services provided by the Islamic State were as follows:

1. *Returning rights and property to their rightful owners;*
2. *Pumping millions of dollars into services that are important to the Muslims;*
3. *The state of security and stability enjoyed by the areas under the Islamic State's authority;*
4. *Ensuring the availability of food products and commodities in the market, particularly bread;*
5. *The reduced crime rate; and*
6. *The flourishing relationship between the Islamic State and its citizens.*

Fourth, for those who are not lured by the romanticized version of the Islamic State, recruiters and propaganda will coerce with threats of apostasy and moral corruption. They manipulate people into questioning their interpretation of their own faith and gaslight recruits into believing that Muslim leaders in the West are the manipulators. For instance, Issue 3 of *Dabiq* cautions:

Living amongst the sinful kills the heart, never mind living amongst
the kuffar!* *Their* kufr† *initially leaves dashes and traces upon*
the heart that over time become engravings and carvings that are

---

* Disbeliever.
† Disbelief.

nearly impossible to remove. They can destroy the person's fitrah* *to a point of no return, so that his heart's doubts and desires entrap him fully.*"[13]

Fifth, for those who arrive in the Islamic State and discover that it is not what they expected, they are threatened with death if they attempt to escape.

For example, on September 2, 2015, distressing images of three-year-old Syrian refugee Alan Kurdi began circulating on the Internet.[14] Human rights activists and reporters felt the images of this poor child, who drowned while attempting to escape the war in Syria, would be a catalyst for international aid to help innocent Syrians find international refuge from the Islamic State militants. While the rest of the world felt gut-wrenching sympathy for this young boy, ISIS used the event as a threat against others who wished to flee (see Image 26):

> *The repeated events of Syrians and Libyans dying on the shores of Turkey, Libya, and Italy, or even on the highways of Austria, is one that should awaken the heart into reflecting upon the issue of* Hijrah†. . . . *It should be known that voluntarily leaving* Dārul-Islām‡ *for* dārul-kufr§ *is a dangerous major sin.*[15]

In their propaganda, ISIS militants spun this story as a threat to drive fear into the people of Syria. The message was simple: if they attempted to leave Syria, Allah would punish them with death.

Last, when threats fail to coerce people into recruitment, ISIS and other terrorist organizations will resort to force, especially against actual Muslims (see Image 27).

For example, in the first issue of ISIS's *Dabiq* magazine, tribal leaders ominously urged "those bearing arms against the Islamic State to repent before they are captured." Thereafter, reports began emerging of fleeing civilians being doused with oil and burned alive in cages.[16]

In response, there was outrage from Islamic religious leaders around the world,

---

* Instinct.
† *Hijrah* is the migration to their self-proclaimed caliphate.
‡ Meaning the "Land of Islam," referring to the Islamic State in Syria.
§ Meaning the "Land of Disbelief," referring to all other lands outside of the "Land of Islam."

denouncing the ISIS interpretation of the Qur'an and their related terrorism. To mitigate the effect of these rebukes from actual Muslim leaders and scholars, ISIS used propaganda to repeatedly assert that any person in opposition to their cause was committing *riddah** or apostasy. Extremist propaganda would repeatedly call for the murder of imams and Islamic scholars who disagreed with their plight, as evidenced by published threats against Hamza Yusuf, Suhaib Webb, Bilal Philips, and Yasir Qadhi.

Ultimately, ISIS wants the world to believe that it represents Islam, even though it doesn't. They try to convince recruits that terrorism is the only tool available to Muslims for protection and retaliation, even though it's not. ISIS leaders attempt to lure marginalized people to territories they control by claiming the Islamic State is a Utopia, even though that couldn't be further from the truth. They attempt to make Muslims, such as converts, especially those who don't have a firm understanding of the religion, doubt their understanding of Islam by accusing them of apostasy if they don't join the terrorist group. Those who already live in the Islamic State, simply by nature of their residency prior to the conflict, and those who are manipulated into traveling there are threatened against attempting to flee. Finally, ISIS has jailed, assaulted, and killed those who challenge their authority, attempt to escape the Islamic State, or fail to join their terrorist group in order to force compliance.

This this how ISIS coerces, defrauds, and forces people into becoming radicalized. This isn't about religion; even a blind woman can see that fact:

> *Every modern war has had its roots in exploitation.*
>
> —Hellen Keller

---

* Abandonment of religious belief.

Through the Eyes of a Terrorist

In my letters with convicted terrorists incarcerated in federal prison, I asked their opinions on a variety of topics because I wanted to better understand how they viewed their own radicalization and the world around them.

For example, following the *Charlie Hebdo* tragedy, I inquired on their opinions of people being killed over blasphemous cartoons. Richard Reid, the shoe bomber who attempted to blow up American Airlines Flight 63 from Paris to Miami, responded from his maximum security prison cell in Florence, Colorado:

> *Hi, yeah, I saw the news on the events in Paris. It's probably best that I don't comment too much on what my exact thoughts are concerning them, but I will say this much—I do not see what happened at Charlie Hebdo as a tragedy. Rather, the tragedy is that people think that it's okay to demean the sacred and belittle that which is more beloved to Muslims than their own souls. For this is how the true Muslim views the Prophet Muhammad—and as the saying goes, "If you play with fire, you might get burned." So, I have no tears for those who insult Islam and belittle the tenets and symbols held true and dear by its people.*

His response to me was covered by NBC News[1] and republished by media outlets around the world, such as the *Daily Mail*[2] and the *Telegraph*[3] in the United Kingdom, *Le Figaro*[4] and *Le Monde*[5] in France, and *Die Welt*[6] in Germany. These news stories about my letter from him eventually made their way to al-Qaeda in the Arabian Peninsula. They had accessed the online articles using The Onion Router (Tor) to conceal their IP address and location. I was shocked to find a quote from his letter to me in Issue 14 of *Inspire* propaganda magazine (see Image 28).

I also asked the convicted terrorists with whom I corresponded about President Donald J. Trump's travel ban, which restricted immigration from Iran, Libya, Syria, Yemen, Somalia, Chad, and North Korea at the time. One of the responses I received came from ISIS recruit Donald Ray Morgan—a North Carolina native who was sentenced to 243 months in federal prison for attempting to provide material support to a designated foreign terrorist organization and possession of a firearm by a felon. For at least eight months in 2014, Morgan had provided support, resources, and services to ISIS and on at least one occasion attempted to travel from Lebanon to Syria to join their fight.[7] In an eleven-page letter,* he replied:

> *I was relieved to see Trump obtain Commander in Disbelief of the United Snakes. He is a man with the courage to not hide under sheepskin, but rather he proudly exposes his wolf heart. I prefer to see the face of the enemy.*
>
> *I make dua [prayer] that he deports ALL Muslims from the U.S. back to Muslim lands and the Islamic State. Muslims who turn away from their religion should be extradited to the Islamic State for prescribed punishment.*
>
> *The [7] seven countries that you mentioned make complete sense on paper, but there are 1.7 billion Muslims worldwide and increasing daily. Many are answering the call of Jihad and a correct adherence to the Qur'an and Sunnah. This means that many Muslims are already in your communities, schools and universities, gyms, jobs etc. Some are like me, patiently waiting in your prison system and are able to teach and speak to a "captive" audience of misguided people that need faith, direction, and purpose. So I ask Allah to make me able to call Islam wherever I may be placed.*
>
> *A ban can't stop that, can it?*

Given Donald Trump's "tough on terrorism" rhetoric, I was intrigued to see an ISIS recruit say he was "relieved" at his election, so I decided to ask other convicted terrorists about their perceptions of Donald J. Trump's presidency in general.

---

* More of which is included in Appendix B.

In reply to my inquiries, I also received correspondence from Kevin James. He was sentenced to sixteen years in federal prison for forming a terrorist group called Jam'iyyat Ul-Islam Is-Saheeh. While James was already incarcerated in a California state prison, he masterminded plans to attack United States military operations, "infidels," and Israeli and Jewish facilities in the Los Angeles area. In one of his letters to me, he wrote:

> First, I don't "think" anything. I don't believe in the U.S. system of governance, its values, democracy, or capitalism anyway. Trump is an American (U.S.) nationalist. He will probably do more for Americans than any U.S. president in the last 70 years. I don't believe he is racist, but he is prejudiced. I send my condolences to you on the election of your new fascist emperor. He will continue on the manifest destiny objectives of the criminals who disobeyed their king and founded this land.
>
> Allah willing, his election will take the blindfold off of the eyes of Muslims who chose to reside here and make them properly learn their Islam and in the least migrate to a Muslim land, leaving the Godless to their own. I like when an honest hater becomes the new U.S. emperor. It was the same with Bush. He woke the Muslim world up from its slumber and I'm sure Trump will do the same. The U.S. cannot defeat Islam. The more it fights, the less it continues to be as it is. Just as the pagan romans could not defeat the believing Christians and the pagan Egyptians could not defeat the believing followers of Moses.
>
> The U.S. was fine when it focused on Communists—two evil powers fighting over this world and its treasures with no hopes for paradise in heaven. But now they both have united to exterminate a people who ONLY desire life in the hereafter and their every action in this life is to secure their place in paradise. This isn't a winnable battle, but U.S. arrogance and greed will not allow it to stop.
>
> Then comes the most arrogant and greedy person in the U.S., its people made their ruler—tacitly approving of the trash that comes from his mouth.

James wasn't the only terrorist who spoke of Donald J. Trump's election as if it were going to be a spark that aroused an Islamic movement. Terrorist recruitment propaganda also contained similar statements following Trump's election (see Image 29). For example, Issue 17 of al-Qaeda's *Inspire* magazine featured sixteen mentions of "Trump," one paragraph included herein:

> *Many Muslims wanted Trump to lose the elections, hoping that Hillary Clinton would be relatively merciful and less antagonistic towards them. This was just a false hope. Have they forgotten what Democrats under Bill Clinton did to Muslims? Have they forgotten the deaths of a million Iraqi children due to the sanctions imposed by Democrats? Have they forgotten the thousands who fell victim to America's "smart" bombs and its drones during Obama's tenure? "Kufr" [Disbelief] is a single nation. In fact, Trump's blunt statements and his hostile stance towards Islam and Muslims may be beneficial in ways that only Allah knows. His rash candidness is a powerful reminder to the Islamic Ummah of the reality of these disbelievers.*[8]

The terrorist perception of President Donald J. Trump reminded me of statements made by the National Socialist Movement—a white supremacy group—following the election of our country's first black President, Barack Obama:

> *President-elect Obama is going to be the spark that arouses the "white movement." Obama's win is our win. We should all be happy of this event.*[9]

David Duke, founder of the Louisiana-based Knights of the Ku Klux Klan and former Grand Wizard, commented that Obama's election was "good in one sense—that it is making white people clear of the fact that that government in Washington, DC, is not our government. . . . We are beginning to learn and realize our positioning. . . . And our position is that we have got to stand up and fight now."

Most white conservatives don't particularly care for any Democratic president, including Barack Obama, but that doesn't mean that they agree with the "white supremacy" sentiments of the National Social Movement or former KKK Grand Wizard David Duke. To that effect, many Muslims may not particularly care for

President Donald J. Trump, but that doesn't mean they agree with sentiments of terrorists, either.

In order to conceal their nefarious intentions, criminal organizations notoriously leech off of legitimate groups or social movements. The KKK hides among conservatives, and anarchists infiltrate liberals. Sex traffickers portray themselves as lovers and faux family to their victims, while ISIS operates under the veneer of Islam. None of these criminal groups truly believe in or care about the pretense they hide behind; it simply allows for more facility in their operation. As such, it is important for us to stop confounding extremist and criminal organizations with legitimate causes and civil actions on both sides; all this does is boost the legitimacy of the former and erroneously label and censure the latter.

Ultimately, most of my correspondences focused on better understanding terrorists' paths to radicalization and their perception of why they committed their respective crimes. Included herein are excerpts from Kevin James and Levar Washington, both of whom were radicalized into terrorism after long histories of delinquency and crime.

James recruited Washington in late 2004, while both were incarcerated at New Folsom Prison. He required Washington to swear an oath of loyalty and obedience to James and their terrorist syndicate Jam'iyyat Ul-Islam Is-Saheeh (JIS).[10]

Washington was released from prison only several weeks after taking the JIS oath. He began recruiting others into the terrorist cell before committing a dozen armed robberies of gas stations in the Los Angeles area to obtain money for their planned attacks. They researched targets—including the "LAX and Consulate of Zion," "Army Recruiting Centers," and a "Military base in Manhattan Beach"—and compiled them into a document called "Modes of Attack." However, their crimes were ultimately prevented by law enforcement, and the men pled guilty to conspiring "to levy war against the government of the United States through terrorism."

Following their conviction, the Assistant United States Attorney with the U.S. Department of Justice who prosecuted their case—Kevin Smith—testified before the U.S. House of Representatives Committee on Homeland Security about the "Threat of Muslim-American Radicalization in U.S. Prisons."[11] I found it troubling that his testimony focused on how to catch and prosecute persons who were radicalized in prison in order to prevent acts of terrorism but omitted any discussion on how to prevent their radicalization in the first place. Moreover, the title of his testimony was even more concerning, considering that it insinuated Muslim Americans were a threat, as opposed to criminal terrorists.

Wanting to learn more about how the men were radicalized and how they rationalized their crimes, I sent inquires to both James and Washington.

From federal prison, Kevin James explained:

> *First, I was never convicted of anything. I took a plea bargain. My mother and beloved best friend in the world passed away in 2006. 14 years she'd waited for my release. I was set to be released in January 2005. I had been in California's Youth Authority from 1992–1995 and state prison from 1995–2005, when the terrorism task force captured me and brought me over to federal custody. She simply couldn't hang on. This made my willingness to fight my case vanish.*
>
> *I don't declare that I'm innocent. My case is different from most all that I've seen to come after mine, in that I was not set up and the charge of declaring war against the U.S. fit. . . . I've met so many arrested on "terrorism" charges from 2006 to now, who did nothing but talk big talk after being instigated by a predator FBI agent. These kids are given 15 to 60 years in prison for "talking." Most weren't learned enough in Islam to know what to do or how. The FBI agents filled their heads with hate and threw them in jail with racists and gang members.*
>
> *I cannot claim innocence of my case, but 60% of those I've met for terrorism cases were totally railroaded.*
>
> *Although I don't claim innocence, proving anything besides my religious sermons on Fridays and a couple books I'd written on the fundamentals of Islam would've been difficult. So, I was included on my student's case.*
>
> *Second, I am not a "convert" as you say, I am a re-vert. My father was Sudani, my mother Creole (African American and French) from Louisiana originally. I was born Muslim, grew up in Southern California, and left Islam to become a graffiti artist then a gang member for a time before returning to Islam. I've worked tirelessly wherever I've been held captive, to speak out against crime, criminals, and gang violence.*

> *The U.S. prison-industrial complex eats this nation's minority*
> *youth and spits them out with no education or vocational training.*
> *If you don't have support from outside, you just live in these oppres-*
> *sive and extremely dangerous institutions and are then, if you have*
> *a release date, spit back out into society and told to behave.*

Levar Washington was less cohesive in his thoughts but nevertheless shared a path to radicalization that was equally rooted in criminality. From federal prison, he wrote:

> *When I was 13 years old, I as hurled into the gauntlet of the*
> *California Correctional System. I was shaped and forged in the steel*
> *crucible, gladiator school—from California Youth Authority, to Los*
> *Angeles County Jail, to the iron cages of Pelican Bay, and Corcoran*
> *SHU.* Behind the buttressed wall, upon the untamed fields, I was*
> *constantly exposed to the fog of war. My savage confrontations are*
> *countless. I assure you that there is nothing I haven't seen, noth-*
> *ing I haven't done, and hitherto, I am unscathed, uninjured, and*
> *unrepentant; primarily because of the infinite Grace of Allah, the*
> *majestic, and secondarily because of my proficient instincts that have*
> *been cultivated amid the killing-ground. Certainly they have never*
> *failed me. On the contrary, they remain my most loyal and sagacious*
> *advisor.*

In addition to the consistent thread of criminality and delinquency across radicalized terrorists prior to their recruitment, I found it interesting that most had no qualms about admitting to the guilt of their convictions; yet they would still comment on what they perceived as issues of entrapment for others. For example, James believed that 60 percent of those he had met with terrorism charges were "totally railroaded." Although he may have been off on the proportion, James wasn't alone in that perception, seeing as a number of media outlets began covering the concerning trend of preemptive prosecution, like in the case of the Duka brothers.

---

* Referring to the Special Housing Unit (SHU) solitary confinement at California State Prison, Corcoran.

Another example may be found in the arrest of Michael Wolfe, who was charged with providing material support of terrorism after he attempted to travel to Syria to join the Islamic State. Unlike the Dukas, he pled guilty and was arrested en route to the airport, but some media outlets suggested that his was another case of borderline entrapment. Over the course of ten months, the FBI used informants to help Wolfe concoct a plan to travel to Syria—something that he may not have been inclined to actually do or been able to do without their assistance. In response to the pressure to protect our country from terrorist attacks, law enforcement began overreaching by building cases off of conjecture and conflating "jihadi fanboys on social media with serious threats to national security,"[12] according to some.

I wrote to Wolfe and asked him about his radicalization. In reply, he explained:

> *Why would I join a terrorist organization or attempt to aid their cause? The short and sweet version—to fight against Bashar al-Assad and the Syrian government. I first became aware of the civil war taking place in Syria in 2012, shortly after entering Islam. When I saw the things the Syrian government was doing to its own men, women, and children, it struck a nerve. Especially since I had my own child on the way. The images reminded me of Nazi Germany. The only difference was that Adolf Hitler carted the Jews off to camps to be killed behind walls. Bashar al-Assad was, and still is, killing the people right in the street. Barrel bombs, Sarin gas, and mass graves for the whole world to see and nobody, to this day, has made even the slightest attempt to stop him.*

Wolfe's reply to me was sent on February 22, 2017. One year later, United States President Donald J. Trump ordered coordinated airstrikes on Syria in retaliation for their chemical attacks against civilians.[13] Wolfe explained that the assaults on the Syrian people hurt him, "not just as a Muslim, but as a human being," and in his opinion, "anyone who is not affected in a similar way is cold and callous." He said he began contemplating how he could aid the Syrian people against their government, but this didn't turn into a plan to travel to Syria and join ISIS until he met an undercover FBI agent named "Rasheed." He clarified:

> *Before meeting with the undercover agent, going overseas was really more of an idea, something that I was running through my head.*

I hadn't actually made any preparations, or taken any steps to join the fight. I had never met anyone who had fought and I had no contacts of my own.

Shortly after meeting Rasheed, however, things started to take shape. He introduced himself as an ex-army ranger with a lot of military experience. He claimed that he traveled a lot doing "security contracting," and he said he had made a lot of useful contacts along the way. He even claimed to have helped people get into conflict areas in the past.

On top of this, his wife—another undercover—claimed to be from Turkey, and they planned on moving there in the near future. They invited my family and I to go with them and told us that her family would help us financially until we became stable. After discussing all of these things, Rasheed explained to me that once in Turkey, he planned on crossing the border into Syria and joining the fight. He claimed that he knew people that could get him into Jabhat al-Nusra, and that he could make arrangements for me as well.

Over the next several months we trained, worked on our plan, and I began obtaining the documents and items I needed for travel. I was paying close attention to the conflict and the various groups involved and came across some damaging information. One of the top officials with al-Nusra released a video statement saying that they were no longer accepting foreign fighters.

I brought this information to Rasheed's attention and he agreed that it may be problematic with our overall objective. So, I made a suggestion, "Why not see if your contact can get us in with the Islamic State?" Of course, he got it done right away.

At this time, the Islamic State were the only ones really open to foreign fighters and although there was in-fighting taking place between the various groups, I felt that I would be able to make clear my position of only coming to fight the Syrian government, not other Muslims. This may have been rather naive of me, but I also had an older, more experienced man with supposed connections, reassuring me every step of the way.

I continued to move forward with my plan under the assumption that I was already assured a spot in the Islamic State and that there would be no issue with only wanting to fight Bashar al-Assad.

On June 17, 2014, my wife and I were arrested in the airport terminal. We watched our children get carted off and soon came to the realization that none of this had been real from the start. Also, shortly after my arrest, the real violence started kicking off. Syria became a bloody, no holds bar, battlefield. The media was having a field day and for about two months I was right in the middle. Every beheading, bombing, and burning falling right on my head.

Not once, in the beginning at least, did the media ever inquire into what my motivation was, what my goal was. No, I was a traitor who never went against his government and a terrorist who never committed an act of terror.

Even now, people look at me with disgust without ever asking why I was doing what I was going. I just wanted to help my brothers and sisters in Syria break free from the grips of tyranny, and I chose what I saw as the best means to help accomplish my end.

Correspondences like these, in combination with my content analyses of extremist propaganda, gave me a better understanding of the radicalization process into terrorism. Again, I couldn't shake the similarities between the conscription tactics used by terrorists and those of human traffickers. At the core of each recruitment process, there was a disjunction between projected and actual motives of these criminals, which possibly explains why their crimes are so difficult to prevent and why many domestic counterterrorism efforts aim at prevention through borderline entrapment.

Ultimately, this exercise reaffirmed my belief that it is important to continue understanding how terrorist organizations recruit so that we can prevent radicalization. After all, our American legacy of counterterrorism has proven:

> *If you know yourself but not the enemy,*
> *for every victory gained you will also suffer a defeat.*
> —Sun Tzu

19

Education Kills Terrorism

The recruitment of ISIS terrorists may have begun as an extremist crusade in Iraq, but it has quickly become a global phenomenon that has taken hold of people from diverse backgrounds, cultures, and belief systems. Although the mainstream public perceives these men and women as nothing more than evil terrorists with psychotic penchants for violence, many members of ISIS have narratives similar to nonterrorists prior to recruitment into extremism.

Recruits in Syria and Iraq are conscripted by the presumption that they will be safer with ISIS than against, and that militants are better able to provide resources to meet the basic physiological needs of the community than the local government. ISIS targets in Western countries join for different reasons. They are drawn to extremism in pursuit of love, belonging, and esteem, as propagandized on social media and in their English language recruitment materials. To some extent, all recruits are manipulated into believing self-actualization can be obtained through the support of ISIS.

Persons radicalized into terrorism from the West also disproportionately suffer from mental illness, emotional trauma, and civil injustices. ISIS recruiters pick up on these issues and respond with gendered solutions. Women tend to be radicalized by romantic partners, who fabricate feelings of "love" during tumultuous periods in life, such as adolescence or midlife crisis. Alternatively, men are more frequently conscripted through appeals to esteem, brotherhood, and the male warrior hypothesis.

ISIS recruiters are cunning individuals who are very capable of making each target believe that he or she is in control, when in reality, they are being led to the edge of a cliff. Winning the war on terror hinges on our ability to prevent average people from being manipulated into joining groups like ISIS.

It is important to note that ISIS defectors often describe becoming disillusioned at some point after being radicalized. This is because they were deceived into joining in the first place. However, if ISIS recruits ever come to the realization that they have been defrauded and are being exploited, it is typically too late. Even planning on going to Syria or Iraq to assist ISIS carries a lengthy federal punishment, more for actually making it there. Therefore, even if recruits live to regret their decision, they have little hope for any semblance of a normal life postradicalization.

Terrorism incidents around the world have increased more than fivefold since 9/11, from 1,881 in 2001 to 10,900 in 2017.[1] Criminologists have described these acts of terrorism as "black swan" events that are difficult to prevent. However, while these crimes are unpredictable, the methods of extremist recruitment are consistent and patterned.

Counterterrorism interventions should prioritize prevention and target locations with high concentrations of socially and economically disenfranchised youth. In addition, we must improve the capacity of law enforcement to police online, where extremists actively recruit. Like so many other criminal enterprises, the final frontier for terrorism is on the Internet. A variety of online platforms, including social media, proliferate the threats, deception, and coercion used to radicalize people from around the world.

There are nonprofits to prevent kids from joining gangs, girls from being sex-trafficked, and immigrants from being exploited, but there is a dearth of organizations dedicated to preventing at-risk youth from being recruited into terrorism. Perhaps our counterterrorism efforts need to become more proactive, as well as strategically reactive.

The parents of children who have been killed fighting for ISIS in Syria continue to stress the importance of prevention. For example, Christianne Boudreau's son, Damian Clairmont, converted to Islam after a troubling period in high school in Calgary, Canada, which included a suicide attempt at age seventeen.[2] He was killed in Syria after joining ISIS in 2014, but his mother wholeheartedly believed that his recruitment and death could have been prevented. "We need to start arming ourselves with the knowledge, the awareness, the education, and to be able to deal with these issues and be able to speak with our children at an early age," Boudreau said.[3] "We do the same thing with sex education, with drugs, and this is just one more thing that our kids are faced with, a challenge."[4]

Terrorist recruitment prevention efforts can begin by conducting risk assessments, as performed for kids in need of other social service interventions. These assessments can be administered by social service providers, counselors, or educators and used as a catalyst for preventive counterterrorism interventions. Appendix A of this book provides a sample instrument, which can be used to assess whether a young person is at risk of being recruited by a criminal organization. Specifically, this tool provides suggestions on how to assess voids in physiological needs, safety, love, belonging, and esteem by asking questions about food security, living stability, physical safety, perceived opportunities for social mobility, and self-worth. Interpreting the results of the survey in the context of the respondent's social media circle of influence can be used to elaborate on whether the minor is at risk of being conscripted into crime, including terrorism.

In addition to identifying kids at risk of radicalization, our counterterrorism efforts should also focus heavily on dismantling the veneer under which they operate. Despite the fact that ISIS leadership consists of godless individuals who are simply opportunists, selfishly pursuing money, power, and reverence, their criminal organization is propagandized as a religions one. ISIS wants the world to believe a bold-faced lie—they represent Islam and commit crimes to protect the Muslim *Ummah*.* Although this couldn't be further from the truth, they have been successful in manipulating much of the non-Muslim world into believing this falsehood. As a result, certain counterterrorism experts have perspectives that actually align with and provide fodder for terrorist propaganda.

For example, Michael Scheuer, former intelligence officer for the Central Intelligence Agency, authored a book in 2004, ironically titled *Imperial Hubris: Why the West Is Losing the War on Terror.* In it, he argued that the greatest danger for Americans confronting extremism is to believe that terrorists attack us for what we are and what we think rather than for what we do—it was a national bestseller.[5] However, he wasn't just talking about terrorists. He believed that the United States was "fighting a worldwide Islamic insurgency—not criminality or terrorism."[6] He unbelievably asserted that "many of the world's 1.3 billion Muslims hate us" and the war bin Laden was waging had "everything to do with the tenants of the Islamic religion."[7]

Former CIA covert officer Bryan Dean Wright had a similar perspective. On June 17, 2016, Fox News published an interview with Wright titled "Terror in America: ISIS & Election 2016."[8] The video opened with a prerecorded interview of President Barack Obama saying: "Islam is a religion that preaches peace, and

---

* Community.

the overwhelming majority of Muslims are peaceful." His statements were followed by a video of Hillary Rodham Clinton, speaking at the Council on Foreign Relations, where she said: "Islam is not our adversary. Muslims are peaceful and tolerant people and have nothing whatsoever to do with terrorism."

Although Obama's and Clinton's statements were 100 percent true, Mr. Wright disagreed, contending that it was time for politicians to stop calling Islam a "religion of peace." In support of his position, he explained that the extremists responsible for the attacks on "Chattanooga" and "Fort Dix" said that the "Islamic faith was inspiring them." Although he admitted the vast majority of Muslims are indeed peaceful, Wright asserted that the attribution of Islam as the inspiration for terrorism plots meant that there was a "sickness in some parts of the Islamic community." He went on to state, "Islam ought to be different" by not "pushing women into the back of the Mosque" and "forcing them to wear a *hijab.*"

How could these law enforcement agents even entertain the idea that Islam is a threat to our national security? Criminals manipulate! That's what they do. The vast majority of sex traffickers tell me that they were "in love" with their victims, and their victims corroborate the same.* According to Mr. Scheuer's and Mr. Wright's reasoning, should I then believe that "love" made them exploit these women in the commercial sex industry? No! It's a subterfuge used to manipulate.

And it isn't only law enforcement. Members of the media also erroneously conflate extremist criminal organizations, such as ISIS and Al-Qaeda, with Islam. Milo Yiannopoulos, for example, has repeatedly perpetuated the falsehood that Islam is "an existential threat."[9] Similarly, Glenn Beck asserts that there are "deadly theological motivations" behind terrorist groups like ISIS and al-Qaeda.[10]

Not only is this type of rhetoric used as fodder for extremist propaganda, but it effectively labels 1.8 billion Muslims—roughly 24 percent of the global population[11]—as criminals. The danger of labeling Muslims as terrorists, when they most certainly are not, is rooted in labeling theory, which suggests that terms used to describe or classify people can stigmatize and influence social networks, thereby affecting the behavior of labeled individuals.[12]

We must correct these fallacies by reaffirming the fact that ISIS and al-Qaeda are criminal organizations, not religious ones. And in order to counter terrorism, we need to focus on combating crime.

---

* A phenomenon known as "trauma bonding."

Leading criminological theory proposes that crime occurs when three things converge in time and space: one, a motivated offender; two, lack of a capable guardian; and three, a suitable target. Historically, much of our efforts to combat crime have focused on incapacitating the motivated offender and implementing certain, swift, and severe punishments in the hope of deterring crime. However, research on policing interventions indicates that these efforts aren't necessarily effective and crime can be better addressed through prevention.

Hot-spot policing, for example, centers on the idea that crime is concentrated to microunits of geography—around 5 percent of street segments contain approximately 50 percent of crime.[13] In response, criminologists have employed mapping and analytics platforms such as ArcGIS to guide police in conducting preventive patrolling at these locations, which results in significant reductions of crime according to research.

Similarly, counterterrorism tactics have focused on implementing certain, swift, and severe punishments for persons who even talk about committing an act of terrorism. We also attempt to prevent terrorism by deploying preventive measures in high-risk areas, such as the use of metal detectors and X-ray machines in airports and fortification of embassies.

However, despite the massive increases in personal, commercial, and governmental expenditures on counterterrorism strategies, as well as a proliferation of programs designed to fight terrorism, there is little scientific knowledge about the effectiveness of most counterterrorism interventions; and available research suggests that interventions either don't work or sometimes increase the likelihood of terrorism and terrorism-related harm.[14]

For example, the use of metal detectors in airports reduces the incidents of plane hijackings, but there may be a displacement effect to other venues for terrorism (e.g., cars, trains, metro rails).[15] This is referred to as "competition and adaptation" or the "cat and mouse" game played between law enforcement and criminals. When law enforcement begins to challenge terrorists' ability to attack a certain target, they will adapt their tactics in order to continue circumventing interventions.

Extremist propaganda acquaints prospective terrorists with a variety of weaponry and targets in their manual for "Open Source Jihad." It also allows militants to virtually train from the comfort of their own home, instead of "risking dangerous travel abroad." Al-Qaeda's *Inspire* magazine, for example, provides instructions on how to "make a bomb in the kitchen of your mom"[16] and how to circumvent metal detection, canine units, and X-ray machines,[17] as well as tactics for destroying buildings,[18] torching parked vehicles and causing road accidents,[19] and derailing trains.[20] For every terrorist detection intervention we devise, they find a way to circumvent it.

Moreover, increasing the severity of punishments for terrorists does not have a statistically discernible effect on the reduction of terrorism.[21] And more important, research suggests intolerance and retaliatory attacks significantly *increase* the number of terrorist incidents in the short run, particularly against the United States, the United Kingdom, and Israel.[22]

Perhaps the reason why our counterterrorism efforts have resulted in displacement, instead of reducing the incidence of terrorism, is because of the high motivation of terrorists. There is a saying among these men that goes, "If it takes me ten centuries to kill my enemy, I will wait 1,000 years for revenge." As long as there are marginalized people to exploit, ISIS will not stop, unless we undermine their ability to recruit and make it clear that their criminal organization has nothing to do with Muslims or Islam. Instead of providing fodder for their radicalization narrative, we need to contradict it and expose the truth.

For example, in his lecture about the four cows, al-Awlaki manufactured an analogy that fit his criminal objective—he claimed that the wolves were non-Muslims in the fable, the black cows were law-abiding Muslims, and the white cow was a "jihadist." He used this analogy to argue that the Muslim community should not have disunity—law-abiding Muslims needed to join with al-Qaeda in order to protect the *Ummah* from the non-Muslim "wolves."

However, through a counterterrorism lens, the message can be diametrically shifted—ISIS are the wolves, non-Muslims are the three black cows, and Muslims are the white cow.* America cannot have disunity in our response to ISIS. All people, Muslim and non-Muslim, must be unified in a coordinated response to these criminals, who have nothing to do with the religion of Islam. This is a message counter to terrorism, but that isn't what we project at present.

Counterterrorism experts, law enforcement, and political leaders largely accept the "motivation of terrorists" as what they propagandize—that they are religious, albeit "extremist." Consistent with al-Awlaki's lecture, the consequences of this misperception have spilled over to the larger Islamic community. Innocent

---

* Incidentally, Muslims are one-fourth of the world's population, while non-Muslims represent three-fourths.

Muslim women are being attacked for wearing *hijabs*, *niqabs* are increasingly being banned,[23] and many public figures continue to perpetuate the erroneous perception that Islam is the impetus for terrorism.

If we want to combat terrorists, we need to dismantle their false narrative, since they are truly driven by money and power, not religion. Not only are the misguided attacks on Muslim people and culture unwarranted, they do nothing to combat terrorism and actually provide fodder for radicalization propaganda.

Second, we must go to great lengths to protect Muslim civilians, especially children. In order to do this, we should provide people who are attempting to flee ISIS in Syria with opportunities for refugee resettlement, offer social services to facilitate the transition, and protect these high-risk migrants from further exploitation. According to the U.S. Department of State's 2018 Trafficking in Persons Report, Syrian refugees are increasingly vulnerable to exploitation, including forced child labor, sex trafficking, begging rings, and transactional marriages of girls in Egypt, Iraq, Jordan, Lebanon, Sudan, Turkey, and Yemen.[24] Families should have the option to escape ISIS, without facing human trafficking victimization thereafter.

Moreover, we need to reassess our foreign policy and practice regarding children in combat zones. For example, following the death of al-Awlaki much of the world was disturbed to find that his sixteen-year-old son and eight-year-old daughter were also killed in airstrikes. White House Press Secretary Robert Gibbs, a senior adviser to President Obama's reelection campaign, was asked about the incidents:

> **Reporter:** *It's an American citizen that is being targeted without due process, without trial. And, he's underage. He's a minor.*
> **White House Press Secretary Gibbs:** *I would suggest that you should have a far more responsible father if they are truly concerned about the well-being of their children. I don't think becoming an al-Qaeda jihadist terrorist is the best way to go about doing your business.*[25]

This is not okay. Saying that a child should have a far more responsible father in order to avoid being killed—really? These kids didn't choose who their father was, where they were born, or how they were raised. Indiscriminately killing them is not an appropriate response, and that needs to cease immediately.

People are not disposable, and children should not be punished for the crimes of their parents.

Third, we must empower marginalized people by reversing the effects of the prison-industrial complex. We can start doing this by decriminalizing* non-violent drug crimes and investing resources in the expansion of mental health services. ISIS invests time, money, attention, and other resources into these communities because they know disenfranchised people are easier to exploit. We need to help these populations more and give them greater opportunities for social mobility. *Big bank takes little bank*—so in order to combat terrorism, America needs to invest more in these communities than the criminals trying to exploit them.

Fourth, it is imperative for us to recognize and address the continued prevalence of racism, Islamophobia, and other forms of discrimination, perhaps beginning with law enforcement agencies. Since police are mostly reactive to information from the communities they serve, they must regain lost trust and rebuild community relationships. Officers should be trained on unconscious bias, diversity and inclusion, and de-escalation tactics. Police must learn to treat all people with dignity and respect. Even if someone is being investigated or arrested for a violation of the law, they are still human and should be given a voice and treated with neutrality. Law enforcement agencies need to refocus their objectives on protecting and serving all communities, while holding officers accountable for unjustified uses of force.

Just because most overt racism ended with the civil rights movement does not under any circumstance mean that discrimination does not persist covertly. Persons of color routinely experience situations of indignity, and we need to recognize this fact. Communities that have been historically disenfranchised must be afforded more opportunities for social mobility. Better schools and social services, vocational training and diversion programs. We must talk about experiences of discrimination in the United States and move forward by making the collective commitment for equality, regardless of the color of someone's skin, nationality, citizenship status, religion, gender, or sexual orientation. We all deserve equivalent opportunities to thrive.

Fifth, we need to be more judicious with word choice. The label of "terrorist"

---

* Decriminalization means reducing the severity of punishment; it is not the same as legalization.

should be applied appropriately to persons who use unlawful violence against civilians in the pursuit of political aims. This term should not be applied to civil rights movements, such as Black Lives Matter,[26] much less to entire faiths.

Moreover, the words *jihad, mujahid,* and *martyr* should stop being used in the context of terrorism. These words are all related to religion, while terrorism is not. Although some might argue that this is a quibble over semantics or a politically correct assault on free speech, words matter, and it is important to separate terrorists and terrorism from the religions and legitimate social movements that they attempt to leech onto.

We must keep in mind that their maligned interpretation of religion is nothing more than a veneer used to rationalize barbarism and murder. In order to prevent radicalization, it is important to dismantle their perverted and distorted interpretation of Islam, which is why, for example, President Barack Obama refused to say "Islamic terrorism"—a decision he was highly criticized for, even though it is the antithesis to the rationale used for radicalization.[27]

Last, in order to have a better standing with the rest of the world, we need to chill with the American hubris. Recognizing our faults, apologizing for them, and correcting them moving forward does not mean that we don't love this country. The reality is, America is no better than any other country, but no country is better than ours!

Ultimately, both terrorism and counterterrorism employ elements of retaliation, which does nothing to deescalate. When they go low, we should go high.[28]

In summation, in order to effectively combat terrorism, we need to identify kids at risk of being recruited by criminal enterprises and invest resources in preventive interventions. It is critical for us to dismantle the erroneous connection between ISIS and Islam and protect Muslims worldwide with our domestic and foreign policies. We must reverse the prison-industrial complex by decriminalizing nonviolent crimes, investing in marginalized communities, and expanding mental health services. It is essential for us to recognize and combat discrimination, repair lost trust, and provide more opportunities for social mobility to communities that have been historically disenfranchised. And finally, it is time for us to improve our relationships with the international community by recognizing our faults, apologizing for them, and learning from our mistakes.

I know what you're thinking, this is all easier said than done, but remember:

A journey of a thousand miles starts from beneath your feet.
—Lao-tzu

APPENDIX A

Needs Assessment Tool to Identify Youth at High Risk of Being Radicalized

The questions below can be incorporated into middle- and high-school health curricula, implemented by counselors, or adopted by direct service providers. In order to reduce the likelihood of social desirability bias, the questionnaire should not have any reference to terrorism or any specific form of crime. Rather, administrators should independently use the interpretation guide below (not presented to the student) to assess whether the adolescent may be at-risk or at-high-risk of being recruited by a criminal enterprise.

Students should be instructed to circle the number that corresponds to their degree of agreement or disagreement with each statement. Alternatively, these questions could be adapted and read aloud in one-on-one environments.

Please emphasize that there are no right or wrong answers in completing this form and discuss the level of confidentiality you are capable of providing to the student respondents. Also, obtain informed parental consent where applicable. Given the sensitive nature of some questions, please utilize this assessment at the sole risk of the administrator.

Questionnaire
Please circle the number that corresponds to your degree of agreement or disagreement with each statement. There are no right or wrong answers in completing this form. If some of the questions seem too personal, you may skip them.

Part A

1. I never skip meals or reduce the size of my meals because there wasn't enough money for food.

Strongly Agree	Agree	Disagree	Strongly Disagree
0	1	2	3

2. I always have enough clean clothing to wear.

Strongly Agree	Agree	Disagree	Strongly Disagree
0	1	2	3

3. I never worry about my living situation.

Strongly Agree	Agree	Disagree	Strongly Disagree
0	1	2	3

4. I always have "a roof over my head."

Strongly Agree	Agree	Disagree	Strongly Disagree
0	1	2	3

5. My family doesn't move around a lot.

Strongly Agree	Agree	Disagree	Strongly Disagree
0	1	2	3

6. I know where I'll be living in six months.

Strongly Agree	Agree	Disagree	Strongly Disagree
0	1	2	3

Part B

1. I feel safe and secure at school.

Strongly Agree	Agree	Disagree	Strongly Disagree
0	1	2	3

2. I feel safe and secure at home.

Strongly Agree	Agree	Disagree	Strongly Disagree
0	1	2	3

3. I feel that my parents adequately protect me from harm.

Strongly Agree	Agree	Disagree	Strongly Disagree
0	1	2	3

4. I feel that the school adequately protects me from harm.

Strongly Agree	Agree	Disagree	Strongly Disagree
0	1	2	3

5. My life generally has routine and structure.

Strongly Agree	Agree	Disagree	Strongly Disagree
0	1	2	3

6. I have never experienced a long period of overwhelming chaos.

Strongly Agree	Agree	Disagree	Strongly Disagree
0	1	2	3

Part C

1. My family loves me.

Strongly Agree	Agree	Disagree	Strongly Disagree
0	1	2	3

2. I have good relationships with my friends.

Strongly Agree	Agree	Disagree	Strongly Disagree
0	1	2	3

3. My parents accept me for who I am.

Strongly Agree	Agree	Disagree	Strongly Disagree
0	1	2	3

4. My friends like me for who I am.

Strongly Agree	Agree	Disagree	Strongly Disagree
0	1	2	3

5. I have never been discriminated against.

Strongly Agree	Agree	Disagree	Strongly Disagree
0	1	2	3

Part D

1. I am successful in life, and my parents recognize me for being so.

Strongly Agree	Agree	Disagree	Strongly Disagree
0	1	2	3

2. I am successful in school, and my teachers recognize me for being so.

Strongly Agree	Agree	Disagree	Strongly Disagree
0	1	2	3

3. I am successful in work, and my boss recognizes me for being so.

Strongly Agree	Agree	Disagree	Strongly Disagree
0	1	2	3

4. I'm satisfied with the responsibility that I have in life.

Strongly Agree	Agree	Disagree	Strongly Disagree
0	1	2	3

5. I'm satisfied with the role that I have in school.

Strongly Agree	Agree	Disagree	Strongly Disagree
0	1	2	3

6. I'm satisfied with my status in life.

Strongly Agree	Agree	Disagree	Strongly Disagree
0	1	2	3

7. I'm satisfied with my reputation in school.

Strongly Agree	Agree	Disagree	Strongly Disagree
0	1	2	3

8. I have high self-esteem.

Strongly Agree	Agree	Disagree	Strongly Disagree
0	1	2	3

Interpretation Guide

Each unsatisfied need may be a deficiency motivator, making the juvenile at risk of being conscripted into crime.

Part A: Physiological Needs:

Respondents who score 12–18 may be at high risk of recruitment through the provision of food/clothing/shelter.

Respondents who score 6–11 may be at risk of recruitment through the provision of food/clothing/shelter.

Respondents who score 0–5 may be at low risk of recruitment through the provision of food/clothing/shelter.

Part B: Safety Needs:

Respondents who score 12–18 may be at high risk of recruitment through the provision of safety.

Respondents who score 6–11 may be at risk of recruitment through the provision of safety.

Respondents who score 0–5 may be at low risk of recruitment through the provision of safety.

Part C: Love/Belonging Needs:

Respondents who score 10–15 may be at high risk of recruitment through the provision of love/belonging.

Respondents who score 5–9 may be at risk of recruitment through the provision of love/belonging.

Respondents who score 0–4 may be at low risk of recruitment through the provision of love/belonging.

Part D: Esteem Needs:

Respondents who score 16–24 may be at high risk of recruitment through improved self-esteem.

Respondents who score 8–15 may be at risk of recruitment through improved self-esteem.

Respondents who score 0–7 may be at low risk of recruitment through improved self-esteem.

To better understand what form of crime a particular young person is at risk of, interpret the findings of this assessment in the context of his or her social media presence. The digital footprint left by those social interactions can provide insight into the types of criminal enterprises that may target them. For example, if they are interacting with persons who hold extremist views of Islam, they may be at risk of being radicalized into ISIS. If they are interacting with anonymous love interests, they could be at risk of sex trafficking or being recruited into terrorism by a romantic partner. If they are associating with gang members, they could be at risk of being recruited into related criminal activity.

While this tool has yet to be validated, the impetus for sharing it is to express the importance of finding new and innovative ways to identify people at risk of being radicalized into terrorism. Preventing criminal recruitment is key to winning the war on terror.

APPENDIX B

A Letter from Donald Morgan

In 2015, an American named Donald Morgan was sentenced to twenty years in federal prison for attempting to travel from Lebanon through Turkey and on to Syria to join ISIS.[1] In a letter from prison, this is how he described his path to radicalization. He called it *"A Path from Falsehood to Truth"*:*

> *I cannot tell you that my life was this pit of turmoil and dysfunction as a child growing up. In fact, it was a very loving, comfortable life with a family that attempted to provide me with every advantage and opportunity to succeed. My parents raised me in a middle-class, southern home. Although not devoutly religious, we participated in the typical holiday events and the occasional Sunday schools before service.*
>
> *As for my social and academic life, I was encouraged by my parents to try all the things I could. I exceled in sports and academics and social life. By all accounts, I was normal and so was my life. I learned at an early age to work hard through a family owned business that I helped in various aspects throughout my life.*
>
> *I had an early interest in being a solider—a Green Beret. My father proudly served in the U.S. Marines during Vietnam and I felt an early sense of Duty, Honor, and Country. I was climbing the ranks in ROTC and slated to be a nominee for the coveted Superior Cadet Award, the highest honor bestowed upon any cadet. Things seemed to be on track.*

---

* Original letter was eleven pages. The following is an abbreviated version.

On December 3, 1984, my father and best friend took his own life with a single gunshot wound to his chest, sitting alone in a parking lot. At 14, my view on life, its value and the hopes of living past 40 years old were changed dramatically. Although I seemed to be strong for my mom and brother, I was not so much.

I continued on, successfully graduating with many achievements and honors from Oak Ridge Military Academy, but my personal struggles were just beginning. After my father's suicide, I didn't see real purpose in life, except to survive and not get hurt in the process.

I would spend years struggling with my own self. I had delayed entry to the U.S. Army and would lose this goal due to a serious accident from a head-on collision. Subsequently, my first year of military college would be ended due to the same injuries and accident. Needless to say, I was at a low point, re-shifting after years of focus to one end goal, a military career. I would recover from my injuries and transfer to university; it would be here that I would be introduced to Islam.

A new elective course was posted called "Contemporary Islam" and I decided to take the* class. The professor was a convert to Islam who resided for seven years in Saudi Arabia studying. She was covered in the hijab *and the black cloak, called the* abayah. *I recall how I felt humbled by her modesty.*

She was teaching an intro to Islam or "Islam for Dummies" at the time, but I quickly realized that the religion and life and path she was describing was what I felt in my heart was missing. I had found what I was seeking.

My first impression with Muslims was watching Palestinian boys fight against oppressive and occupational forces of the Zionist IDF with merely a rock and a sling-shot. This impression of one's willingness to fight for their faith with no regard to life and limb would come to me again 10 years later.

I jumped at the chance to approach the professor after the course was over and proudly announce that I wanted to be Muslim. The religion of Islam was simple yet encompassing and complete, and I knew that it was the Straight Path.

---

* Name of professor was redacted from the original letter.

She explained to me the declaration of faith, "There is no god worthy of worship except Allah alone without partner and Muhammad is His Messenger"—the first step and pillar of Islam and becoming a Muslim. She went to explain that a Muslim doesn't have girlfriends, use drugs or alcohol, gamble, listen to music, etc. She looked me in my eyes and asked me, "Are you ready to submit to the will of Allah and turn away from all of these things?" At that moment, I knew that I could not. More importantly, I didn't want to make a mockery of such a serious step by doing it without any true intention to be sincere.

May Allah reward and bless the Professor. Ameen. I would not become Muslim that day, but Islam was in my heart.

Growing up and in my family there was and is much diversity of people. So, in spite of a false assumption, the south is not quite as racist or segregated as many portray it and not like I've seen in northern cities. I did experience my share of racism and klan marches and being told to choose a black friend or a white friend. However, by my university years, this was not an issue for me, but the strain of discrimination existed not from whites only, but blacks as well.

This is the beauty of the Qur'an that it teaches us that racism, tribalism, nationalism CAN NOT exist in Islam nor the heart of a true Muslim.

I was approached by some great guys to attend an interest meeting for a fraternity, Phi Beta Sigma. It is a predominately black fraternity, but I was welcomed and loved and cherish those brothers to this day.

I "went over" Fall '91.

I had become sort of an activist, protester type. Much like people today, except instead of burning down the CVS, I, along with other PBS bros, ate lunch with high-risk kids and offered to do after-school tutoring. I guess in the way of other Sigma, Huey P. Newton.

After a few run-ins with some law enforcement officers and their clearly racist overtones not only to the blacks with me but also towards me, I decided to beat them by taking their place.[2] It also served as a substitute of a long lost dream to be a solider, but after a few years I realized that I would not be making a difference and resigned.

I began to feel the pains of depression and by 1996 I had earned a felony charge for discharging a weapon during a fight at a bar, and I spent 25–39 months in prison to give it some thought.

Fortunately, I had my heart waiting for me upon my release, and surely all would be well.

I began my career in sales and finance, and rose quickly in rank and compensation. Although I was driven and successful at my career; I was proving horrible as a husband, intimate friend, and loving father. I was angry inside, very untrusting and very good at hiding much of it. I had come to the conclusion that material things, which I was great at obtaining, were an acceptable substitute for real love, affection, and friendship. Material things meant "I love you" and more often "I'm sorry."

I was chasing and loving this creation and my desires, but I was void of faith, morals, and peace in my heart. Perhaps on the outside most days, I appeared to be winning or happy, but on the inside I was angry, sad, and depressed, and even dying. I pursued everything this world had to offer—fancy cars, clothes, watches, drugs, and sex, but none of it in any amount made me happy. It seemed the more I got of it, the more I felt worse. I didn't know it at the time but Allah was testing me with this life and the creation and I was failing.

By the Mercy of Allah, someone came into my life at this very low point, and I climbed out of the hole that I created for myself.

In June 2008, at Tariq Mosque in Toronto, I took my shaha-dah* *becoming Muslim. Of course, true to my professor's advice, Islam was to be entered with a sincere heart and willingness to alter and change your life to please Allah, not yourself. As I try to impress upon the Muslims in here, "It is not enough to say that you are Muslim, you must BE a Muslim."*

From 2008 until 2010, I struggled with my own self and trying to learn my religion and all the components that it entailed, such as Arabic, abstaining from all the stuff I liked (drugs, women, etc.),

---

* The Muslim profession of faith.

praying five times a day, etc. I made excuse after excuse to the point that by 2010, I was Muslim by name alone.

In fact, I was that Muslim drinking a beer, but didn't want bacon to be on my burger. Pretense not content—a problem with most Muslims in the world today and truly with most societies as a whole.

In 2010, I was in the final preparations of a bodybuilding competition and would eat approximately seven times per day. A person who was very close to me at this time said, "It's Ramadan. You're Muslim, right? Aren't you supposed to be fasting? Even bad Muslims fast!" A sword through my heart would have hurt less.

This was the moment that I took my religion as serious as my workout regiment, my business, and all the things that seem to get in front of my faith. I began to commit myself to truly learn and apply my religion to my life. It was the start of my shedding this life and the creation for the promise of the Rewards of Paradise.

Step by step, I grew until 2012 when I met amazing brothers and sisters around the world who helped guide and teach me. After fasting for Ramadan, I was fully committed to devote my life to Allah, Islam, and Jihad.

Unfortunately, I could have never anticipated the backlash that I would face from my wife, family, coworkers and friends. On the one hand, I had beautiful brothers like Iftikhar Jaman[3] giving me love and aid—may Allah reward his death as a Martyr and grant him the highest levels of Paradise—and on the other side were those closest to me, accusing me of being extreme and fanatical. They insisted that I should be more flexible in my religion, to accept other deviances and false gods they chose to follow in worship. They were calling me to their immorality and disbelief so as not to upset them!! I never realized how far gone most people are in their disbelief of their Creator until I began to shed their ways and beliefs and speak out against them.

I was speaking out on social media, creating videos calling those to Islam, sharing other's lectures and videos and warning the enemies of Islam. I began to organize funds and coordinate efforts that resulted in opening a new Islamic Center and Mosque. I was actively preparing to walk away from a 13-year career in sales and finance. How could I sit in the comforts of my home safe while my brothers and sisters were risking their lives to raise the banner of Islam? It was time to make hijrah, *leave this immoral land for the land of the Muslims.*

After surviving a horrible experience in the airport, my wife and I were on our way to our home in Beirut. It is worth noting that at the airport, the DHS and TSA disrespected my wife and me by throwing my Qur'an on the ground, calling me a follower of a religion of killing and extremism. It was to the point that one of the TSA agents boldly stepped up and denounced the way I was being treated and they finally eased their attacks and allowed me on the plane. I never spoke about it. It was a significant moment.

From Beirut and its borders, I was able to coordinate convoys and supplies and recruit soldiers to fight for the cause of Allah.

On June 29, 2014, the Caliph (Muslim Leader) Abu-Bakr al-Baghdadi, may Allah protect him and guide him, declared in his sermon during Friday prayers that the Islamic State was established. I immediately pledged my allegiance and loyalty to him and the Islamic State—a pledge that I continue to give inside these prison walls."

So here is brief and concise story about me—a boy struggling with life and faith who became a man who found Peace and Truth in Islam. It may not be so exciting or a tale of a monster or evil deranged madman, but I am grateful to Allah for guiding me to the Straight Path and allowing me to be Muslim.

The U.S. Government and others like the media call me a terrorist or an extremist, but I am not concerned about that. What I care about is that all I do is for the Sake of Allah and that He rewards me with Martyrdom. In'sha'Allah.

I'll await your reply, if you send one.

*Abu Umar al-Amriki**

---

* Morgan uses this Arabic name, which translates to Abu Umar the American.

ACKNOWLEDGMENTS

As always, I am sincerely grateful for my family. Beyond all others, they have been my inspiration and support throughout my scholarship and career.

To my beautiful and kindhearted daughter, Destiny—all of my passion for social justice begins with you. My path in life was arduous at times, but you were my first inspiration for success and made me want to make the world a better place. Everything I have and everything I have become is because of you. Thank you. I love you more than you will ever know.

For my mother, Belinda, you have sacrificed so much to be there for me when I needed you. For every barrier that I thought was insurmountable, you taught me to persevere. You showed me the meaning of unconditional love and how to be selfless. Words cannot express how fortunate I feel to have you as my mom.

My littlest ones—Mia, Rio, and Nicolas—you are the reason why I smiled through every adversity I have ever faced. Each of you, with your own special personality and talents, brought and continue to bring such incredible joy to my life. I don't think you will ever know how important this was for me, especially given my difficult and disheartening area of research. I can't wait to see who you become and the greatness you will bring to this world. I love you very much, and I am so lucky to be your mom.

And to my husband, Luis. I couldn't have chosen a better man to be the father of my children. You are amazing, and I feel privileged to have you as my partner. We have faced our own challenges, but your support has never wavered. You will never know how much I truly care for you and how thankful I am for everything you do for our family.

Although it goes without saying, I owe a very special debt of gratitude to my literary agents, Ronald Goldfarb and Gerrie Sturman. You believed in me and continue to champion my work. Because of you and your advocacy, this book was connected with an extremely talented editor—Jon Arlan from Skyhorse, who has been so incredibly patient and persevering throughout the publication process. Thank you all so much for everything you do and all of your support. Words cannot express how truly appreciative I am to know each of you.

Last, but certainly not least, to any person who has ever felt marginalized— Please do not fall for the silver tongue of the criminal organizations that *will* target you. Know that you *are* valued and we can work together to make sure your rights are protected and needs are met. If you ever feel like giving up or giving in to crime, please read this poem. During times of despair, it makes me feel unconquerable, and I hope it makes you feel the same, too:

> *Out of the night that covers me,*
> *Black as the Pit from pole to pole,*
> *I thank whatever gods may be*
> *For my unconquerable soul.*
> *In the fell clutch of circumstance*
> *I have not winced nor cried aloud.*
> *Under the bludgeonings of chance*
> *My head is bloody, but unbowed.*
> *Beyond this place of wrath and tears*
> *Looms but the Horror of the shade,*
> *And yet the menace of the years*
> *Finds, and shall find, me unafraid.*
> *It matters not how strait the gate,*
> *How charged with punishments the scroll,*
> *I am the master of my fate,*
> *I am the captain of my soul.*
> —"Invictus" by William Ernest Henley, 1875

NOTES

Author's Note

1 BBC. 2009. Religions: Islam: Jihad. BBC. Retrieved on July 8, 2018, from http://www
   .bbc.co.uk/religion/religions/islam/beliefs/jihad_1.shtml.
2 In line with Muslim scholars, such as Dr. Waleed El-Ansary. Hagerty, Barbara Bradley.
   March 18, 2010. Is The Bible More Violent Than The Quran? National Public Radio.
   Retrieved on July 27, 2018, from https://www.npr.org/templates/story/story.php?storyId
   =124494788.

Introduction

1 Mehlman-Orozco, Kimberly. September 29, 2016. What we see, when we imagine a
   criminal. The Hill. Retrieved on September 30, 2018, from http://thehill.com/blogs
   /pundits-blog/civil-rights/298574-what-we-see-when-we-imagine-a-criminal.
2 Madriz, Esther I. (1997). Images of Criminals and Victims: A Study on Women's Fear
   and Social Control. Journal of Gender and Society. Retrieved on April 1, 2018, from:
   http://journals.sagepub.com/doi/pdf/10.1177/089124397011003005.
3 Rinehart Kochel, Tammy, Wilson, David B., and Mastrofski, Stephen D. (2011). Effect
   of Suspect Race on Officers' Arrest Decisions. Criminology. Retrieved on November 25,
   2017, from https://onlinelibrary.wiley.com/doi/full/10.1111/j.1745–9125.2011.00230.x.
4 Suleiman, Imam Omar. November 1, 2017. What "Allahu Akbar" really means. CNN.
   Retrieved on January 28, 2018, from https://www.cnn.com/2017/11/01/opinions/allahu-
   akbar-meaning/index.html.

PART ONE

Chapter One: Drawing Parallels

1 This is a pseudonym and not the actual name of the student.
2 Timing slightly altered in order to further protect the identity of the student.
3 Cornell Law School. 18 U.S. Code § 2339A - Providing material support to terrorists.
   Retrieved on January 10, 2018, from: https://www.law.cornell.edu/uscode/text/18/2339A.
4 List based on Maslow's Hierarchy of Needs, which is a theory used to explain what drives
   human motivation.
5 Godlasky, Anne. November 6, 2017. When is it terrorism? When is it a hate crime? USA
   Today. Retrieved January 23, 2018, from: https://www.usatoday.com/story/news/nation
   /2017/11/06/when-terrorism-definition/835288001/.
   Vidino, Lorenzo and Hughes, Seamus. November 2015. ISIS in America: From Retweets

to Raqqa. George Washington University Program on Extremism contains a list of 71 individuals charged for ISIS-related activities as of November 12, 2015.

6   As of May 27, 2018, a list of 580 persons convicted of terrorism or terrorism-related crimes 9/11/2001–12/31/2014 can be found here: https://web.archive.org/web/20160906022314/ http:/www.sessions.senate.gov/public/_cache/files/e93b5041-aee9-4289-acd2 -ee46822c402e/06.14.16-doj-nsd-list.pdf.

7   https://www.bop.gov/inmateloc/,

8   Elliott, Michael. February 16, 2002. The Shoe Bomber's World. Time. Retrieved on November 1, 2017, from http://content.time.com/time/world/article/0,8599,203478,00.html.

9   The *Telegraph*. December 26, 2001. Mosque leader warns over extremist converts. The *Telegraph*. Retrieved on January 10, 2018, from: http://www.telegraph.co.uk/news /1366320/Mosque-leader-warns-over-extremist-converts.html.

Chapter Two: Archetype

1   9/11 Memorial. FAQ About 9/11. Retrieved on January 6, 2018, from: https://www.911 memorial.org/sites/default/files/FAQ%20about%20911_2.pdf.

2   Trivedi, Bijal P. September 13, 2001. Why Symbols Become Targets. National Geographic Today. Retrieved on January 6, 2018, from: https://news.nationalgeographic .com/news/2001/09/0913_TVsymbol.html.

3   Taliban. (August, 2010). War on Roads. In Fight Magazine, No. 20. Retrieved from: https://azelin.files.wordpress.com/2010/08/the-islamic-emirate-of-afghanistan-releases -in-fight-magazine-20.pdf.

4   Ibid.

5   Kelley, Michael B. (August 20, 2014). One Big Question Surrounds the Murder of US Journalist James Foley By ISIS. Business Insider. Retrieved January 7, 2018, from: http: //www.businessinsider.com/how-did-isis-kidnap-james-foley-2014-8.

6   Callimachi, Rukmini. (August 20, 2014). Before Killing James Foley, ISIS Demanded Ransom From U.S. The *New York Times*. Retrieved on January 7, 2018, from https: //www.nytimes.com/2014/08/21/world/middleeast/isis-pressed-for-ransom-before-killing -james-foley.html.

7   Fredericks, Bob. (February 26, 2015). ISIS militant "Jihadi John" unmasked as middle-class Brit. The *New York Post*. Retrieved on January 7, 2018, from https://nypost.com /2015/02/26/isis-militant-jihadi-john-revealed-as-middle-class-brit/.

8   Charlton, Corey. (September 25, 2017). The Devil's Lair: ISIS "Beatles" gang of British killers—including Jihadi John—seen unmasked together for the first time in chilling footage. *The Sun*. Retrieved on January 7, 2018, from https://www.thesun.co.uk/news /4542748/isis-beatles-gang-of-british-killers-including-jihadi-john-seen-unmasked -together-for-the-first-time-in-chilling-footage/.

9   Chester, Tim. (March 2, 2015). Jihadi John: A "bullied" loner and model employee before ISIS. Mashable. Retrieved on January 7, 2018, from: http://mashable.com/2015/03/02 /jihadi-john-mohammed-emwazi/#wlOhpgunPqqc.

10 Burke, Sarah and Jamieson, Alastair. (November 13, 2015). "Jihadi John": From Would-Be Soccer Star to Face of ISIS. NBC News. Retrieved on January 7, 2018, from https://www .nbcnews.com/storyline/isis-uncovered/jihadi-john-would-be-soccer-star-face-isis -n462721.

11 Ibid.

12 Onyanga-Omara, Jane. (March 2, 2015). ISIL defector says "Jihadi John" was cold loner. Retrieved on January 7, 2018, on: https://www.usatoday.com/story/news/world /2015/03/02/jihadi-john-cold-loner/24249249/.

13 NBC News. (March 1, 2015). "Jihadi John": Emails Suggest Mohammed Emwazi Had Suicidal Thoughts. Retrieved on January 7, 2018, from: https://www.nbcnews.com /storyline/isis-terror/jihadi-john-emails-suggest-mohammed-emwazi-had-suicidal -thoughts-n315051.
14 Al-Qaeda. (Spring 2014). Shattered: A Story About Change. *Inspire*. Issue 12.

Chapter Three: Entrapped

1   Kocieniewski, David. May 9, 2007. 6 Men Arrested in a Terror Plot Against Fort Dix. The *New York Times*. Retrieved on October 18, 2017, from https://www.nytimes .com/2007/05/09/us/09plot.html.
2   Parry, Wayne. May 8, 2007. 6 Charged in Plot to Attack Army Post. The *Washington Post*. Retrieved on October 18, 2017, from http://www.washingtonpost.com/wp-dyn /content/article/2007/05/08/AR2007050800454_pf.html.
3   Temple-Raston, Dina and Norris, Michele. May 8, 2007. Six Accused of Plot to Attack Fort Dix. NPR. Retrieved on August 27, 2017, from https://www.npr.org/templates/story /story.php?storyId=10080637.
4   Ripley, Amanda. December 6, 2007. The Fort Dix Conspiracy: Preventing terrorist strikes that may never happen is a messy business. How a Circuit City clerk, the FBI and an ex-con landed five men in jail on charges of plotting to attack a military base. *TIME*. Retrieved on May 12, 2017, from http://content.time.com/time/subscriber/article /0,33009,1692025–3,00.html.
5   The sixth defendant, Agron Abdullahu, pleaded guilty to weapons charges for aiding and abetting the Duka brothers and was sentenced to only 20 in federal prison. Since he was not connected directly with the plot against Fort Dix, the moniker for the group changed from the "Fort Dix Six" to the "Fort Dix Five." Department of Justice Press Release. April 28, 2009. Three Brothers Sentenced to Life Prison Terms for Conspiring to Kill U.S. Soldiers. U.S. Department of Justice. Retrieved on July 10, 2017, from https://www .justice.gov/opa/pr/three-brothers-sentenced-life-prison-terms-conspiring-kill-us-soldiers.
6   Department of Justice Press Release. Two Additional Defendants Sentenced for Conspiring to Kill U.S. Soldiers. April 29, 2009. U.S. Department of Justice. Retrieved on August 10, 2017, from https://www.justice.gov/opa/pr/two-additional -defendants-sentenced-conspiring-kill-us-soldiers.
7   The first question was "Why did you do what you are convicted of?"
8   Referring to the Facebook post, which later became known as the "manifesto" of Christopher Dorner, a former Los Angeles police officer who went on a killing spree in 2013. http://laist.com/2013/02/07/christopher_dorners_manifesto_in_fu.php.
9   He was referring to a 32-year-old Christian, conservative, Norwegian man—Anders Behring Breivik—who was convicted of bombing and gunning down seventy-seven people in and around Oslo and sentenced to only twenty-one years in prison. Libell, Henrik Pryser. (March 15, 2016). Anders Behring Breivik, Killer in 2011 Norway Massacre, Says Prison Conditions Violate His Rights. The *New York Times*. Retrieved on May 1, 2018, from https://www .nytimes.com/2016/03/16/world/europe/anders-breivik-nazi-prison-lawsuit.html.
10 Bergen, Peter. 2016. *United States of Jihad: Who Are America's Homegrown Terrorists, and How Do We Stop Them?* Broadway Books.
11 Ax, Joseph. December 3, 2015. U.S. appeals court clears New York's "cannibal cop" of all charges. Reuters. Retrieved August 4, 2017, from https://www.reuters.com/article /new-york-crime-cannibal/u-s-appeals-court-clears-new-yorks-cannibal-cop-of-all -charges-idUSL1N13S1M420151203.
12 Bergen, Peter. (2016). *United States of Jihad: Investigating America's Homegrown Terrorists*. Crown.

PART TWO

Chapter Four: Sister of Terror

1   Mehlman-Orozco, Kimberly. 2017. Projected heroes and self-perceived manipulators: understanding the duplicitous identities of human traffickers. Trends in Organized Crime.
2   Fisher, Helen. 2008. The brain in love. TED Talk. Retrieved on May 1, 2018, from https://www.ted.com/talks/helen_fisher_studies_the_brain_in_love/transcript?language=en.

Chapter Five: Jihad Jane

1   Johnson, Carrie. March 10, 2010. JihadJane, an American woman, faces terrorism charges. The *Washington Post*. Retrieved on April 10, 2017, from http://www.washingtonpost.com/wp-dyn/content/article/2010/03/09/AR2010030902670.html.
2   Khan, Huma, Cohen, Emily, and Ryan, Jason. March 10, 2010. "Jihad Jane's" Arrest Raises Fears About Homegrown Terrorists. ABC News. Retrieved on April 25, 2017, from https://abcnews.go.com/GMA/Politics/jihad-jane-arrest-colleen-larose-raises-fears-homegrown/story?id=10056187.
3   Shiffman, John. December 7, 2012. Jane's Jihad: The exclusive story of Colleen LaRose, the American-born woman who came to be considered the new face of terrorism. Reuters Special Report. Retrieved January 12, 2018, from http://graphics.thomsonreuters.com/12/12/JihadJaneAll.pdf.
4   Ibid.
5   Thomas, Pierre, Krolowitz, Benjamin, and Clarke, Susan. Mary 12, 2010. Exclusive: "Jihad Jane's" Ex-Husband Says Suspect Was Bible-Carrying Churchgoer. ABC News. Retrieved on April 4, 2018, from https://abcnews.go.com/GMA/jihad-jane-husband-speaks-terror-suspect/story?id=10080443.
6   CNN. March 10, 2010. Kurt Gorman Interview. CNN. Retrieved January 7, 2017, from https://www.youtube.com/watch?v=UrKblyA9zs8.
7   CNN. March 10, 2010. Police report: "Jihad Jane" attempted suicide in 2005. CNN. Retrieved on April 1, 2018, from http://news.blogs.cnn.com/2010/03/10/police-report-jihad-jane-attempted-suicide-in-2005/.
8   Shiffman, John. December 7, 2012. Jane's Jihad: The exclusive story of Colleen LaRose, the American-born woman who came to be considered the new face of terrorism. Reuters Special Report. Retrieved January 12, 2018, from http://graphics.thomsonreuters.com/12/12/JihadJaneAll.pdf.
9   Ibid.
10 United States of America v. Colleen R. LaRose a.k.a. Fatima LaRose a.k.a. Jihad Jane. March 4, 2010. Indictment. Retrieved on May 1, 2017, from https://media.nbcphiladelphia.com/documents/JihadJane.pdf.
11 Shiffman, John. December 7, 2012. Jane's Jihad: The exclusive story of Colleen LaRose, the American-born woman who came to be considered the new face of terrorism. Reuters Special Report. Retrieved January 12, 2018, from http://graphics.thomsonreuters.com/12/12/JihadJaneAll.pdf.
12 Ibid.
13 Mehlman-Orozco, Kimberly. 2017. Projected heroes and self-perceived manipulators: understanding the duplicitous identities of human traffickers. Trends in Organized Crime.
14 Royal, Mickey. 1998. *The Pimp Game: Instructional Guide.* Mikail Sharif.

Chapter Six: White Widow

1   BBC News. September 26, 2013. Profile: Samantha Lewthwaite. BBC News. Retrieved
    May 1, 2018, from http://www.bbc.com/news/uk-24204517.

2   The *Daily Telegraph*. March 1, 2012. Soldier's daughter who turned to Islam. The
    Daily Telegraph. Retrieved on May 1, 2017 from: https://www.pressreader.com/uk
    /the-daily-telegraph/20120301/282913792420188.

3   The *Daily Mail*. September 25, 2013. Samantha Lewthwaite's grandmother suf-
    fers stress, hospitalized over granddaughter's notoriety. The *Daily Mail*. September
    25, 2013. Retrieved on May 1, 2017, from https://www.standardmedia.co.ke/mobile
    /?articleID=2000094263&story_title=samantha-lewthwaite-s-grandmother
    -suffers-stress-hospitalised-over-granddaughter-s-notoriety&pageNo=2.

4   "Judgment in Appeal of Crown v. el-Faisal, Supreme Court of Judicature, Court
    of Appeal." March 4, 2004. Retrieved January 1, 2018, from https://web.archive
    .org/web/20120519051947/http://nefafoundation.org/miscellaneous/FeaturedDocs
    /RoyalCourtsofJustice_AlFaisal.pdf.

5   Laville, Sandra, Gillan, Audrey, and Aslam, Dilpazier. July 14, 2005. "Father figure"
    inspired young bombers: Leeds Police evacuate streets close to radical youth center.
    The *Guardian*. Retrieved on Jun 2, 2017, from https://www.theguardian.com/uk/2005
    /jul/15/july7.uksecurity6.

6   Al Jazeera. Mohammed Sidique Khan's Martyrdom Video. Retrieved from: https://www
    .youtube.com/watch?v=jHXLaio8G3I.

7   BBC News. July 3, 2015. 7 July London bombings: What happened that day? BBC
    News. Retrieved on June 8, 2017, from http://www.bbc.com/news/uk-33253598.

8   BBC News. September 23, 2005. Widow of bomber "abhors" attack. BBC News.
    Retrieved on July 10, 2017, from http://news.bbc.co.uk/2/hi/uk_news/4273804.stm.

9   O'Brien, Deirdre. April 1, 2012. Revealed: The teenage years of 7/7 bomber's wife
    Samantha Lewthwaite now hunted as the White Widow terror suspect. *Mirror*.
    Retrieved on November 22, 2017, from https://www.mirror.co.uk/news/uk-news
    /revealed-teenage-years-77-bombers-778081.

10 Peters, Justin. September 24, 2013. Did a British Mother of Three Really Mastermind
    the Nairobi Mall Attack? Slate. Retrieved on June 2, 2017, from http://www.slate.com
    /blogs/crime/2013/09/24/samantha_lewthwaite_white_widow_did_she_really_mastermind
    _the_nairobi_mall.html.

11 Rouse, Alisha. May 17, 2015. White Widow has "masterminded 400 murders": British
    jihadi allegedly planned Kenyan university attack that left 148 dead after rising fast
    through Al Shabaab's ranks. The *Daily Mail*. Retrieved on July 1, 2018, from http:
    //www.dailymail.co.uk/news/article-3085770/White-Widow-Samantha-Lewthwaite
    -masterminded-400-murders.html.

12 Associated Press. September 26, 2013. "White Widow" Samantha Lewthwaite wanted
    by Interpol. CBC. Retrieved on June 2, 2017, from http://www.cbc.ca/news/world
    /white-widow-samantha-lewthwaite-wanted-by-interpol-1.1870005.

13 Lewthwaite, Samantha. October 23, 2013. "White Widow wrote love poem to Osama."
    The *New York Post*. Retrieved on July 3, 2017, from https://nypost.com/2013/10/23
    /white-widow-wrote-epic-love-poem-to-osama-bin-laden/.

14 Gaidi Taani. Issue 3. Retrieved on January 30, 2018, from https://azelin.files.wordpress
    .com/2013/03/gaidi-mtaani-issue-3.pdf.

15 Gaidi Taani. Issue 1. Retrieved on January 28, 2018, from https://azelin.files.wordpress
    .com/2012/04/gaidi-mtaani-issue-1.pdf.

16 The Islamic Supreme Council of America. N.d. Jihad: A Misunderstood Concept
    from Islam—What Jihad is, and is not. Retrieved on July 20, 2018, from http:

//islamicsupremecouncil.org/understanding-islam/legal-rulings/5-jihad-a-misunder-stood-concept-from-islam.html?start=9.

The Oxford Islamic Studies Online. N.d. Jihad. The Oxford Dictionary of Islam. Retrieved on July 20, 2018, from http://www.oxfordislamicstudies.com/article/opr/t125 /e1199.

BBC. August 3, 2009. Jihad. BBC. Retrieved on July 20, 2018, from http://www.bbc .co.uk/religion/religions/islam/beliefs/jihad_1.shtml.

17 BBC News. September 26, 2013. Profile: Samantha Lewthwaite. BBC News. Retrieved May 1, 2018, from http://www.bbc.com/news/uk-24204517.

18 "Believe nothing you hear, and only one half that you see," idiom originally attributed to Edgar Allan Poe but given as a piece of advice from a convicted sex trafficker interviewed for Dr. Kimberly Mehlman-Orozco's first book, *Hidden in Plain Sight: America's Slaves of the New Millennium.*

19 If anyone were to be taken hostage, the correctional officers would not negotiate with the prisoner for release.

Chapter Seven: Black Widow

1 News Corp Australia Network. October 23, 2013. The love story that led Naida Asiyalova to detonate a suicide bomb aboard a Russian public bus. Retrieved on October 18, 2017, from: https://www.news.com.au/world/the-love-story-that-led -naida-asiyalova-to-detonate-a-suicide-bomb-aboard-a-russian-public-bus /news-story/68811d31845584197cff5560da2a7de1.

2 Herszenhorn, David M. October 21, 2013. Suicide Bomber Strikes Bus in Southern Russia. The *New York Times*. Retrieved on June 26, 2017, from https://www.nytimes .com/2013/10/22/world/europe/deadly-bombing-hits-bus-in-southern-russia.html.

3 RT. October 21, 2013. Militant's wife behind Volgograd suicide blast. Retrieved on June 2, 2018, from https://www.rt.com/news/volgograd-blast-militant-wife-518/.

4 News Corp Australia Network. October 23, 2013. The love story that led Naida Asiyalova to detonate a suicide bomb aboard a Russian public bus. Retrieved on October 18, 2017, from: https://www.news.com.au/world/the-love-story-that-led-naida -asiyalova-to-detonate-a-suicide-bomb-aboard-a-russian-public-bus/news -story/68811d31845584197cff5560da2a7de1.

5 Cullison, Alan. November 19, 2013. Meet the Rebel Commander in Syria That Assad, Russia and the U.S. All Fear. The *Wall Street Journal*. Retrieved on August 14, 2018, from https://www.wsj.com/articles/no-headline-available-1384899732.

6 History. Boston Marathon Bombing. Retrieved on March 26, 2017, from https://www .history.com/topics/boston-marathon-bombings.

7 Harding, Luke. June 19, 2010. Dagestan: My daughter the terrorist. The *Guardian*. Retrieved on Jun 29, 2017, from https://www.theguardian.com/world/2010/jun/19 /dagestan-suicide-bombers-terrorism-russia.

8 Ash, Lucy. November 24, 2011. Dagestan—the most dangerous place in Europe. BBC News. Retrieved on June 1, 2018, from https://www.bbc.com/news/magazine-15824831.

9 Fisher, Max. April 19, 2013. 9 Questions about Chechnya and Dagestan you were too embarrassed to ask. The *Washington Post*. Retrieved on November 1, 2017, from https://www.washingtonpost.com/news/worldviews/wp/2013/04/19/9-questions-about-chechnya-and-dagestan-you-were-too-embarrassed-to-ask/?noredirect=on&utm_term= .2f0aeea8abfe.

10 Ibid.

11 Womack, Helen. August 11, 1999. Dagestan moves to state of holy war. Independent.

Retrieved on July 1, 2017, from https://www.independent.co.uk/news/dagestan-moves
-to-state-of-holy-war-1112053.html.

12 Yuzik, Yulia. October 24, 2013. Russia's New Black Widows: The deadly and mysterious
new breed of female suicide bomber. Foreign Policy. Retrieved on January 17, 2018, from
http://foreignpolicy.com/2013/10/24/russias-new-black-widows/.

13 Ibid.

14 Keller, Bill. June 21, 1998. The Caucasian War. The *New York Times*. Retrieved on
November 21, 2017, from https://www.nytimes.com/1998/06/21/books/the-caucasian
-war.html.

15 Yuzik, Yulia. October 24, 2013. Russia's New Black Widows: The deadly and mysterious
new breed of female suicide bomber. Foreign Policy. Retrieved on January 17, 2018, from
http://foreignpolicy.com/2013/10/24/russias-new-black-widows/.

16 Keller, Bill. June 21, 1998. The Caucasian War. The *New York Times*. Retrieved on
November 21, 2017, from https://www.nytimes.com/1998/06/21/books/the-caucasian
-war.html.

17 Herszenhorn, David M. October 21, 2013. Suicide Bomber Strikes Bus in Southern
Russia. The *New York Times*. Retrieved on June 26, 2017, from https://www.nytimes
.com/2013/10/22/world/europe/deadly-bombing-hits-bus-in-southern-russia.html.

18 The *Siberian Times*. October 22, 2013. Siberian "extremist" was married to
the Volgograd "suicide bomber". The *Siberian Times*. Retrieved on October 2, 2017,
from http://siberiantimes.com/other/others/news/siberian-extremist-was-married-to-the
-volgograd-suicide-bomber/.

19 News Corp Australia Network. October 23, 2013. The love story that led Naida
Asiyalova to detonate a suicide bomb aboard a Russian public bus. Retrieved on
October 18, 2017, from: https://www.news.com.au/world/the-love-story-that-led-naida
-asiyalova-to-detonate-a-suicide-bomb-aboard-a-russian-public-bus/news-story
/68811d31845584197cff5560da2a7de1.

20 Stewart, Will. October 21, 2013. The horrifying moment a woman suicide bomber kills
six and injures 30 in Russian bus blast: "Black widow" may have had terminal disease.
Daily Mail. Retrieved April 7, 2017, from http://www.dailymail.co.uk/news/article
-2470371/Russian-bus-blast-Black-widow-suicide-bomber-kills-6.html.

21 Cornell, Svante E. 1999. International Reactions to Massive Human Rights Violations:
The Case of Chechnya. *Europe-Asia Studies*, Vol. 51, No. 1.

22 Rybina, Julia and Sergeev, Nikolay. August 30, 2012. Suicide blast kills sheikh, aims
to shatter peace in Dagestan. Russia Beyond. Retrieved on November 17, 2017, from
https://www.rbth.com/articles/2012/08/30/suicide_blast_kills_sheikh_aims_to_shatter
_peace_in_dagestan_17803.html.

23 Ibid.

24 Islam.ru. n.d. SHAYKH SAID-AFANDI AL-CHIRKAWI. Retrieved on April 11,
2018, from http://www.islam.ru/en/node/4.

25 Modern-day northern Saudi Arabia.

26 Ryan, Michael. 2013. *Decoding Al-Qaeda's Strategy: The Deep Battle Against America*.
Columbia University Press.

27 PBS. N.d. A Chronology: The House of Saud. Frontline. Retrieved on June 1, 2018,
from: https://www.pbs.org/wgbh/pages/frontline/shows/saud/cron/.

28 Islam.ru. n.d. SHAYKH SAID-AFANDI AL-CHIRKAWI. Retrieved on April 11,
2018, from http://www.islam.ru/en/node/4.

29 Alexandrova, Lyudmila. August 30, 2012. Bomber who killed Dagestani theologian was
Russian actress married to Wahhabi. TASS Russian News Agency. Retrieved on March
17, 2018, from http://tass.com/opinions/762854.

30 RT. August 30, 2012. Female suicide bomber in Muslim cleric attack identified as actress. Retrieved on March 3, 2018, from https://www.rt.com/news/afandi-dagestan-suicide-bomber-897/.

31 Islam.ru. n.d. SHAYKH SAID-AFANDI AL-CHIRKAWI. Retrieved on April 11, 2018, from http://www.islam.ru/en/node/4.

32 The *Moscow Times*. June 22, 2018. "Black Widow" Bomber Was Actress, Dancer. Retrieved on June 1, 2018, from https://themoscowtimes.com/articles/black-widow-bomber-was-actress-dancer-17421.

33 Dronzina, Tatyana and Houdaigui, Rachid El. 2010. Contemporary Suicide Terrorism: Origins, Trends and Ways of Tackling It. NATO Science for Peace and Security Series. Vol. 101.

34 Nemtsova, Anna. September 6, 2012. Russia's Female Menaces. The Daily Beast. Retrieved on June 7, 2017, from https://www.thedailybeast.com/russias-female-menaces.

Chapter Eight: Terror Teens

1 Konrad, Kerstin, Firk, Christine, and Uhlhaas, Peter. (2013). Brain Development During Adolescence: Neuroscientific Insights Into This Developmental Period. Deutsches Arzteblatt International.

2 Moffitt, Terri E. (1993). Adolescence-limited and life-course-persistent antisocial behavior: a developmental taxonomy. Psychological Reviews, 100, 4: 674–701.

3 Calterwood, Imogen. October 4, 2015. Teenage "terror twins" who fled Britain to join ISIS tried to recruit their whole family telling brothers: "We might seem evil to you, but we will all be happy in the afterlife." *Daily Mail*. Retrieved on April 10, 2018, from http://www.dailymail.co.uk/news/article-3259363/Teenage-terror-twins-fled-Britain-join-ISIS-tried-recruit-family-telling-brothers-evil-happy-afterlife.html.

4 YouTube. August 12, 2013. MAB Quran Competition 1434 2013 Ahmed Halane Winner of Category 5 Half of the Quran.

5 Quilliam. February 16, 2016. Ahmed Halane: What I never told my Arabic classmate – Alexandra Bissoondath. Retrieved on June 1, 2017, from https://www.quilliaminternational.com/ahmed-halane-what-i-never-told-my-arabic-classmate/.

6 The Qur'an forbids sex outside of marriage, and a hadith in Sahih al-Bukhari forbids prostitution.

7 Shane, Scott. August 27, 2015. The Lessons of Anwar al-Awlaki. The *New York Times Magazine*. Retrieved on June 1, 2018, from https://www.nytimes.com/2015/08/30/magazine/the-lessons-of-anwar-al-awlaki.html.

8 Quilliam. February 16, 2016. Ahmed Halane: What I never told my Arabic classmate —Alexandra Bissoondath. Retrieved on June 1, 2017, from https://www.quilliaminternational.com/ahmed-halane-what-i-never-told-my-arabic-classmate/.

9 Gye, Hugo. March 11, 2015. "Terror twin" who became a jihadi bride was caught with "ISIS picture" on her college computer SIX MONTHS before she went to Syria. The *Daily Mail*. http://www.dailymail.co.uk/news/article-2988377/Terror-twin-ISIS-picture-computer-six-months-went-Syria.html.

10 Saltman, Erin Marie and Smith, Melanie. (2015). "Till Martyrdom Do Us Part": Gender and the ISIS Phenomenon. Institute for Strategic Dialogue. Retrieved on January 18, 2018, from https://www.isdglobal.org/wp-content/uploads/2016/02/Till_Martyrdom_Do_Us_Part_Gender_and_the_ISIS_Phenomenon.pdf.

11 Ibid.

12 Saltman, Erin Marie and Smith, Melanie. (2015). "Till Martyrdom Do Us Part": Gender and the ISIS Phenomenon. Institute for Strategic Dialogue. Retrieved on January 18,

2018, from https://www.isdglobal.org/wp-content/uploads/2016/02/Till_Martyrdom _Do_Us_Part_Gender_and_the_ISIS_Phenomenon.pdf.

13 Russell, Ben and Webb, Sam. October 5, 2015. "Terror twins" who fled UK to join ISIS "tried to get family to join them." *Mirror*. Retrieved on June 1, 2018 from https://www .mirror.co.uk/news/uk-news/terror-twins-who-fled-uk-6576393.

14 de Freytas-Tamura, Kimiko. December 27, 2014. Double Blow for Parents of Jihadists: Losing Children, Then Their Community. The *New York Times*. Retrieved on June 11, 2017, from https://www.nytimes.com/2014/12/28/world/double-blow-for-parents-of -jihadists-losing-children-then-their-community.html.

15 Ibid.

16 Person in Need of Supervision.

17 Child in Need of Services/Supervision.

18 de Freytas-Tamura, Kimiko. December 27, 2014. Double Blow for Parents of Jihadists: Losing Children, Then Their Community. The *New York Times*. Retrieved on June 11, 2017, from https://www.nytimes.com/2014/12/28/world/double-blow-for-parents-of -jihadists-losing-children-then-their-community.html.

19 Shellenbarger, Sue. January 16, 2018. How Tech Experts Monitor Their Teens on Social Media. The *Wall Street Journal*. Retrieved February 19, 2018, from https://www.wsj .com/articles/is-your-child-social-media-savvy-1516111365.

20 Mehlman-Orozco, Kimberly. 2017. *Hidden in Plain Sight: America's Slaves of the New Millennium*. ABC-Clio.

21 Deuteronomy, Chapter 13: "You shall not desire him, and you shall not hearken to him; neither shall you pity him, have mercy upon him, nor shield him. But you shall surely kill him, your hand shall be the first against him to put him to death, and afterwards the hand of all the people."

22 Editors of Encyclopaedia Britannica. N.d. Khārijite. Encyclopedia Britannica. Retrieved on April 1, 2018, from https://www.britannica.com/topic/Kharijite.

23 Elias, Abu Amina. N.d. Hadith on Khawarij: The Kharijites come with beautiful preaching but evil deeds. Daily Hadith Online. Retrieved on June 1, 2018, from https://abuaminaelias.com/dailyhadithonline/2014/09/18/hadith-on-khawarij-the -kharijites-come-with-beautiful-preaching-but-evil-deeds/.

24 *Ibid*.

25 Elias, Abu Amina. N.d. Hadith on Rebels: In the last days, violent young rebels with foolish dreams will terrorize the Muslims. Daily Hadith Online. Retrieved on June 1, 2018, from https://abuaminaelias.com/dailyhadithonline/2012/04/04/hadith-on-rebels- in-the-last-days-violent-young-rebels-with-foolish-dreams-will-terrorize-the-muslims/.

26 Engel, Pamela. September 17, 2016. This is the name ISIS hates being called more than "Daesh." Business Insider. Retrieved on July 17, 2017, from http://www.businessinsider .com/isis-khawarij-2016-9.

27 Sullivan, Lena. March 30, 2016. Twisted woman Jaelyn Delshaun Young tried to join evil ISIS with her husband after converting to Islam. Georgia Newsday. Retrieved on July 24, 2018, from https://www.georgianewsday.com/news/national/395582-twisted-woman -jaelyn-delshaun-young-tried-to-join-evil-isis-with-her-husband-after-converting-to -islam.html.

28 Sehmer, Alexander. November 25, 2015. Isis teen "poster girl" Samra Kesinovic "beaten to death" as she tried to flee the group. Independent. Retrieved on July 24, 2018, from https://www.independent.co.uk/news/world/europe/isis-teenage-poster-girl-samra -kesinovic-beaten-to-death-by-group-as-she-tried-to-flee-killings-a6747801.html.

Chapter Nine: Grandma Terror

1   Wethington, Elaine. 2000. Expecting Stress: Americans and the "Midlife Crisis." Motivation and Emotion 24 (2): 85–103.

2   Ibid.

3   Lake, Emma. November 13, 2017. Never-before-seen pictures show "White Widow" Sally Jones drinking and smoking in the 1990—when she was a "pagan who would rant about Chistians." *The Sun*. Retrieved on June 2, 2018, from https://www.thesun.co.uk /news/4866682/never-before-seen-pictures-white-widow-sally-jones/.

4   Biali, Susan. 2012. Too Much Time Online Makes You Moodier, Lonelier and Obsessed: Research confirms fears about the impact of the internet on our Brain. *Psychology Today*. Retrieved on August 19, 2018, from https://www.psychologytoday.com/us/blog /prescriptions-life/201207/too-much-time-online-makes-you-moodier-lonelier-and -obsessed.

5   Express. September 2, 2014. British jihadist once proudly revelled in being "sexy babe" with "big knockers." Retrieved on June 7, 2016, from https://www.express.co.uk/news /uk/506240/British-jihadist-woman-proud-of-being-sexy-babe.

6   Born on December 19, 2004, according to Gillman, Ollie. September 12, 2014. New picture emerges of British jihadist Sally Jones with partner and new-born baby taken ten years before she joined ISIS. The *Daily Mail*. Retrieved on July 27, 2018, from http://www .dailymail.co.uk/news/article-2753864/New-picture-emerges-British-jihadist-Sally -Jones-partner-new-born-baby-taken-ten-years-joined-ISIS.html.

7   Express. September 2, 2014. British jihadist once proudly revelled in being "sexy babe" with "big knockers." Retrieved on June 7, 2016, from https://www.express.co.uk/news /uk/506240/British-jihadist-woman-proud-of-being-sexy-babe.

8   Hunter, Chris. September 8, 2014. "Why I joined Islamic State": Chatham mum Sally Jones speaks of jihadist mission after moving to Syria with husband Junaid Hussain. KentOnline. Retrieved on November 21, 2017, from http://www.kentonline.co.uk /medway/news/jihadist-sally-jones-23110/.

9   Al-Bahri, Ahmad. July 15, 2014. In Raqqa, an All-Female ISIS Brigade Cracks Down on Local Women. News Deeply. Retrieved on October 1, 2017, from https://www.newsdeeply.com/syria/articles/2014/07/15/in-raqqa-an-all-female-isis -brigade-cracks-down-on-local-women.

10 Curry, Colleen. December 22, 2014. A British Mother Reportedly Left Welfare Behind and Is Now Helping Recruit for the Islamic State. Vice News. Retrieved on June 7, 2016, from https://news.vice.com/article/a-british-mother-reportedly-left-welfare-behind-and -is-now-helping-recruit-for-the-islamic-state.

11 Kern, Soeren. September 21, 2014. Britain's Female Jihadists. Retrieved on December 5, 2017, from https://www.gatestoneinstitute.org/4714/britain-female-jihadists.

12 *Syria*.

13 Malik, Shiv. February 21, 2015. Lured by Isis: how the young girls who revel in brutality are offered cause. The *Guardian*. Retrieved on August 13, 2017, from https://www .theguardian.com/world/2015/feb/20/push-pull-lure-western-women-isis.

14 Sengupta, Kim. February 27, 2015. Dozens of jihadis in fighting in Syria using the name "al-Britani." Independent. Retrieved on January 7, 2017, from https://www.independent .co.uk/news/world/middle-east/dozens-of-jihadis-in-fighting-in-syria-using-the-name -al-britani-10076635.html.

15 Shephard, Michelle. October 17, 2014. Islamic State militants luring Western women as wives. The *Star*. Retrieved on March 26, 2016, from https://www.thestar.com/news /world/2014/10/17/islamic_state_militants_luring_western_women_as_wives.html.

16 Rusbridge-Thomas, Annabel. August 16, 2015. Kent mother Sally Jones lived off Borough Green church handouts before fleeing to join Islamic State in Syria. KentOnline. Retrieved on November 2, 2017, from http://www.kentonline.co.uk/sevenoaks/news /jihadi-sally-lived-off-church-41764/.

17 Campbell, Alexia Fernandez. December 6, 2015. Why ISIS Recruiting in America Reached Historic Levels. The Atlantic. Retrieved on May 1, 2017, from https://www.theatlantic.com /politics/archive/2015/12/why-isis-recruiting-in-america-reached-historic-levels/433560/.

18 Quote puts an ISIS-twist on Rudyard Kipling's poem *The Young British Soldier*:
"When you're wounded and left on Afghanistan's plains,
And the women come out to cut up what remains,
Jest roll to your rifle and blow out your brains
An' go to your Gawd like a soldier."
Adams, Sam. September 27, 2014. British ISIS militant becomes grandmother while "waging jihad" in Syria. *Mirror*. Retrieved on May 11, 2017, from https://www.mirror .co.uk/news/world-news/british-isis-militant-becomes-grandmother-4333441.

19 http://www.dailymail.co.uk/news/article-3068723/The-British-jihadi-fighting-ISIS -Syria-groomed-Texas-Muhammed-cartoon-gunmen-terror-group-s-attack-soil.html. https://www.cnn.com/2015/05/06/us/who-is-junaid-hussain-garland-texas-attack /index.html.

20 Lanier, Candice. August 27, 2015. Killed in Airstrike: Top ISIS Hacker On Pentagon Hit List Who Threatened Attacks on US Military. Medium. Retrieved on February 11, 2018, from https://medium.com/@CandiceLanier/killed-in-airstrike-top-isis-hacker-on -pentagon-hit-list-who-threatened-attacks-on-us-military-cac9e67dc940.

21 Reynolds, Leda. October 6, 2015. From punk rocker to jihadi: UK gran who is now the world's most wanted female terrorist. *Express*. Retrieved on July 1, 2018, from https://www.express.co.uk/news/world/610060/Sally-Jones-ISIS-Islamic-State -terrorist-grandmother-punk-rocker.

22 Lanier, Candice. August 27, 2015. Killed in Airstrike: Top ISIS Hacker On Pentagon Hit List Who Threatened Attacks on US Military. Medium. Retrieved on February 11, 2018, from https://medium.com/@CandiceLanier/killed-in-airstrike-top-isis-hacker-on -pentagon-hit-list-who-threatened-attacks-on-us-military-cac9e67dc940.

23 Moore, Jack. October 7, 2015. ISIS SYMPATHIZER RELEASES ADDRESS OF NAVY SEAL ON BIN LADEN MISSION. *Newsweek*. Retrieved on April 14, 2018, from https://www.newsweek.com/isis-sympathizer-releases-address-navy-seal-bin -laden-mission-380802.

24 Cain, Kathryn. August 26, 2016. TERROR TOT: Horrific ISIS video shows British child—dubbed Abu Abdullah al-Britani—"shooting prisoner in the head" in Syria. *The Sun*. Retrieved on September 28, 2017, from https://www.thesun.co.uk/news/1680684 /horrific-isis-video-shows-british-child-executing-prisoners-in-syria/.

25 The age of criminality is only ten-years-old in the UK. Mays, Alex. August 27, 2016. Horrific ISIS Video Shows Young "British Boy" Executing Prisoner. Unilad. Retrieved on September 26, 2017, from https://www.unilad.co.uk/news/horrific-isis-video -shows-young-british-boy-executing-prisoner/.

26 Ellery, Ben. August 27, 2016. "That's my child!" Father says blue-eyed British boy "killer" seen executing a captured prisoner in Syria is the son he had with Sally Jones who "brainwashed" the youngster and took him to join ISIS. Daily Mail. Retrieved on June 2, 2016, from http://www.dailymail.co.uk/news/article-3761804/That-s-son-Father-identifies -British-boy-killer-seen-executing-captured-prisoner-Syria.html.

27 MacAskill, Ewen. October 12, 2017. British ISIS member Sally Jones "killed in airstrike with 12-year-old son. The *Guardian*. Retrieved on April 17, 2018,

from https://www.theguardian.com/world/2017/oct/12/british-isis-member-sally-jones-white-widow-killed-airstrike-son-islamic-state-syria.

28 Steinbuch, Yaron. November 16, 2017. White Widow's orphan son, 12, is alive and training with ISIS. The *New York Post*. Retrieved on November 21, 2017, from https://nypost.com/2017/11/16/white-widows-orphan-son-12-is-alive-and-training-with-isis/.

29 Nelson, Sara. April 7, 2017. Sally Jones: British Jihadi Bride Who Fled UK To Join ISIS "Desperate To Return Home." The *Huffington Post*. Retrieved on July 1, 2018, from https://www.huffingtonpost.co.uk/entry/sally-jones-british-jihadi-bride-who-fled-uk-to-join-isis-desperate-to-return-home_uk_595b628be4b0da2c73252567.

30 Sanghani, Radhika. July 3, 2013. Top 40 signs of a midlife crisis revealed. The *Telegraph*. Retrieved February 26, 2017, from https://www.telegraph.co.uk/news/newstopics/howaboutthat/10156725/Top-40-signs-of-a-midlife-crisis-revealed.html.

31 *Inspire* magazine, Issue 1. Retrieved on July 2, 2018 from https://azelin.files.wordpress.com/2010/06/aqap-inspire-magazine-volume-1-uncorrupted.pdf.

32 Ibid.

33 In 2010, cartoonists of television show *South Park* were threatened with death for depicting the Prophet Muhammad in an episode. The Everybody Draw Mohammed Day event was in response and intended to support artists threatened with violence for drawing representations of the Prophet Muhammad by flooding the Internet with cartoons, because it would be unrealistic for every person to be murdered.

34 Khalil, Shauqi Abu. 2003. Atlas of the Qur'an: Places. Nations. Landmarks. Darussalam.

35 Bunting, Tony. N.d. Battle of Badr. Encyclopedia Britannica. Retrieved on April 25, 2017, from https://www.britannica.com/event/Battle-of-Badr.

36 Poole, Patrick. May 28, 2015. Indiana Grandma Now ISIS Supporter "Jihad Kathie," Living and Inciting Violence in Germany. PJ Media. Retrieved on April 6, 2018, from https://pjmedia.com/blog/indiana-grandma-now-isis-supporter-jihad-kathie-living-and-inciting-violence-in-germany/.

37 Nelson, Sara. July 19, 2017. Sally Jones: Petition To Ban British ISIS Bride From UK Reaches 15,000. The *Huffington Post*. Retrieved on July 27, 2018, from https://www.huffingtonpost.co.uk/entry/sally-jones-petition-to-ban-british-isis-bride-from-uk-reaches-15000_uk_596f5326e4b00db3d0f4858c.

PART THREE

Chapter Ten: Brother of Terror

1 Bouzar, Dounia and Flynn, Carol Rollie. September 5, 2017. ISIS Recruiting: It's Not (Just) Ideological. Foreign Policy Research Institute. Retrieved on July 20, 2018, from https://www.fpri.org/article/2017/09/isis-recruiting-not-just-ideological/.

2 Ibid.

3 Cottee, Simon and Bloom, Mia. September 8, 2017. The Myth of the ISIS Female Suicide Bomber: She is almost entirely fictitious—so why are some people so keen to believe otherwise? *The Atlantic*. Retrieved on December 28, 2017, from https://www.theatlantic.com/international/archive/2017/09/isis-female-suicide-bomber/539172/.

4 Saltman, Erin Marie and Smith, Melanie. 2015. "Till Martyrdom Do Us Part": Gender and the ISIS Phenomenon. Institute for Strategic Dialogue. Retrieved October 19, 2017, from https://www.isdglobal.org/wp-content/uploads/2016/02/Till_Martyrdom_Do_Us_Part_Gender_and_the_ISIS_Phenomenon.pdf.

5 Ibid.

6 Paraszczuk, Joanna. January 29, 2015. Why Western Women Join ISIS. Business

Insider. Retrieved on July 26, 2018, from https://www.businessinsider.com/why
-western-women-join-isis-2015-1.

7   Saltman, Erin Marie and Smith, Melanie. 2015. "Till Martyrdom Do Us Part": Gender
and the ISIS Phenomenon. Institute for Strategic Dialogue. Retrieved October 19, 2017,
from https://www.isdglobal.org/wp-content/uploads/2016/02/Till_Martyrdom_Do_Us
_Part_Gender_and_the_ISIS_Phenomenon.pdf.

8   Huckerby, Jayne. December 7, 2015. Why Women Join ISIS. *TIME*. Retrieved on
November 21, 2017, from http://time.com/4138377/women-in-isis/.

9   Vugt, Mark Van. September 20, 2014. ISIS and the Real Reason Why Young
Muslim Men Join the Jihad. *Psychology Today*. Retrieved on April 1, 2017, from
https://www.psychologytoday.com/us/blog/naturally-selected/201409/isis-and-the
-real-reason-why-young-muslim-men-join-the-jihad.

10 McDonald, Melissa M., Navarrete, Carlos David, and Mark Van Vugt. 2012. Evolution
and the psychology of intergroup conflict: the male warrior hypothesis. Philosophical
Transactions of the Royal Society of London Biological Sciences. 367 (1589): 670–
679. Retrieved on April 7, 2018, from https://www.ncbi.nlm.nih.gov/pmc/articles
/PMC3260849/.

11 Ibid.

12 Bouzar, Dounia and Flynn, Carol Rollie. September 5, 2017. ISIS Recruiting: It's Not
(Just) Ideological. Foreign Policy Research Institute. Retrieved on July 20, 2018, from
https://www.fpri.org/article/2017/09/isis-recruiting-not-just-ideological/.

Chapter Eleven: Tactics of a Desert Lion

1   Huda. July 23, 2018. The 5 Muslim Daily Prayer Times and What They Mean.
Thought Co. Retrieved July 28, 2018, from https://www.thoughtco.com/islamic
-prayer-timings-2003811.

2   Center of Islamic Shi'a Studies. N.d. Shia praying differences. Center for Islamic
Shi'a Stuides. Retrieved on June 29, 2018, from http://shiastudies.org/article/
shi-a-prayer-rituals.

3   Dakake, David. N.d. Some Misappropriations of Quranic Verses. Islamic Research
Institute. Retrieved on April 25, 2018, from http://karamah.org/wp-content/uploads
/2011/10/Some-Misappropriations-of-Quranic-Verses.pdf.

4   U.S. Department of State. June 30, 2016. Human Trafficking in Conflict Zones.
Office to Monitor and Combat Trafficking in Persons. Retrieved on April 7, 2017, from
https://2009–2017.state.gov/j/tip/rls/fs/2016/259137.htm.

5   U.S. Department of State. 2015. Trafficking in Persons Report, 2015. Office to Monitor
and Combat Trafficking in Persons. Retrieved on April 7, 2017, from https://www.state
.gov/j/tip/rls/tiprpt/countries/2015/243543.htm.

6   Ibid.

7   Agence France Presse. August 28, 2013. New face prompts Iraq militancy fears.
News 24. Retrieved on April 11, 2018, from https://www.news24.com/World/News
/New-face-prompts-Iraq-militancy-fears-20130828.

8   Boyle, Darren and Gayle, Damien. June 14, 2014. Unmasked: The smiling chief executioner
who dares to bare his face in gruesome videos because he revels in the notoriety of being
a Jihadist poster boy. The *Daily Mail*. Retrieved on October 27, 2017, from http://www
.dailymail.co.uk/news/article-2658182/Unmasked-The-public-face-ISIS-terror-army
-threatening-destroy-Iraq.html.

9   Hall, John. June 8, 2015. Pictured, the most feared policeman in the world: Jihadi in
charge of religious police in ISIS capital behind countless beheadings, crucifixions and
amputations. The *Daily Mail*. Retrieved on October 1, 2017, from http://www.dailymail

.co.uk/news/article-3112378/Pictured-feared-policeman-world-Jihadi-charge-religious
-police-ISIS-capital-countless-beheadings-crucifixions-amputations.html.

10 Gibbons-Neff, Thomas and Warrick, Joby. May 9, 2016. Notorious Islamic State
leader killed in airstrike, Pentagon says. The *Washington Post*. Retrieved on May 22,
2018,   from   https://www.washingtonpost.com/news/checkpoint/wp/2016/05/09
/notorious-islamic-state-leader-killed-in-airstrike-pentagon-says/?noredirect=on&utm
_term=.081b107e9eb4.

11 Parlapiano, Alicia. June 27, 2018. The Travel Ban Has Been Upheld.
Here Are Some of Its Effects So Far. The *New York Times*. Retrieved on July 27, 2018,
from   https://www.nytimes.com/interactive/2018/06/27/us/politics/trump-travel-ban
-effects.html.

12 Taylor, Adam. November 16, 2015. The Islamic State wants you to hate refugees. The
Washington Post. Retrieved on January 1, 2017, from https://www.washingtonpost.com
/news/worldviews/wp/2015/11/16/the-islamic-state-wants-you-to-hate-refugees/?utm
_term=.af5d8b7342f0.

13 Nichols, Chris. February 1, 2017. MOSTLY TRUE: Odds of fatal terror attack in
U.S. by a refugee? 3.6 billion to 1. Politifact. Retrieved on June 1, 2017, from https:
//www.politifact.com/california/statements/2017/feb/01/ted-lieu/odds-youll-be-killed
-terror-attack-america-refugee/.

14 Mosher, Dave and Gould, Skye. March 25, 2018. The odds that a gun will kill the average American may surprise you. Business Insider. Retrieved on July 1, 2018 from https:
//www.businessinsider.com/us-gun-death-murder-risk-statistics-2018-3.

15 Nichols, Chris. February 1, 2017. MOSTLY TRUE: Odds of fatal terror attack in
U.S. by a refugee? 3.6 billion to 1. Politifact. Retrieved on June 1, 2017, from
https://www.politifact.com/california/statements/2017/feb/01/ted-lieu/odds-youll
-be-killed-terror-attack-america-refugee/.

16 Mosher, Dave and Gould, Skye. March 25, 2018. The odds that a gun will kill the average American may surprise you. Business Insider. Retrieved on July 1, 2018, from https:
//www.businessinsider.com/us-gun-death-murder-risk-statistics-2018-3.

17 Ibid.

Chapter Twelve: Terrorist for Hire

1   NPR Staff. November 17, 2011. The Arab Spring: A Year Of Revolution. NPR. Retrieved
on January 7, 2016, from https://www.npr.org/2011/12/17/143897126/the-arab-spring-a
-year-of-revolution.

2   Ibid.

3   Ibid.

4   Chrisafis, Angelique and Black, Ian. January 14, 2011. Zine al-Abidine Ben Ali forced to flee
Tunisia as protesters claim victory. The *Guardian*. Retrieved on April 10, 2017, from https:
//www.theguardian.com/world/2011/jan/14/tunisian-president-flees-country-protests.

5   CNN Wire Staff. June 20, 2011. Ousted Tunisian strongman convicted of corruption
charges. CNN. Retrieved on November 21, 2016, from http://www.cnn.com/2011
/WORLD/africa/06/20/tunisia.ben.ali/index.html.

6   Abdessalem, Rafik. January 18, 2014. Tunisia: A pioneer of Arab democracy. Aljazeera.
Retrieved on August 24, 2017, from https://www.aljazeera.com/indepth/opinion
/2014/01/tunisia-pioneer-arab-democracy-2014117827634794.html.

7   ISIS. 2011. The Tsunami of Change. *Inspire*.

8   International Labor Organization (ILO). November, 2017. Unemployment, youth total
(% of total labor force ages 15–24) (modeled ILO estimate). The World Bank. Retrieved
on June 7, 2018, from https://data.worldbank.org/indicator/SL.UEM.1524.ZS.

9   Stirgus, Eric. September 14, 2012. Unemployment rate comparable to Great Depression, congressman says. Politifact. Retrieved on June 7, 2016, from https://www.politifact.com/georgia/statements/2012/sep/14/phil-gingrey/unemployment-rate-comparable-great-depression-cong/.

10 Caryl, Christian. July 15, 2018. Why Does Tunisia Produce So Many Terrorists? Foreign Policy. Retrieved on July 27, 2018, from https://foreignpolicy.com/2016/07/15/why-does-tunisia-produce-so-many-terrorists-nice-france-truck-terrorist-attack/.

11 Zarocostas, John. March 17, 2015. More than 7,000 Tunisians said to have joined Islamic State. McClatchy. Retrieved on April 27, 2018, from https://www.mcclatchydc.com/news/nation-world/world/article24781867.html.

12 Caryl, Christian. July 15, 2018. Why Does Tunisia Produce So Many Terrorists? Foreign Policy. Retrieved on July 27, 2018, from https://foreignpolicy.com/2016/07/15/why-does-tunisia-produce-so-many-terrorists-nice-france-truck-terrorist-attack/.

13 Macdonald, Geoffrey and Waggoner, Luke. January 27, 2017. Why are so many Tunisians joining the Islamic State? The *Washington Post*. Retrieved on June 7, 2018, from https://www.washingtonpost.com/news/monkey-cage/wp/2017/01/27/why-are-so-many-tunisians-joining-the-islamic-state/?utm_term=.b74a2a567f03.

14 Ibid.

15 Agnew, Robert. 1992. Foundation for a General Strain Theory of Crime and Delinquency. Criminology. 30, 1.

16 Georgy, Michael. November 29, 2016. Exclusive: Jailed Islamic State suspects recall path to jihad in Iraq. Reuters. Retrieved on June 1, 2018, from https://www.reuters.com/article/us-mideast-crisis-mosul-prisoners-exclus-idUSKBN13O1QZ.

17 Ibid.

18 Dosky, Reber. December 7, 2017. The Sex Slaves of ISIS. *The Atlantic*. Retrieved on April 7, 2018, from https://www.theatlantic.com/video/index/547802/yazidi-female-prisoners-isis/.

19 For example, in the trial of Rances Ulices Amaya (gang name "Murder").

20 Raghavan, Chitra and Doychak, Kendra. 2015. Trauma-coerced Bonding and Victims of Sex Trafficking: Where do we go from here? *International Journal of Emergency Mental health and Human Resilience*, Vol. 17, No. 2, pp. 583–587.

21 Mehlman-Orozco, Kimberly. 2017. *Hidden in Plain Sight: America's Slaves of the New Millennium*. ABC-Clio.

22 United Nations. December 10, 1948. The Universal Declaration of Human Rights. United Nations. Retrieved on July 31, 2018, from http://www.un.org/en/universal-declaration-human-rights/.

Chapter Thirteen: Ginger Jihadi

1   Milo. February 10, 2017. MILO: Dear Netflix People, Stop Race-Baiting. Breitbart. Retrieved on July 7, 2017, from https://www.breitbart.com/milo/2017/02/10/milo-dear-netflix-sod-off/.

2   Piquero, Alex R. 2008. Disproportionate Minority Contact. *The Future of Children*. 18,2: 59–79.

3   Mitchell, Ojmarrh. 2005. A Meta-Analysis of Race and Sentencing Research: Explaining the Inconsistencies. *Journal of Quantitative Criminology*. 21,4: 439–466.

4   Shapiro, Ben. August 19, 2015. Why White People Seek Black Privilege. Breitbart. Retrieved on June 7, 2017, from https://www.breitbart.com/big-government/2015/08/19/why-white-people-seek-black-privilege/.

5   Bokhari, Allum and Yiannopoulos, Milo. March 29, 2016. An Establishment Conservative's

Guide To The Alt-Right. Breitbart. Retrieved on June 7, 2018, from https://www.breit bart.com/tech/2016/03/29/an-establishment-conservatives-guide-to-the-alt-right/.

6 Milo. September 19, 2016. FULL TEXT: "How To Destroy The Alt Right" By MILO. Breitbart. Retrieved on June 7, 2017, from https://www.breitbart.com/milo/2016/09/19 /milo-destroy-alt-right-speech/.

7 Milo. December 16, 2016. FULL TEXT: MILO on "Master Baiters: The Leftists Keeping America's Race War Alive." Breitbart. Retrieved on June 7, 2018, from https://www.breit bart.com/milo/2016/12/13/full-text-master-baiters-leftists-keeping-race-war-alive/.

8 Yiannopoulos, Milo and Wilson, Jeremy. September 9, 2014. Ginger Jihadis: Why Redheads are Attracted to Radical Islam. Breitbart. Retrieved on August 1, 2018, from https://www.breitbart.com/london/2014/09/09/ginger-jihadis-why-redheads-are -attracted-to-radical-islam/.

9 Guéguen, Nicolas. September 8, 2012. Hair Color and Courtship: Blond Women Received More Courtship Solicitations and Redhead Men Received More Refusals. *Psychological Studies.* 57,4: 369–375.

10 Persaud, Raj and Furnham, Adrian. September 25, 2012. Hair Colour and Attraction— Is the Latest Psychological Research Bad News for Redheads? The *Huffington Post*, UK Edition. Retrieved on June 7, 2018, from https://www.huffingtonpost.co.uk/dr-raj -persaud/redheads-psychology_b_1911771.html.

11 Hunter, Margaret. 2007. The Persistent Problem of Colorism: Skin Tone, Status, and Inequality. Sociology Compass: 237–254. Retrieved on July 27, 2018, from https:// inside.mills.edu/academics/faculty/soc/mhunter/The%20Persistent%20Problem%20 of%20Colorism.pdf.

12 Carter, Jarrett L. April 11, 2013. Bringing Back the Brown Paper Bag Test to HBCUs. The *Huffington Post*. Retrieved on July 7, 2018 from https://www.huffingtonpost.com /jarrett-l-carter/bringing-back-the-brown-p_b_3059700.html.

13 Byrd, Ayana D. and Tharps, Lori L. *Hair Story: Untangling the Roots of Black Hair in America*. St. Martins Press.

14 Yiannopoulos, Milo and Wilson, Jeremy. September 9, 2014. Ginger Jihadis: Why Redheads are Attracted to Radical Islam. Breitbart. Retrieved on June 7, 2018, from https://www.breitbart.com/london/2014/09/09/ginger-jihadis-why-redheads -are-attracted-to-radical-islam/.

15 Ibid.

16 Ibid.

17 Spillett, Richard. November 2, 2015. Ginger-haired "Muslim patrol" member jailed for trying to enforce sharia law on the streets of London blames the internet for turning him into an extremist. The *Daily Mail*. Retrieved on July 1, 2018, from http://www.dailymail .co.uk/news/article-3300168/Muslim-patrol-member-blames-internet-turning-extremist .html.

18 Leech, Robb. My Brother The Terrorist. Daily Motion. Retrieved on June 7, 2018, from https://www.dailymotion.com/video/x2g3owf.

19 Gillman, Ollie. August 17, 2016. "Some brains needs washing": What vile hate preacher Anjem Choudary told brother of convicted Muslim convert Richard Dart. The *Daily Mail*. Retrieved on July 7, 2018, from http://www.dailymail.co.uk/news/article-3744787/Some -brains-needs-washing-vile-hate-preacher-Anjem-Choudary-told-brother-convicted -Muslim-convert-Richard-Dart.html.

20 Saul, Heather. October 21, 2014. Australian jihadist Abdullah Elmir vows Isis will fight "until black flag is on the top of Buckingham Palace." Independent. Retrieved on September 26, 2016, from https://www.independent.co.uk/news/world/middle-east

/australian-teenage-jihadist-abdullah-elmir-vows-isis-will-fight-until-black-flag-is-on
-top-of-9808983.html.

21 The Australian. October 22, 2014. Terrorists "groomed" teen jihadist Abdullah Elmir like
pedophiles. Retrieved on July 8, 2018, from https://www.theaustralian.com.au/national
-affairs/terrorists-groomed-teen-jihadist-abdullah-elmir-like-pedophiles/news-story
/eb8141b9a2c72a015313a15875cb647f.

22 Staff writers. December 10, 2015. "Ginger Jihadi" Abdullah Elmir reportedly killed
in Syria. News.Au.Com. Retrieved on October 11, 2017, from https://www.news
.com.au/national/ginger-jihadi-abdullah-elmir-reportedly-killed-in-syria/news-story
/feea3707e522c35e39e7be3370d56bde.

23 Cullison, Alan. November 19, 2013. Meet the Rebel Commander in Syria That Assad,
Russia and the U.S. All Fear. The *Wall Street Journal*. Retrieved on February 26, 2017,
from https://www.wsj.com/articles/no-headline-available-1384899732.

24 Ibid.

25 Moore, Jack. March 9, 2016. Isis's Minister of War Omar the Chechen Targeted in U.S.
Air Strike. *Newsweek*. Retrieved on March 17, 2017, from https://www.newsweek.com
/isiss-minister-war-omar-chechen-targeted-us-air-strike-434966.

26 Michael, Tom. December 27th 2016. KILLED FOR "MAGIC" ISIS thug with bizarre
bright ginger beard orders Syrian pensioner's head to be hacked off after accusing him
of being a WIZARD. The *Sun*. Retrieved on April 11, 2017, from https://www.thesun
.co.uk/news/2482974/isis-pensioner-head-off-syria-wizard/.

27 Gillespie, Tom. January 29, 2016. "Ginger Jihadi" who groomed six-year-old son with
ISIS propaganda is jailed for spreading hate. The *Sun*. Retrieved on October 20, 2017,
from https://www.thesun.co.uk/archives/news/258361/ginger-jihadi-who-groomed-six
-year-old-son-with-isis-propaganda-is-jailed-for-spreading-hate/.

28 Duell, Mark. June 13, 2017. "Ginger jihadi" who radicalized himself online in his Welsh
valleys home is jailed for 28 months for downloading ISIS terror manuals. The *Daily Mail*.
Retrieved on April 30, 2018, from http://www.dailymail.co.uk/news/article-4600592
/Ginger-jihadi-radicalised-jailed.html.

29 Matthews, Alex. May 1, 2018. TERROR CHARGE Ginger "jihadi" was "planning
large-scale terror attack on Oxford Street and Madame Tussauds using vehicle." The *Sun*.
Retrieved on June 7, 2018, from https://www.thesun.co.uk/news/6185002/ginger-jihadi
-was-planning-large-scale-terror-attack-on-oxford-street-and-madame-tussauds-using
-vehicle/.

30 Yiannopoulos, Milo. September 27, 2016. FULL TEXT: 10 Things Milo Hates
About Islam. Breitbart. Retrieved on August 1, 2018, from https://www.breitbart.com
/milo/2016/09/27/10-things-milo-hates-islam/.

31 Popularized in United States by Mark Twain and attributed to the British Prime Minister
Benjamin Disraeli.

32 Huston, Warner Todd. April 30, 2015. Second Prisoner in Baltimore Police Van
with Freddie Gray Speaks Out. Breitbart. Retrieved on June 7, 2018, from https://www
.breitbart.com/big-government/2015/04/30/second-prisoner-in-baltimore
-police-van-with-freddie-gray-speaks-out/.

33 Breitbart News. May 1, 2015. Live Updates—Baltimore Curfew, Night 4: Freddie
Gray's Arresting Officers Indicted. Breitbart. Retrieved on July 7, 2018, from
https://www.breitbart.com/big-government/2015/05/01/live-updates-baltimore-curfew
-night-4-freddie-grays-arresting-officers-indicted/.

34 Islamic State. July, 2014. The Return of Khilafah. Dabiq, Issue 1. Retrieved on June 2, 2016,
from https://azelin.files.wordpress.com/2014/07/islamic-state-22dc481biq-magazine
-122.pdf.

35 Hooper, Simon. December 19, 2013. Black Britons confront "radical Islam." Aljazeera.
    Retrieved on July 8, 2018, from https://www.aljazeera.com/indepth/features/2013/12
    /black-britons-confront-radical-islam-2013121871456382764.html.
36 Pew Research Center. July 24, 2017. U.S.-born Muslims more likely to be converts
    to the faith. Religious Beliefs and Practices. Retrieved on July 7, 2018, from http:
    //www.pewforum.org/2017/07/26/religious-beliefs-and-practices/pf_2017-06-26
    _muslimamericans-06-02/.
37 Reddie, Richard. October 5, 2009. Why are black people turning to Islam? The
    Guardian. Retrieved on July 7, 2018, from https://www.theguardian.com/commentisfree
    /belief/2009/oct/05/black-muslims-islam.
38 Hooper, Simon. December 19, 2013. Black Britons confront "radical Islam." Aljazeera.
    Retrieved on July 8, 2018, from https://www.aljazeera.com/indepth/features/2013/12
    /black-britons-confront-radical-islam-2013121871456382764.html.
39 Baker, Abdul Haqq. August 19, 2013. Islam's ability to empower is a magnet to black
    British youths. The *Guardian*. Retrieved on July 8, 2018, from https://www.theguardian
    .com/commentisfree/2013/aug/19/islam-empower-magnet-black-british-youths.
40 Hooper, Simon. December 19, 2013. Black Britons confront "radical Islam." Aljazeera.
    Retrieved on July 8, 2018, from https://www.aljazeera.com/indepth/features/2013/12
    /black-britons-confront-radical-islam-2013121871456382764.html.
41 Alexander, Michele. 2010. *The New Jim Crow: Mass Incarceration in the Age of
    Colorblindness*. The New Press.
42 The Sentencing Project. 2013. Report of The Sentencing Project to the United Nations
    Human Rights Committee: Regarding Racial Disparities in the United States Criminal
    Justice System. Retrieved on July 8, 2018, from http://sentencingproject.org/wp-content
    /uploads/2015/12/Race-and-Justice-Shadow-Report-ICCPR.pdf.

Chapter Fourteen: Orphans of ISIS

1   Sage, Adam. January 8, 2015. "We have avenged Muhammad. We have killed Charlie
    Hebdo". The *Times*. Retrieved on July 18, 2017 from https://www.thetimes.co.uk
    /article/we-have-avenged-muhammad-we-have-killed-charlie-hebdo-77j0vzh8lcl.
2   Al-Qaeda. 2015. Assassination Operations. Inspire, Issue 14. Retrieved on June 2, 2016,
    from https://azelin.files.wordpress.com/2015/09/inspire-magazine-14.pdf.
3   Al-Qaeda. 2013. We are All Usama. Inspire, Issue 10. Retrieved on June 2, 2016, from
    https://azelin.files.wordpress.com/2013/03/inspire-magazine-issue-10.pdf.
4   Kirkpatrick, David D. September 11, 2012. Anger Over a Film Fuels Anti-American
    Attacks in Libya and Egypt. The *New York Times*. Retrieved on November 21, 2016, from
    https://www.nytimes.com/2012/09/12/world/middleeast/anger-over-film-fuels-anti
    -american-attacks-in-libya-and-egypt.html.
5   Ibid.
6   Ibid.
7   Ibid.
8   Kessler, Glenn. October 21, 2015. Fact-checking the Benghazi attacks. The
    Washington Post. Retrieved on November 23, 2017, from https://www.washingtonpost
    .com/news/fact-checker/wp/2015/10/21/fact-checking-the-benghazi-attacks-2/?utm_term
    =.9cb6b4c4f831.
9   Thiessen, Marc. A. September 19, 2016. Hillary Clinton, who tells dreadful lies. The
    Washington Post. Retrieved on September 28, 2017, from https://www.washingtonpost
    .com/opinions/hillary-clinton-who-tells-dreadful-lies/2016/09/19/cd38412e-7e6a-11e6
    -9070-5c4905bf40dc_story.html?utm_term=.e16b886de799.

10 Jyllands-Posten. September 30, 2005. The Face of Muhammad. KulturWeekend. Retrieved on September 26, 2017, from http://multimedia.jp.dk/archive/00080/Avisside _Muhammed-te_80003a.pdf.

11 Anderson, John Ward. January 31, 2006. Cartoons of Prophet Met With Outrage. The *Washington Post.* Retrieved on March 26, 2016, from http://www.washingtonpost.com /wp-dyn/content/article/2006/01/30/AR2006013001316.html.

12 Hundevadt, Kim. March 11, 2008. The Cartoon Crisis—how it unfolded. Jyllands-Posten: International. Retrieved on June 7, 2017, from https://jyllands-posten.dk /international/ECE3931398/The-Cartoon-Crisis—how-it-unfolded/.

13 Ibid.

14 Times Online. February 6, 2006. Timeline: the Muhammad cartoons. *The Times* UK. Retrieved on April 1, 2018, from https://www.thetimes.co.uk/article/timeline-the -muhammad-cartoons-lhhfjbt3m29.

15 Kite, Melissa. 2006. Muslim protests are incitement to murder, say Tories. The *Telegraph.* Retrieved on August 14, 2018, from https://www.telegraph.co.uk/news/uknews/1509664 /Muslim-protests-are-incitement-to-murder-say-Tories.html.

16 Ibid.

17 Foreign Staff. May 4, 2015. Prophet Mohammed cartoons controversy: timeline. The *Telegraph.* Retrieved on April 1, 2018, from https://www.telegraph.co.uk/news/worldnews /europe/france/11341599/Prophet-Muhammad-cartoons-controversy-timeline.html.

18 Ibid.

19 Al-Qaeda. 2010. May Our Souls Be Sacrificed for You! Inspire, Issue 1. Retrieved on June 1, 2017, from https://azelin.files.wordpress.com/2010/06/aqap-inspire-magazine -volume-1-uncorrupted.pdf.

20 Spiegel Online. March 28, 2008. "The Cartoon Must Not Be Used Against Muslims as a Whole." Spiegel Online. Retrieved on April 1, 2018, from http://www.spiegel.de /international/europe/interview-with-muhammad-cartoonist-westergaard-the-cartoon -must-not-be-used-against-muslims-as-a-whole-a-544052.html.

21 BBC News UK. February 9, 2006. Dutch MP backs Muhammad cartoons. BBC News. Retrieved on April 1, 2016, from http://news.bbc.co.uk/2/hi/europe/4698528.stm.

22 Mills, Jen. February 22, 2016. Renewed $600,000 fatwa issued to kill British author Salman Rushdie. Metro UK. Retrieved on June 25, 2017, from https://metro.co.uk/2016/02/22 /renewed-600000-fatwa-issued-to-kill-british-author-salman-rushdie-5710279/.

23 Al-Shabaab. 2015. May Our Mothers Be Bereaved of Us Should We Fail to Avenge Our Prophet. Gaidi Mtaani, Issue 7. Retrieved on June 2, 2017, from https://azelin.files.word press.com/2015/02/gaidi-mtaani-issue-7.pdf.

24 ISIS. 2015. From Hypocrisy to Apostasy: The Extinction of the Grayzone. Dabiq, Issue 7. Retrieved on June 7, 2018, from https://jihadology.net/2015/02/12/al-ḥayat -media-center-presents-a-new-issue-of-the-islamic-states-magazine-dabiq-7/.

25 Sabin, Lamiat. January 12, 2015. Former teacher of Kouachi brothers says they were "not intelligent enough to resist extremism." Independent. Retrieved on June 7, 2018, from https://www.independent.co.uk/news/world/europe/former-teacher-of-kouachi-brothers -says-they-were-not-intelligent-enough-to-resist-extremism-9973318.html.

26 Samuel, Henry. January 19, 2015. Charlie Hebdo killers "traumatised by mother"s suicide." The *Telegraph.* Retrieved on June 7, 2018, from https://www.telegraph.co.uk/news /worldnews/europe/france/11354847/Charlie-Hebdo-killers-traumatised-by-mothers -suicide.html.

27 Bronstein, Scott. January 14, 2015. Cherif and Said Kouachi: Their path to terror. CNN. Retrieved on July 1, 2018, from https://www.cnn.com/2015/01/13/world/kouachi -brothers-radicalization/index.html.

28 Kutner, Max. January 8, 2015. Meet Farid Benyettou, the Man Who Trained Paris Attack Suspect Cherif Kouachi. *Newsweek*. Retrieved on June 1, 2018, from https://www.newsweek.com/meet-farid-benyettou-man-who-trained-paris-attack-suspect-cherif-kouachi-298028.

29 Ibid.

30 Daniel, Gregory and Agasse, Antoine. July 16, 2018. Mentor of 2015 jihadist attackers expelled by France to Algeria. The Times of Israel. Retrieved on August 1, 2018, from https://www.timesofisrael.com/mentor-of-2015-jihadist-attackers-expelled-by-france-to-algeria/.

Chapter Fifteen: Cubs of the Caliphate

1   ISIS. 2015. From the Battle of Al-Ahzab to the War of Coalitions. Dabiq, Issue 11. Retrieved on June 1, 2018, from https://azelin.files.wordpress.com/2015/09/the-islamic-state-e2809cdc481biq-magazine-11e280b3.pdf.

2   Svirsky, Meira. 2017. He Made Me Alive With His Blood. Clarion Project. Retrieved on March 17, 2017, from https://clarionproject.org/warning-graphic-video-isis-children-4/.

3   United Nations. 2002. Optional Protocol on the Involvement of Children in Armed Conflict. Retrieved on November 27, 2017, from https://childrenandarmedconflict.un.org/tools-for-action/opac/.

4   Ibid.

5   U.S. Department of State. 2018. Child Soldiers Prevention Act List. Trafficking in Persons Report, 2018. Retrieved on July 10, 2018, from https://www.state.gov/j/tip/rls/tiprpt/2018/282577.htm.

6   Ibid.

7   U.S. Department of State. 2018. Trafficking in Persons Report, 2018. Retrieved on July 10, 2018, from https://www.state.gov/documents/organization/282798.pdf.

8   Associated Press. July 15, 2015. Scores of ISIL child soldiers "killed" in Syria in 2015. Aljazeera. Retrieved on September 28, 2017, from https://www.aljazeera.com/news/2015/07/scores-isil-child-soldiers-killed-syria-2015-150715132745980.html.

9   ISIS. 2015. Shari'ah Alone Will Rule Africa. *Dabiq*, Issue 8. Retrieved on June 1, 2017, from https://azelin.files.wordpress.com/2015/03/the-islamic-state-e2809cdc481biq-magazine-8e280b3.pdf.

10 ISIS. 2017. The Ruling on the Belligerent Christians. Rumiyah, Issue 9. Retrieved on July 12, 2018, from https://azelin.files.wordpress.com/2017/05/rome-magazine-9.pdf.

11 Rudaw. December 11, 2016. Iraqi army denies it killed, drove tank over a "child soldier." Rudaw. Retrieved on June 1, 2018, from http://www.rudaw.net/english/middleeast/iraq/111120165.

12 LiveLeak. N.d. ISIL Child Soldier Captured and Killed by Iraqi Forces. Live Leak. Retrieved on June 30, 2018, from https://www.liveleak.com/view?i=def_1478876431.

PART FOUR

Chapter Sixteen: Counterterrorism

1   History.com. n.d. Osama bin Laden. History.com Retrieved on January 26, 2018, from https://www.history.com/topics/osama-bin-laden.

2   Ibid.

3   Ibid.

4   Moran, Michael. 1998. Bin Laden comes home to roost: His CIA ties are only the beginning of a woeful story. NBC News. Retrieved on January 11, 2018, from http://www.nbcnews.com/id/3340101/t/bin-laden-comes-home-roost/#.W2w0sS2ZPEo.

5   Ibid.
6   History.com. n.d. Osama bin Laden. History.com Retrieved on January 26, 2018, from https://www.history.com/topics/osama-bin-laden.
7   Nance, Malcolm. 2016. *Defeating ISIS: Who They Are, How They Fight, What They Believe.* Skyhorse.
8   Moran, Michael. 1998. Bin Laden comes home to roost: His CIA ties are only the beginning of a woeful story. NBC News. Retrieved on January 11, 2018, from http://www.nbcnews.com/id/3340101/t/bin-laden-comes-home-roost/#.W2w0sS2ZPEo.
9   Insight Crime and Center for Latin American and Latino Studies. N.d. MS13 in the Americas: How the World's Most Notorious Gang Defies Logic, Resists Destruction. U.S. Department of Justice. Retrieved on July 20, 2018, from https://www.justice.gov/eoir/page/file/1043576/download.
10 Denvir, Daniel. 2017. Deporting people made Central America's gangs. More deportation won't help. The *Washington Post*. Retrieved on June 1, 2018, from www.washingtonpost.com.

Chapter Seventeen: *Rumiyah*

1   Electronic Frontier Foundation. N.d. Content Blocking. EFF. Retrieved on July 17, 2018, from https://www.eff.org/issues/content-blocking.
2   Ibid.
3   Mehlman-Orozco, Kimberly. 2015. TOR and the Bitcoin: An Exploration into Law Enforcement Surveillance Capability Online. The Diplomatic Courier. Retrieved on March 26, 2015, from https://www.diplomaticourier.com/2015/03/19/tor-and-the-bitcoin-an-exploration-into-law-enforcement-surveillance-capability-online/.
4   Al-Qaeda. 2010. May Our Souls be Sacrificed for You! Inspire. Retrieved on June 1, 2017 from https://azelin.files.wordpress.com/2010/06/aqap-inspire-magazine-volume-1-uncorrupted.pdf.
5   Tor. N.d. About Tor. Retrieved on July 19, 2018 from https://www.torproject.org/about/overview.html.en.
6   *Ibid.*
7   Mehlman-Orozco, Kimberly. 2017. *Hidden in Plain Sight: America's Slaves of the New Millennium.* ABC-Clio.
8   Al-Qaeda. 2011. Who & Why. *Inspire*, Issue 11. Retrieved on August 25, 2017, from https://azelin.files.wordpress.com/2013/05/inspire-magazine-issue-11.pdf.
9   Friedersdorf, Conor. 2012. How Team Obama Justifies the Killing of a 16-Year-Old American. *The Atlantic*. Retrieved on July 1, 2017, from https://www.theatlantic.com/politics/archive/2012/10/how-team-obama-justifies-the-killing-of-a-16-year-old-american/264028/.
10 Browne, Ryan. 2017. Daughter of Anwar Al-Awlaki reported killed in Yemen raid. CNN. Retrieved on July 7, 2017, from https://www.cnn.com/2017/01/31/politics/yemen-raid-daughter-al-qaeda-leader/index.html.
11 Al-Qaeda. 2012. Winning on the Ground. *Inspire*, Issue 9. Retrieved on July 7, 2017, from https://azelin.files.wordpress.com/2012/05/inspire-magazine-9.pdf.
12 ISIS. 2015. From Hypocrisy to Apostasy: The Extinction of the Grayzone. *Dabiq*, Issue 7. Retrieved on June 26, 2017, from https://azelin.files.wordpress.com/2015/02/the-islamic-state-e2809cdc481biq-magazine-722.pdf.
13 ISIS. 2016. A Call to Hijrah. *Dabiq*, Issue 3. Retrieved on August 25, 2017 from https://azelin.files.wordpress.com/2016/07/the-islamic-state-e2809cdacc84biq-magazine-322.pdf.

14 Walsh, Bryan. 2015. Alan Kurdi's Story: Behind The Most Heartbreaking Photo of 2015. *TIME*. Retrieved on April 16, 2017, from http://time.com/4162306/alan-kurdi -syria-drowned-boy-refugee-crisis/.

15 ISIS. 2015. From the Battle of Al-Ahzab to the War of Coalitions. *Dabiq*, Issue 11. Retrieved on June 25, 2017, from https://azelin.files.wordpress.com/2015/09/the-islamic -state-e2809cdc481biq-magazine-11e280b3.pdf.

16 Robinson, Julian. 2017. ISIS burn 12 people alive including a family of four after forcing them into metal cages and dousing them with oil when they tried to flee in Iraq. The *Daily Mail*. Retrieved on July 1, 2018, from http://www.dailymail.co.uk/news/article-4661166 /ISIS-burn-12-people-alive-cages-trying-escape.html.

Chapter Eighteen: Through the Eyes of a Terrorist

1 Siegel, Stephanie. 2015. Shoe-Bomber Has "Tactical Regrets" Over Failed American Airlines Plot. NBC News. Retrieved on February 3, 2015, from https://www.nbcnews.com/news /us-news/shoe-bomber-has-tactical-regrets-over-failed-american-airlines-plot-n296396.

2 Boyle, Louise. 2015. Shoe-bomber Richard Reid claims God meant for him to fail in blowing up a passenger jet as he says Charlie Hebdo attack was not a tragedy. The *Daily Mail*. Retrieved on April 1, 2017, from http://www.dailymail.co.uk/news/article-2937804 /Shoe-bomber-Richard-Reid-claims-God-wanted-fail-blowing-passenger-jet.html.

3 Sherwell, Philip. 2015. Failed "shoe bomber" Richard Reid describes "tactical regrets" that mass murder mission failed. The *Telegraph*. Retrieved on April 1, 2017, from https: //www.telegraph.co.uk/news/worldnews/northamerica/usa/11388442/Failed-shoe -bomber-Richard-Reid-describes-tactical-regrets-that-mass-murder-mission-failed.html.

4 Blin, Simon. 2015. Pour Richard Reid, son projet d'attentat-suicide était "conforme à la loi coranique". *Le Figaro*. Retrieved on April 1, 2017, from http://www.lefigaro.fr/inter-national/2015/02/04/01003-20150204ARTFIG00184-pour-richard-reid-son-projet-d -attentat-suicide-etait-conforme-a-la-loi-coranique.php.

5 *Le Monde*. 2015. Richard Reid, le djihadiste « Shoe Bomber », ne se repent pas. *Le Monde*. Retrieved on April 1, 2017, from https://www.lemonde.fr/international/article /2015/02/04/richard-reid-djihadiste-non-repenti_4569242_3210.html.

6 Remke, Michael. 2015. Nach One-Night-Stand wurde „Dschihad-Jane" radikal. *Die Welt*. Retrieved on April 1, 2017, from https://www.welt.de/vermischtes/article136433722 /Nach-One-Night-Stand-wurde-Dschihad-Jane-radikal.html.

7 U.S. Department of Justice Press Release. 2015. North Carolina Man Sentenced to Serve 243 Months in Prison for Attempting to Provide Material Support to a Designated Foreign Terrorist Organization. U.S. Department of Justice. Retrieved on June 1, 2017, from https://www.justice.gov/opa/pr/north-carolina-man-sentenced-serve-243-months-prison -attempting-provide-material-support.

8 Al-Qaeda. 2017. Train Derail Operations. *Inspire*, Issue 11. Retrieved on June 19, 2018, from https://azelin.files.wordpress.com/2017/08/inspire-magazine-17.pdf.

9 Preston, Mark. 2009. White supremacists watched in lead up to Obama administra-tion. CNN. Retrieved on November 26, 2016, from http://www.cnn.com/2009 /POLITICS/01/16/obama.white.supremacists/.

10 U.S. Attorney's Office. 2009. Man Who Formed Terrorist Group that Plotted Attacks on Military and Jewish Facilities Sentenced to 16 Years in Federal Prison. Federal Bureau of Investigation. Retrieved on November 11, 2016, from https://archives.fbi.gov/archives /losangeles/press-releases/2009/la030609ausa.htm.

11 Smith, Kevin. 2011. The Threat of Muslim-American Radicalization in U.S. Prisons. Testimony presented before the U.S. House of Representatives Committee on Homeland

Security. Retrieved on November 11, 2016, from https://homeland.house.gov/files/
Testimony%20Smith_1.pdf.

12 Knefel, John. 2015. The FBI Keeps Arresting Hapless Jihadi Fanboys and Calling Them
ISIS Recruits. *The New Republic*. Retrieved on June 1, 2017, from https://newrepublic
.com/article/121360/fbi-keeps-overhyping-threat-would-be-isis-recruits.

13 Gordts, Eline and Frej, Willa 2018. Trump Orders Strikes On Syria In Retaliation For
Chemical Attack. The *Huffington Post*. Retrieved on July 7, 2018, from https://www
.huffingtonpost.com/entry/trump-strikes-syria-retaliation-chemical-attack_us
_5acc7508e4b07a3485e7e642.

Chapter Nineteen: Education Kills Terrorism

1   Global Terrorism Database. N.d. Global Terrorism Database. University of Maryland.
Retrieved on August 11, 2018, from https://www.start.umd.edu/gtd/search/Results
.aspx?start_month=0&end_month=12&start_year=2017&end_year=2017&start
_day=0&end_day=31.

2   Newton, Paula. 2015. Son died fighting for ISIS, mom wants to fight propaganda.
CNN. Retrieved on April 7, 2016, from https://www.cnn.com/2015/02/19/world/canada
-isis-fighter-mother/index.html.

3   Ibid.

4   Ibid.

5   Scheuer, Michael. 2004. *Imperial Hubris: Why the West is Losing the War on Terror.*
Potomac Books.

6   Ibid.

7   Ibid.

8   Fox News. 2016. Former CIA officer: Stop calling Islam a "religion of peace." Fox News.
Retrieved on August 10, 2018, from https://www.youtube.com/watch?v=zmNdt-7CMjU.

9   Milo. 2016. FULLTEXT: 10 Things Milo Hates About Islam. Brietbard. Retrieved on August
1, 2018, from https://www.breitbart.com/milo/2016/09/27/10-things-milo-hates-islam/.

10 Beck, Glenn. 2015. *It IS About Islam: Exposing the Truth About ISIS, Al Qaeda, Iran, and
The Caliphate.* Threshold Editions.

11 Lipoka, Michael. 2017. Muslims and Islam: Key findings in the U.S. and around the
world. Pew Research Center. Retrieved on August 10, 2018, from http://www.pewresearch
.org/fact-tank/2017/08/09/muslims-and-islam-key-findings-in-the-u-s-and-around-the
-world/.

12 Bernburg, Jon Gunnar, Krohn, Marvin D., and Rivera, Craig J. 2006. Official Labeling,
Criminal Embeddedness, and Subsequent Delinquency: A Longitudinal Test of
Labeling Theory. Journal of Research in Crime and Delinquency. Volume 43, Number
1: 67–88. Retrieved on July 8, 2017, from https://s3.amazonaws.com/academia.edu
.documents/40159827/Official_Labeling_Criminal_Embeddedness_20151118
-18713-76rjua.pdf?AWSAccessKeyId=AKIAIWOWYYGZ2Y53UL3A&Ex-
pires=1534034249&Signature=SIHgGx6USulLVus2v%2BSj0feolco%3D&re-
sponse-content-disposition=inline%3B%20filename%3DOfficial_Labeling_Criminal_
Embeddedness.pdf.

13 Weisburd, David. 2018. Hot Spots of Crime and Place-Based Prevention. *Criminology &
Public Policy.* Volume 17, Issue 1: 5–25.

14 Lum, Cynthia, Kennedy, Leslie W., and Sherley, Alison J. 2006. The effectiveness of
counter-terrorism strategies. Campbell Collaboration. Retrieved on August 1, 2018, from
https://campbellcollaboration.org/library/effectiveness-of-counter-terrorism-strategies
.html.

15 Ibid.

16 Al-Qaeda. 2010. May Our Souls Be Sacrificed for You! *Inspire*, Issue 1. Retrieved on June 1, 2017 from https://azelin.files.wordpress.com/2010/06/aqap-inspire-magazine-volume -1-uncorrupted.pdf.

17 Al-Qaeda. 2010. $4,200. *Inspire*, Issue 3. Retrieved on August 14, 2018, from https: //azelin.files.wordpress.com/2010/11/inspire-magazine-3.pdf.

18 Al-Qaeda. 2010. The Ruling on Dispossessing: The Disbelievers Wealth in Dar Al-Harb. *Inspire*, Issue 4. Retrieved on August 14, 2018, from https://azelin.files.wordpress .com/2011/01/inspire-magazine-4.pdf.

19 Al-Qaeda. 2013. We are All Usama. *Inspire*, Issue 10. Retrieved on June 2, 2016, from https://azelin.files.wordpress.com/2013/03/inspire-magazine-issue-10.pdf.

20 Al-Qaeda. 2017. Train Derail Operations. *Inspire*, Issue 11. Retrieved on June 19, 2018, from https://azelin.files.wordpress.com/2017/08/inspire-magazine-17.pdf.

21 Lum, Cynthia, Kennedy, Leslie W., and Sherley, Alison J. 2006. The effectiveness of counter-terrorism strategies. Campbell Collaboration. Retrieved on August 1, 2018, from https://campbellcollaboration.org/library/effectiveness-of-counter-terrorism-strategies .html.

22 Ibid.

23 Samuel, Sigal. 2018. Banning Muslim Veils Tends to Backfire—Why Do Countries Keep Doing It? *The Atlantic*. Retrieved on August 10, 2018, from https://www.theatlantic .com/international/archive/2018/08/denmark-burqa-veil-ban/566630/.

24 U.S. Department of State. 2018. Trafficking in Persons Report, 2018. Retrieved on July 10, 2018, from https://www.state.gov/documents/organization/282798.pdf.

25 Friedersdorf, Conor. 2012. How Team Obama Justifies the Killing of a 16-Year-Old American. *The Atlantic*. Retrieved on July 1, 2017, from https://www.theatlantic .com/politics/archive/2012/10/how-team-obama-justifies-the-killing-of-a-16-year-old -american/264028/.

26 Martin, Michel. 2018. Labeled A "Terrorist," A Black Lives Matter Founder Writes Her Record. NPR. Retrieved on June 7, 2018, from https://www.npr.org/2018/01 /27/578980821/labeled-a-terrorist-a-black-lives-matter-founder-writes-her-record.

27 Diaz, Daniella. September 29, 2016. Obama: Why I won't say "Islamic terrorism." CNN.

28 Obama, Michelle. 2016. Michelle Obama: "When they go low, we go high." MSNBC. Retrieved on August 10, 2018, from http://www.msnbc.com/rachel-maddow-show /michelle-obama-when-they-go-low-we-go-high.

Appendix B: A Letter from Donald Morgan

1 Ferran, Lee. May 13, 2015. American Wannabe ISIS Fighter Donald Morgan Gets 20 Years in Prison. ABC News. Retrieved on August 9, 2018, from https://abcnews .go.com/International/american-wannabe-isis-fighter-donald-morgan-20-years /story?id=31009777.

2 Donald Ray Morgan was a former Rowan County Sheriff's deputy and was once a reserve East Spencer police officer. Walker, Shavonne. 2015. Former Rowan resident sentenced to 20 years for trying to join terrorist group ISIS. *Salisbury Post*. Retrieved on June 1, 2018, from https://www.salisburypost.com/2015/05/13/former-rowan-resident -sentenced-to-20-years-for-trying-to-join-terriorist-group-isis/.

3 British man who gained a cult following before being killed while fighting in Syria. Darshna, Soni. 2014. "Our brother died a martyr fighting in Syria." Channel 4. Retrieved on August 7, 2018, from https://www.channel4.com/news/iftikhar-jaman-syria-death -isis-jihad-british-portsmouth.

INDEX